Capital Formation in West Germany

# Capital Formation in West Germany

Karl W. Roskamp

Wayne State University

Wayne State University Press, Detroit 1965

---

*Wayne State University*
*Center for Economic Studies*
*Monograph Number 3*

*To the Memory of Jan and Anna Röskamp*

# Contents

Abbreviations                                                          17
Preface                                                               19
Introduction                                                          23

## I. West German Economic Conditions—1948              27
   a. Food and Industrial Production in the German
       Federal Republic, 1945–1948
   b. Changes in Population and Labor Force
   c. Capital Equipment and Production Levels
   d. International Trade
   e. Financial Disorganization
   f. The 1948 Currency Reform
   g. Doctrine of the "Social Market Economy"
   h. Summary

## II. Capital Formation, 1948–1960                       53
   a. Composition and Growth of Gross National
       Product
   b. Developments in Gross Domestic Capital
       Formation

## III. Sources of Savings for Capital Formation          82
   a. Individual Savings
   b. Public Policy and Individual Savings

    c. Business Savings
    d. Public Policy, Tax Incentives and Business Savings
        *Accelerated Depreciation in Business*
        *Accelerated Depreciation in Housing*
        *Loans as Capital Incentives*
        *Tax Exemptions on Retained Earnings*
        *Taxes and the Capital Market*
        *Taxes and Exports*
    e. Government Savings
    f. Social Security Savings
    g. Bank Credit
    h. Foreign Funds
    i. Summary of the Government's Contribution to Savings

IV. The Government's Influence on the
    Structure of Capital Formation                  162
        a. Production Bottlenecks
        b. Residential Construction
        c. Shipbuilding
        d. Agriculture
        e. Communication and Transport
        f. Capital Investments in Social and Cultural
           Institutions
        g. Public Guideposts to Private Investments

V. Equity, Government and Capital Formation        208
        a. Tax Burden Distribution—1950
            *Income Distribution*
            *Tax Allocation by Income Brackets*
            *General Turnover Tax*
            *Tobacco Tax*
            *Assessed Individual Income Tax*
            *Immediate Aid Levy*
            *Wage Tax*
            *Corporate Income Tax*
            *Local Tax on Business*
            *Local Real Estate Tax*

*Other Taxes*

*Incidence of Tax Structure*

b. Distribution of Contributions to Social
   Insurance

c. Total Burden Distribution, 1950

d. Total Burden Distribution after 1950

e. Distribution of Benefits from Public
   Investments

f. Tax Exemption Distribution

g. Summary
   Appendix Tables to Chapter V      253

VI. Lessons from the West German Experience      263
   Bibliography      269
   Index      283

# Tables

## A. Tables in Text

*Table* 1 Gross Investment in West German Industry 1936–1945 by Industry Groups    37

*Table* 2 Money Supply—December 1948    46

*Table* 3 West German Gross National Product—Current and 1954 Constant Prices, Implicit Price Trend in G.N.P. and Growth Rates of G.N.P.    63

*Table* 4 National Product by Industrial Origin. Current Prices    65

*Table* 5 Percentage Distribution of Uses of G.N.P. 1949–1960    67

*Table* 6 Uses of Gross National Product 1949–1960    68

*Table* 7 National Income Aggregates, 1948 2d half—1960    69

*Table* 8 Price Indexes to Capital Formation in West Germany 1949–1960    73

*Table* 9 Marginal Capital Output Ratios for West German Economy and Industry 1950–1960    76

*Table* 10 Structure of Gross Domestic Capital Formation, 1948 2d half—1960    78

*Table* 11 Components of Gross Domestic Capital Formation, 1948 2d half—1960    80

*Table* 12 Gross Investment in Equipment as % of Private Gross Domestic Investment—West Germany and United States    81

*Table 13*  Gross Investment and Gross Savings, 1948 2d half—1960  84

*Table 14*  Components of Net Capital Formation, 1948 2d half—1960  88

*Table 15*  Components of Individual Savings, 1948 2d half—1960  92

*Table 16*  Tax-Favored Savings Deposits, Fixed Interest Securities and Premiums for Savings in Building Associations 1949–1960  102

*Table 17*  Tax Deductions by Persons under Capital Accumulation Agreements. Estimated Budget Losses through Deductions by Savers in Building Associations 1949–1959  105

*Table 18*  Increase in Assets in Business Sector 1948 2d half—1960  112

*Table 19*  Financing of Increases in Business Assets 1948 2d half—1960  114

*Table 20*  Financing of Increase in Business Assets, Percentage Distribution of Sources of Funds, 1950–1960  116

*Table 21*  Comparison of Corporate Financing—West Germany and United States. Percentage Distribution of Increase in Assets and Sources of Financing  120

*Table 22*  Deductions under various Paragraphs for Accelerated Depreciation by Business  128

*Table 23*  Deductions by Business for Tax-exempt Loans, Retained Earnings, Export Aids, and Interest on Tax-Favored Securities, 1949–1957  133

*Table 24*  Total Business Deductions and Budget Losses, 1949–1957  136

*Table 25*  Alternative Estimates of Net Government Savings, 1948–1957  142

*Table 26*  Estimate of Influence of Surpluses and Deficits on Government Income and Products Transaction Account on Sources and Uses for Gross Private Investment, 1949–1957  144

*Table 27*  Gross Investments, Loans and Subsidies for Investments Granted by Government 1948 2d half—1958  146

| | | |
|---|---|---:|
| *Table 28* | Percentage Distribution of Government Loans by Economic Sectors in 1955 | 148 |
| *Table 29* | Savings of the Social Insurance System, 1948 2d half—1957 | 150 |
| *Table 30* | Increases in West German Social Security System Assets, 1950–1958 | 152 |
| *Table 31* | Changes in Main Assets and Liabilities of Banking System 1950–1960 | 153 |
| *Table 32* | Foreign Aid Received by West Germany to December, 1954 | 156 |
| *Table 33* | Government Contribution to Total Gross Savings. Government Gross Savings as Percentages of Total Gross Savings | 159 |
| *Table 34* | Contribution of Government to Total Net Savings. Government Net Savings as Percentage of Net Domestic Capital Formation | 160 |
| *Table 35* | Production, Investments and Employment in Coal Mining, 1949–1956 | 170 |
| *Table 36* | Production, Investments and Employment in the Iron and Steel Industry, 1949–1956 | 172 |
| *Table 37* | Production and Investments in Electric Power Sector | 174 |
| *Table 38* | Residential Construction in West Germany 1949–1959 | 179 |
| *Table 39* | Public Aid to Residential Construction 1949–1960 | 180 |
| *Table 40* | Reconstruction of Merchant Fleet 1949–1956 | 183 |
| *Table 41* | Development of West German Agriculture 1949–1959 | 188 |
| *Table 42* | Public Aid to Agriculture 1949–1960 | 189 |
| *Table 43* | Development in Transport and Communication 1949–1956 | 191 |
| *Table 44* | Extent of Public Influence on Gross Investment in Transportation and Communication 1949–1956 | 192 |
| *Table 45* | Indexes to Development in Transportation and Communication, 1949–1956 | 193 |
| *Table 46* | Development of Public Expenditures for Social and Cultural Purposes and Local | |

|            | Services by all Levels of Government 1925– 1957 | 198 |
| *Table 47* | Gross Investments in Fixed Assets in Social and Cultural Institutions 1949–1957 | 200 |
| *Table 48* | Public Funds Used in the Financing of Gross Investments in Fixed Assets in Social and Cultural Institutions, 1949–1957 | 202 |
| *Table 49* | Distribution by Income Brackets of: Households, Income, Taxes Paid, Tax Exemptions and Tax Benefits to favor Capital Formation, 1950 | 213 |
| *Table 50* | Estimated Distribution of Tax Burden in 1950 | 223 |
| *Table 51* | Estimated Effective Tax Rates in West Germany 1950 (Without Contributions to Social Insurance) | 225 |
| *Table 52* | Estimated Distribution of Contributions to Social Insurance by Income Brackets in 1950. Contributions to Old Age Insurance and Unemployment Insurance | 228 |
| *Table 53* | Summary Tables: Distribution of Tax Burden and Contributions to Social Insurances in 1950. Household Income, Tax Burden, Contributions to Social Insurances, and Effective Tax Rates | 231 |
| *Table 54* | Total Tax Revenue as Percentage of Personal Income 1950–1959 | 233 |
| *Table 55* | Total Tax Revenue (Cash Receipts) all Government Levels, 1950–1960 | 235 |
| *Table 56* | Changes in Tax Structure: Yield of Taxes as Percentage of Total Tax Revenue, 1950–1960 | 236 |
| *Table 57* | Changes in Yields of Various Taxes 1950–1960 | 237 |
| *Table 58* | Percentage Distribution of Income Tax Payers by Income Brackets: 1950, 1954, and 1957 | 238 |
| *Table 59* | Distribution of Gross Investments by Government in West Germany by Economic Sectors, 1949–1955 | 242 |

*Table 60*   Distribution of Benefits from Government Investments in 1950. Excess of Benefits over Burden in Income Brackets 244

*Table 61*   Distribution of Tax Exemptions to Favor Capital Formation and Number of Taxpayers by Income Brackets 1950 and 1954 245

*Table 62*   Distribution of Benefits from Government Investment and Tax Exemptions in 1950. Excess of Total Benefits over Burden in Income Brackets 246

## B. Tables in Appendix to Chapter V

*Appendix Table 1*   Estimate of Number Distribution of Households by Income Brackets 254

*Appendix Table 2*   Estimate of Household Incomes and Expenditures 255

*Appendix Table 3*   Household Structure in West Germany in 1950 256

*Appendix Table 4*   Total Tax Revenue at all Government Levels 1950 256

*Appendix Table 5*   Estimated Distribution of Tax Payments for 1950 258

*Appendix Table 6*   Estimated Distribution of Taxes Paid by Income Brackets 259

*Appendix Table 7*   Estimated Effective Tax Rates 260

*Appendix Table 8*   Basic Distributions Used for Tax Allocation 261

*Appendix Table 9*   Estimate of Distribution of Deductions and Tax Benefits by Income Brackets 262

# Abbreviations

| | |
|---|---|
| B D L | Bank Deutscher Länder |
| B F M | Bundesfinanzministerium |
| B. G. BL. | Bundesgesetzblatt |
| C.D.U. | Christlich–Demokratische Union |
| D.I.W. | Deutsches Institut für Wirtschaftsforschung, Berlin |
| DM | Deutsch Mark—unit of currency in the German Federal Republic after the Currency Reform of 1948 |
| ECA | Economic Cooperation Act |
| E.R.P. | European Recovery Program |
| E.St. D.V. | Einkommensteuerdurchführungsverordnung |
| E.St. G. | Einkommensteuergesetz |
| F.D.P. | Freie Demokratische Partei |
| F.R. | German Federal Republic |
| GARIOA | Government Aid and Relief in Occupied Areas |
| G.D.R. | German Democratic Republic |
| G.m.b. H. | Gesellschaft mit beschränkter Haftung |
| G.N.P. | Gross National Product |
| H. Y. | Half Year |
| I.F.O. | Institut für Wirtschaftsforschung München |
| J.E.I.A. | Joint Export Import Agency |
| K.G. | Kommandit Gesellschaft |
| L.A. | Lastenausgleich |
| M.R. | Monthly Report |
| N.N.P. | Net National Product |

| | |
|---|---|
| OEEC | Organization for European Economic Cooperation |
| O.H.G. | Offene Handelsgesellschaft |
| Para | Paragraph |
| RM | Reichsmark—unit of currency in Germany before the Currency Reform of 1948 |
| St.B.A. | Statistisches Bundesamt |
| St.H.B. | Statistisches Handbuch |
| St.B.R.D. | Statistik der Bundesrepublik Deutschland |
| St.J.B. | Statistisches Jahrbuch |
| S.P.D. | Sozialdemokratische Partei Deutschlands |
| U.K. | United Kingdom |
| U.S. | United States |
| Wi. und Stat. | Wirtschaft und Statistik |

# Preface

WHEN THIS STUDY was begun in the summer of 1958, the intention was to explore the role of government in the rapid capital formation of post-war West Germany. On this only relatively little information was available at that time. It was difficult to obtain an overall picture of public efforts to further capital formation and the country's economic growth. Originally it was intended to cover fiscal and monetary policy as well as the developments in the resurging capital market.

A preliminary study of a large number of documents during a first visit to West Germany in 1958 revealed, however, that the most decisive public influence on capital formation was implemented through fiscal policy. This being the case, the study was subsequently more and more directed towards an investigation of developments in the fiscal area. Other areas were dealt with to such an extent only as was necessary to provide a general picture of the various phases of the West German economic growth and to bring into sharper focus the effects of specific fiscal measures.

Within the fiscal area itself an attempt was made to analyze essentially three problems. The first was to explore to what extent fiscal policy helped to generate the necessary amount of savings for the country's rapid capital formation. The second problem was to investigate how fiscal policy was used to channel resources into production sectors. Finally, the last and most tempting but also the most difficult problem was to make a quantitative estimate as to who had paid and who had benefited from public capital formation.

It is hoped that the result of this study will contribute to a better understanding of the West German Social Market Economy.

I am indebted to many persons without whose help the writing of this book would have been impossible. My special thanks go to Professor Richard A. Musgrave of Princeton University and Professor Wolfgang F. Stolper of the University of Michigan. Both gave me their valuable advice on many difficult problems and they read all of the manuscript. Equally I should like to thank Professor Harvey E. Brazer of the University of Michigan, Professor Harold J. Barnett of Washington University in St. Louis, Professor Romney Robinson of Brandeis University, Professor Richard Eckaus of MIT, Professors Marian Krzyzaniak and David Felix both of Wayne State University, and Dr. Horst Mendershausen of Rand Corporation, who were kind enough to give their advice on specific subjects, or who read part of the manuscript. Professor A. J. Heidenheimer of the University of Florida went through the whole manuscript and made valuable suggestions.

In West Germany, I thank Professor Knut Borchardt of the Wirtschaftshochschule Mannheim who read the manuscript and helped to improve it in various ways. Professor Paul Senf of the University of Saarbrücken advised on West German budgetary procedures. Professor Gerhard Zeitel of the Wirtschaftshochschule Mannheim, who had done pioneering work on the incidence of the West German tax structure, gave his advice on some tax problems, and Dr. Egon Baumgart of the Deutsche Institut für Wirtschaftsforschung in West Berlin provided valuable information on investments by economic sectors.

It is a special pleasure to thank the many West German officials in the various ministries and in the West German central bank for their invaluable aid. Unfortunately, they are too numerous to mention individually. All of them gave me the benefit of their intimate knowledge of West German institutions and postwar economic developments.

It is not necessary to stress that none of the above persons is responsible for the views expressed in this book. For these, only the author is to blame.

I further gratefully acknowledge the generous aid which I received from the Ford Foundation. A faculty research fellowship permitted me to devote one academic year to the preparation of this book.

Part of Chapter 5 of this book was published as an article in *National Tax Journal* in 1963. I am thankful to the publishers of this journal who gave their kind permission to reprint it in this book.

Finally my thanks go to the secretarial staff of the Department of Economics of Wayne State University in Detroit for having typed and retyped the manuscript.

# Introduction

ECONOMIC GROWTH has become a major focus of interest during recent years. Underdeveloped countries are emerging while industrialized societies are making vigorous efforts to accelerate their economic growth rates. For a large part of the human population, which still lives at a subsistence level but hopes to escape from poverty, economic growth offers the only solution. For many developed countries, economic expansion has become, during these days of a prolonged cold war between two ideologies, a matter of national survival. We do not need to dwell upon the obvious importance of an adequate rate of economic growth.

The analysis of historical growth patterns suggests that a combination of specific factors is necessary to permit an economy to grow. These are, in essence: the desire for economic growth, the ability to use and transform existing resources efficiently, and a distribution of the final product which will avoid both the negation of expansion incentives and, on the other hand, an explosion of the system because of social discontent. Economic growth is a sociological as well as a technological process, requiring continuous adjustments in both the social fabric and the structure of production. Some of these adjustments are instantaneous. Others may involve a long period of time. Many of them can be left to free market forces, but some require the interference of public authorities if acceptable solutions are to be achieved.

23

The advanced Western countries are mixed economies in which the government sector plays an important role. These countries rely basically on a free market system, but their governments have an important influence on the patterns of economic growth. Governments can increase incentives for entrepreneurs, persuading them to take larger risks. They can impose penalties if the public interest requires it. In certain sectors of the economy, governments may assume the entrepreneurial function directly if this will contribute to the welfare of the public. Governments can strongly influence the allocation of resources to either investment or consumption and are not limited merely to causing changes in total volumes. There are many devices by which public action can alter the composition of these aggregates, especially that of capital formation. Because economic growth is a long-run process, some critical decisions are involved which lie far beyond the time horizon of private entrepreneurs. Examples of these are education, the building and maintenance of roads and waterways, and the support of basic research which will not pay off in the foreseeable future.

In short, governments in developed countries with free market economies are not, and cannot be, neutral with respect to economic growth. They have great opportunities and responsibilities to provide the necessary framework within which a free market system can provide socially acceptable solutions and generate economic growth.

This study provides an analysis of a Western government's economic policy measures with respect to capital formation during a period of strong economic growth. The experience of West Germany since World War II can yield new insights concerning the growth process.

The West German experience was unique, largely characterized by a bouncing back to levels of production which had previously been attained. It was thus significantly different from what one might call the normal growth of other Western countries; but, it also had little similarity to the pattern of economic growth in underdeveloped countries. The student of economic growth may therefore consider this case too peculiar for general application; yet it does provide some pertinent lessons for other countries.

West Germany's postwar economic growth process was an event for which no simple explanation can be given. Most writers have emphasized the role of market forces in this process. This has had the unfortunate effect of camouflaging the important contribution of government to this rapid economic expansion.[1] A study of the government's influence on economic growth and, more specifically, its influence on capital formation may therefore fill in a gap. We believe that West German economic growth provides an extremely interesting case because of its particular, and evidently successful, interaction of market forces and public policy.

---

[1] *See,* for instance: Egon Sohmen, "Competition and Growth: West Germany," *American Economic Review,* December, 1959, p. 986 and comments on this article by Karl W. Roskamp, A. I. MacBean and W. G. Shepherd, and R. G. Opie, "Competition and Growth—The Lessons of West Germany," *American Economic Review,* December, 1960, p. 1015.

# I. West German Economic Conditions, 1948

WEST GERMANY'S economic growth began with a currency reform in 1948. It has been said that after this date a new and vigorous economy emerged from the ashes of the war like the mythical bird, Phoenix.

This facile analogy is unfortunately of little aid to a diagnosis of the economic conditions prevailing in West Germany in 1948. To judge the performance of its economy since 1948, one has to understand the point of departure. What were those ashes like? Leaving mythology aside, what had actually happened to the factors of production, entrepreneurial initiative, trade, and the financial system since the cataclysm in 1945? To set the stage for our later analysis, we must first review events preceding the 1948 currency reform—a measure which had a major impact on the economic expansion of the '50's.

Of course, the growth process did not start from zero. Much of the productive capacities survived the ravages of war. Also available were the talents of a gifted industrious nation. On the other hand, severe structural dislocations had created problems which cannot be ignored. By selecting a number of specific subjects, it is possible to clarify the rather intricate developments in the German economy during and after the war, and to isolate those factors which primarily determined the later growth process. We shall first describe West Germany's productive resources—land, labor, natural resources, and capital stock—as they existed in 1948. After this, we shall examine West Germany's international trade, its financial system, and the currency reform in 1948. Even the most detailed description of these factors cannot, however, furnish a complete picture of the West German economy in 1948. For this, an additional investigation of the political and sociological changes following the war would be necessary. This is beyond the scope of this book, and it should be admitted that the economist, though fully recognizing the importance of these influences, is generally glad to leave the analysis of such matters to colleagues in other branches of social science.

a. *Food and Industrial Production in the German Federal Republic—1945–1948*

As a consequence of the war, the Germany of 1937 was split into several parts. The largest part constitutes what is now the German Federal Republic (F.R.) or West Germany, and consists of the former U.S., U.K., and French zones of occupation. The Russian zone of occupation became the German Democratic Republic (G.D.R.) or East Germany. The eastern districts beyond the Oder-Neisse line are now under Polish or Russian administration. Berlin received special status as a four-power city. This postwar division of Germany became a highly controversial political issue involving all the great political powers.

The division of Germany meant the loss of large eastern agricultural areas. Before the war, Eastern Germany (beyond the Oder-Neisse line) shipped substantial quantities of agricultural surpluses to Western Germany and to Berlin. Germany had long since ceased to be self-sufficient in its food supply, however. At the eve of World War II, in spite of all attempts to become autarkic, it could only produce about 89% of its food consumption.[1] The degree of self-sufficiency varied for the different areas. It was highest in the districts beyond the Oder-Neisse line and lowest in Western Germany. The division of Germany made

---

[1] Bruno Gleitze, "Ostdeutsche Wirtschaft," Berlin: Duncker und Humblot, 1956, p. 167.

the food supply in the west, where the degree of self-sufficiency was much below the average of the Reich, especially precarious. An aggravating factor was that in the years immediately after the war the crops in West Germany were far below prewar averages. This was due to a lack of fertilizers and other agricultural inputs.

In the prewar years (1935–1938 average), Western Germany had produced about 14 million tons of grains, compared to only 8.3 million tons in 1946. The lack of an adequate postwar fodder supply caused a substantial drop in the number of pigs—Germany's most important source of meat. Pig production fell from 11 million pigs before the war to 5.3 million in 1945.[1]

The most pressing problem in West Germany after the war was to achieve an adequate food supply. The food shortage became more acute due to the influx of refugees. To ameliorate the grave situation, the Allies imported large amounts of grains, starches, and pulses into West Germany. Expressed in grain values, these imports amounted for the combined U.S.–U.K. zones (Bizone) to 958,000 tons in 1945, 1.7 million tons in 1946, and 4.15 million tons in 1947.[2] In spite of these imports, which prevented mass starvation, the food supply of the population was highly insufficient. Before the war, an intake of 2,400 calories per day for a person not working was considered adequate. In 1947 and part of 1948 (until June), the normal consumer ("Normal Verbraucher") received between 1,218 and 1,552 calories per day.[3] The situation was somewhat better for the agricultural population, but the city population could only try to supplement its meager supplies of rationed food with unrationed vegetables and the like.

The division of Germany thus created a drastic shortage of food supplies in West Germany. Any West German government would have to make immediate efforts to solve this problem.

The partition of Germany had equally far-reaching conse-

[1] Hans Schlange Schöningen, *Im Schatten des Hungers* (Hamburg, Berlin: Paul Paray, 1955), p. 303.

[2] Grain values are defined as the food value of 1 kg. of wheat or rye.

[3] *Deutschland Jahrbuch 1949*, Essen: West Verlag, 1949, p. 137.

quences on industrial production. In 1936, more than 60% of total industrial production was located in Western Germany.[1] Some types of industries were, however, concentrated in specific areas. For instance, most of the heavy metallurgical industry was located in the west, especially in the Ruhr district, and in the now-Polish Upper Silesian area. The heavy chemical industry and several light industries were, on the other hand, chiefly in the German Democratic Republic. As a result, the division of Germany led to disproportions in industrial capacities in the individual sections. A large part of the early efforts in both West and East Germany were aimed at eliminating these disproportions and regaining prewar production levels. This was easier for the West Germans since it is less difficult to build up light industries when heavy ones exist. Also, international trade made up for shortages. The East Germans, on the other hand, found that they had to make substantial investments in heavy industries to complement their structure of production.[2]

Here, we may mention that the division of the country also affected transportation and communications. The traditionally heavy East-West traffic ended and the new emphasis became North-South. More attention will be given this problem in Chapter IV.

b. *Changes in Population and Labor Force*

One of the largest migrations of people in history occurred when more than 10 million Germans from eastern and southeastern Europe moved into West Germany. This movement started before the end of the war, when large numbers of East Germans sought to escape the advancing Red Army. It ended, at least temporarily, on August 13, 1961, when the East German government began to erect the wall dividing East and West Berlin. Thus, for about 16 years there had been a major exodus from the east, although the reasons for this changed. The first wave of

---

[1] Gleitze, *op. cit.*, p. 170.
[2] For a detailed discussion of the economy of East Germany, see: Wolfgang F. Stolper with the assistance of Karl W. Roskamp, *The Structure of the East German Economy* (Cambridge, Mass., Harvard University Press, 1959).

refugees, not wishing to fall into Russian hands, reached the western part of Germany at the end of the war. Immediately after the war, the German population was expelled from the areas now under Polish and Russian administration beyond the Oder-Neisse line, and from Czechoslovakia, Hungary, and Rumania. These two movements brought more than 7.5 million people into West Germany by 1950, whereas East Germany and Berlin had an influx of 4.1 million. Then, from 1950 until the middle of 1959, about 3 million people left East Germany, among them 1 million from districts further east. Thus, more than 10 million people were absorbed in West Germany from 1945 through 1959. In 1936, there lived in its area, and in West Berlin, 40.9 million people, or 60.8% of the population of the Reich. This population increased to 42.1 million in 1939, and after the war took its toll it was 41.0 million. By 1951, the same area had more than 50.2 million inhabitants. This was an increase unique in Europe.[1]

There was, of course, a great shortage of housing. Before the war, West Germany had about 10.8 million dwelling units. Of these, 2.3 million were destroyed during the war. In West Berlin, another 300,000 were ruined.[2] Simply to house the indigenous population was very difficult. The situation became desperate when the large number of refugees arrived. Overcrowding of apartments caused varied sorts of social friction and discontent. A large scale residential construction program was imperative.

The influx of refugees did not lead to a parallel increase in the labor force. In spite of the fact that the population had increased by about 7 million by 1948, the labor force was about the same as in 1939. In that year, 51.2% of the population belonged to the labor force, compared with only 43.5% in 1948.[3] Structurally, there were significant changes. The war losses were extremely

---

[1] Friedrich Edding, *The Refugees as a Burden, a Stimulus, and a Challenge to the West German Economy* (The Hague: Martinus Nijhoff, 1951), p. 9.

[2] Präsident des Bundesausgleichsamtes, "10 Jahre Lastenausgleich," Bad Homburg, n.d., p. 16.

[3] *The European Recovery Program*, Joint Report of United States and United Kingdom Military Governors. No. 2. Dec., 1948, p. 89.

heavy in the age groups between 20 and 40 years. The quality of the labor force had also deteriorated. Though one could find all kinds of personal abilities among them, many refugees came from agricultural districts and often had to acquire industrial skills before they could again find employment.

The integration of refugees into the economic process was made more difficult because many had first found shelter in agricultural areas where war destruction had been least. The states of Lower Saxonia, Schleswig-Holstein, and Bavaria had received a relatively high percentage of refugees. In many of the rural areas no employment could be found for the newcomers and, in places where employment could be offered, no dwelling units were available. This was one of the grave scructural problems faced by West Germany in 1948.[1]

A few words must be said about the attitudes of workers and entrepreneurs between 1945 and the 1948 currency reform. During this time, there was little incentive to work for money. Because of the severe inflation, money could not buy very much. Food was rationed. To obtain an apartment, or even a single room, one had to expect a long and tedious fight with various local commissions. For clothing, one had to rely on old household reserves, if there were any. Only a few services could be purchased freely. Those who were lucky had employers who paid part of their wages in commodities such as butter and fats, which were extremely scarce. Employment by Allied occupiers was desirable because one could then expect occasionally to receive some cigarettes or small amounts of tea or coffee. Such items had an extremely high value on the black market and were very often demanded as an addition to the normal purchasing price of goods and services. This became a habit in many sectors of the economy. Often, for example, money alone could not procure a railroad freight car, but a few hundred cigarettes added to the price would work a miracle and, in spite of any difficulties, a car would appear.

A large number of people did work only for money, however,

1 Edding, *op. cit.*, p. 10. See also: *Wi. und Stat.* Vol. 3, 1951, p. 436.

and had no or little possibility of obtaining any such compensation in kind. Many people wanted to hold onto their regular jobs until better days arrived. Others had no connection with black markets and would not consider participating in such illicit activities. Also, a formal certificate of employment was necessary in order to obtain ration cards. In some rare cases, persons had insufficient money to purchase even the meager ration allowances.

Real incomes were low in these years, but they were low for everyone except, perhaps, for some large farmers who profited from the rapid improvement in terms of trade in favor of agriculture. For a large part of the population there occurred a substantial levelling of the difference in real income. One was poor but everyone was poor. There was no way to get rich. Even the shrewdest black marketeer could not hope to get very far. If his operations became too large, he would come into conflict with the authorities and end up in prison.

No estimates of the real income distribution exist for these years. The prevailing inflation no doubt changed the distribution in the direction of greater equality. It acted as a mollifying element and lessened the differences between "haves" and "have nots." This was, in retrospect, a highly desirable development. It reduced to a considerable extent the amount of social friction connected with the absorption of the large numbers of refugees. If the influx of millions of destitute people into West Germany had occurred under tight money conditions and in a society where, under an effective price system, large differences in income and property would have been conspicuous, the social repercussions might have been much more severe.

In this context it is useful quickly to review the attitudes of workers and entrepreneurs with respect to productive efforts in the pre-currency-reform period.

Because of the rapid inflation, many workers had a kind of money illusion and they felt richer than they actually were. Inflation had removed part of the restraints normally imposed by a well-functioning price system. Other restraints, legal and administrative, imposed by Allied and German authorities, were felt, but they affected owners of real assets more than the broad masses. When finally, in 1948, after the currency reform, a normally working price system reappeared, many of the illusions created by the postwar inflation soon vaporized and the real situation of workers became painfully clear. Labor was the abundant factor of production in the first years after 1948 and real wages remained rather low for a long time.

The situation for entrepreneurs during these years was different. West Germany remained basically capitalistic. In contrast to the Soviet zone of occupation, private property rights were not interfered with. The old prewar entrepreneurs were still active and could exercise their skill and intiative within the limits set by a tight price control and allocation system. There was, in addition, an influx of aggressive entrepreneurial talent. Among the refugees were many people with great entrepreneurial abilities. These soon began to compete with the old established group. All of the refugee entrepreneurs had seen better days and later they made great efforts to regain their old social positions.

Yet, between 1945 and 1948 it was impossible for even the most gifted entrepreneur to reconstruct. In many cases the only achievement was a reasonable food supply, clothing, and a decent home. Those who could still produce had no great incentive to sell their products for money. It was feared that this was a waste of the few existing assets still held, because very often new raw materials—or labor services—could not be purchased for money alone. A good deal of all production went, therefore, into hoarding. This was evidently in the self-interest of entrepreneurs but, at the same time, highly asocial in view of the urgent needs of millions of deprived people, especially the refugees. Yet the practice did not cause great concern. Psychologically, there was in those days a slow process of reorientation towards rugged individualism. The war and the postwar events had been shocking. The collapse of the state and the evident uselessness of all the sacrifices which had been made, led to the idea that ultimately each man had to fend for himself. The better he did this, the better off he was. There was no apparent general concern for equity in a country where one man was chased from his home and soil (as was the case with refugees) whereas the other man kept everything and there was no recourse. The premium was on individual effort and one's own efficiency. Nothing else counted. Such attitudes were widely prevalent before the currency reform and they were carried over into the 1950's.

### c. *Capital Equipment and Production Levels*

Industrial production was deplorably low at the time of the currency reform in 1948. It was estimated to be only about 55% to 50% of the 1936 level.[1] The 1936 industrial production was not the highest that the German economy had achieved. Industrial production in 1944—which was, of course, overwhelmingly war production—was about one-third higher than in 1936.[2]

However, it seems that industrial capacity was not a limiting factor to West German production in 1948. Perhaps most restraining was the inadequate supply of raw materials. Another obstacle was the lack of incentive to work because of repressed inflation and tight price controls. Finally, the Allies had imposed limitations on production. Although these were no actual handicap under the circumstances prevailing between 1945 and 1948, they did have a psychological impact.

The choice of the year 1936 as a base year for comparisons with production after the war is often made because this year is considered the last "normal" one before the war. The armament program under the Hitler regime was then just beginning.[3] Another reason is that there exist excellent statistical data about industrial production for this year.[4] Comparisons between 1936 and postwar years have, however, a disadvantage in that they ignore the changes which occurred in the West German economy between 1936 and 1945, especially in its capital stock. The result

[1] *Deutschland Jahrbuch, 1949, op cit.,* p. 173, 174. H. C. Wallich, *Mainsprings of German Revival* (New Haven: Yale University Press, 1955), p. 35.

[2] Gleitze, *op cit.,* p. 169, figures refer to Reich.

[3] D.I.W. *Die deutsche Industrie im Kriege, 1939–1945* (Berlin: Duncker und Humblot, 1954), p. 17.

[4] *Die deutsche Industrie,* Gesamtergebnisse der amtlichen Produktionsstatistik, Schriftenreihe des Reichsamtes für Wehrwirtschaftliche Planung, Berlin, 1939.

is that growth rates after the currency reform are generally over estimated, while the achievements of the German economy before and during the war are underestimated. It should be noted that there were rapid increases in the output of some industries between 1936 and 1945. These occurred especially in mining, production of electricity, the chemical industry, iron and steel making, machine building, and the metal goods industries.[1] To achieve higher production in these industries, large investments were made until the end of the war. According to a German estimate, gross investments in industry amounted to 39.8 billion RM between 1936 and 1945. Of this, more than 34.0 billion RM were invested in basic products industries and in investment goods industries.[2]

Destruction during the war and later dismantling decreased these capacities. Netherthless, the remaining capacity was, in many cases, substantially above that in 1936. All told, West German industry actually had, in 1946, a greater industrial capacity than in 1936. True, much of this was war-oriented because most of the war-time investment served the armament industry. A large part of it, however, could be converted for civil production, especially in basic industries.[3] There was, to the benefit of the F.R., a large "spill-over" from the prewar and war years as far as industrial capacity was concerned. This occurred because the Nazis had greatly increased capacity and much of it was damaged slightly if at all during the war. In addition, the western Allies, in contrast to the Russians in East Germany, did not significantly decrease industrial capacity for civil production by dismantling plants.

---

1 Gleitze, *op. cit.,* pp. 169–173.

2 *Wochenberichte,* Deutsches Institut für Wirtschaftsforschung, Berlin, August 1957, p. 124.

3 Opinions and estimates differ as to the extent of capacity losses in the war and post-war years. See: Rolf Krengel, *Anlagevermögen, Produktion und Beschäftigung der Industrie im Gebiet der Bundesrepublik von 1924 bis 1956* (Berlin: Duncker und Humblot, 1958); Ernst Eisendrath, *Anlagevermögen und Dekapitalisation der deutschen Industrie,* p. 126 (Berlin: Duncker und Humblot, 1950); Harmsen Report, *Am Abend der Demontage, Bremer Ausschuss für Wirtschaftsforschung,* p. 26 (Bremen: Truien Verlag, 1951).

TABLE 1.

Gross Investment in West German Industry from 1936
to the End of World War II by Industry Groups[1]

(1950 Prices—Millions of RM)

| Industry | |
| --- | --- |
| Basic Products | 25,548 |
| Investment Goods | 8,597 |
| Consumption Goods | 3,067 |
| Food, Drink and Tobacco | 2,213 |
| Others (Kleinbetriebe) | 398 |
| Total Industry | 39,823 |

[1] Calculated from "Wochenbericht" D.I.W., August 1957, p. 124.

### d. *International Trade*

The German economy is an open economy. Foreign trade was
always an absolute necessity even in the years immediately prior
to World War II, in spite of great efforts to become autarkic.
Traditionally, Germany imported foodstuffs and industrial raw
materials. It paid for these with the export of finished industrial
products. In 1936, 36% of all imports were foodstuffs and stimu-
lants, 37% industrial raw materials. The rest consisted of semi-
finished (17.8%) and finished (9.2%) industrial products.[1] The
textile industry, the food, drink and tobacco industries, and the
oils and fats industries were heavily dependent on raw material
imports.

The export/import pattern of Western Germany in 1936 was
somewhat different from that of Germany as a whole. It imported
12% of its agricultural products and 12% of its industrial raw
materials. It exported 18% of its industrial production but no
agricultural products. Germany as a whole exported a small
amount of agricultural products in 1936.

In 1938, Germany had imported, in spite of all efforts to become self-sufficient, about 4 million tons of grain for both human

[1] *Statistisches Handbuch von Deutschland 1928–1944*, p. 392–394, Herausgegeben vom Länderrat des amerikanischen Besatzungsgebietes, München 1949.

consumption and fodder.[1] Most of this went to Western Germany. After the war, the loss of agricultural surplus areas beyond the Oder-Neisse and the huge rise in population increased the dependence of West Germany on food imports, especially grains and fats.

German industries had always depended on the import of raw materials, some of which had a strategic importance. The division of the country increased this dependence greatly.

If West Germany's economy was to revive and grow, integration with the world economy was imperative and great efforts had to be made to obtain the goods needed through international trade. Germany as a whole, which, in a larger and more diversified area had a much better balanced economy than West Germany, could not achieve self-sufficiency before the war. To hope that the latter could be self-sufficient was completely unrealistic. Nevertheless, a special feature of the West German economy in the first postwar years up to 1948–49 was a high degree of enforced self-sufficiency. The occupying powers were very reluctant to permit West Germany to engage in international trade. During 1945–48 this was probably due to uncertainty about the political future of Germany. The question of German reparations and the future level and pattern of production were not yet settled. Proclamation No. 2 of the Allied Control Council had actually forbidden Germans to engage in foreign trade. All foreign transactions had to go through Allied channels. A special Joint Export Import Agency (J.E.I.A.) which had a foreign trade monopoly was later set up in West Germany. J.E.I.A. had the difficult task of trying to sell German exportable goods because direct negotiations between German exporters and foreign importers were forbidden. The procedure was difficult and the volume traded was small. There was, during this period, a remarkable change in the commodity composition of exports. Before the war, 97% of Germany's exports consisted of industrial products—mostly finished goods and some raw materials.[2] After

1 IFO Institut, München, *Fünf Jahre Deutsche Mark* (Berlin: Duncker und Humblot, 1953), p. 104.
2 *The European Recovery Program, op. cit.*, No. 2. Dec. 1948, p. 63–65.

the war this pattern was completely reversed. West Germany began to export mainly raw materials—the traditional coal exports and the not-so-traditional export of timber.[1] The output of finished manufactured goods was so low that even had there been no restriction no great amount of exports could have been made.

### e. *Financial Disorganization*

The years immediately after World War II were marked by a complete disorganization of finance. As a result of war financing, the money supply had increased enormously. It is estimated that the total money supply at the end of the war, including time deposits, amounted to 298 billion RM, or 173 billion RM exclusive of time deposits. This compares with 56.4 billion RM including time deposits and 29.1 billion RM without them in 1938. The immediate postwar money supply (here including time deposits) for rump Germany (U.S., U.K., French, and Russian zone of occupation) was about 173 billion RM. The difference between 298 billion RM and 173 billion RM is explained by the fact that 70 billion RM were immediately blocked by Russian authorities in the Soviet zone of occupation or were destroyed in liberated areas or declared void in the area east of the Oder-Neisse. These 173 billion RM included, however, about 12 billion RM of military scrip. The money supply of West Germany including time deposits must have been about 133 billion RM.[2]

The results of this tremendous oversupply of money are well known. Very soon there were two price levels, one for rationed goods and one for goods traded in black markets. The cost of living index (for goods legally traded) rose from 112 in October, 1945, to 131 in May, 1948.[3] That this increase was not larger was due to a surprisingly well-functioning price control system,

---

[1] Ludwig Erhard with the assistance of Dr. von Maltzan, *Germany's Comeback in the World Market* (New York: Macmillan, 1954), pp. 74–75.

[2] All figures for the period before the currency reform in 1948 are from an article by Eduard Wolf in *Die deutsche Wirtschaft zwei Jahre nach dem Zusammenbruch* (Berlin: Albert Nauck, 1947).

[3] OMGUS, "Report of Military Governor," Statistical Annex XVII, July 1948, p. 49.

established before and during the war and maintained by the Allies during and after 1945 in an attempt to keep prices at a pre-occupational level.[1] It is estimated that about 90% of all transactions were legal and the subject to price control.

The black markets were another story. The volume of transactions in these markets was relatively small, but prices were substantially higher. They ranged from 100 times the legal prices for butter, cigarettes, and coffee to 10 times the legal prices for electrical equipment. It is probably not too erroneous to assume that average black market prices were about 50 times as high as legal prices. In spite of the relatively small volume of black market transactions, they absorbed a considerable part of the excess money supply. On the whole, both price levels remained fairly constant, but black market prices declined slightly toward 1948 as production increased.

As a result of the financial disorganization, a substantial amount of all transactions—up to 50% according to some estimates—took the form of a highly inefficient and clumsy bilateral exchange. It has been argued that bilateral exchange was often the chief means of survival for business and individuals before the currency reform. It was nevertheless costly, inefficient, and intensely disliked. In short, money had, to a large extent, lost its function and the distortions in prices were serious.

As far as public finance is concerned, the Allies had substantially increased tax rates in 1946, especially for the personal income tax. These tax rates were the highest Germany had ever seen. Although they were of no great importance during the time of repressed inflation, the West German government objected strongly to them after the currency reform. Fiscal policy was, nevertheless, not very effective against the inflation. Budgetary receipts at all government levels amounted in 1947–48 to 16.3 billion RM. In 1949–50, after the currency reform, they amounted to 19.1 billion DM.[2]

---

[1] Horst Mendershausen, "Prices, Money and the Distribution of Goods in Postwar Germany," *The American Economic Review*, June 1949, p. 646–658.

[2] "Postwar Monetary and Fiscal Policies in West Germany," p. 34, O.I.R. Report no. 5171, Department of State, unclassified.

## f. *The 1948 Currency Reform*

There was general agreement on the need for a currency reform in West Germany after World War II. Some German experts had secretly discussed this problem even before the war ended. According to Sauermann there seem to have been about 30 different plans for a reform which were carefully studied in formulating the program which the United States Government submitted to the Allied Control Council in 1946.[1] This plan was called, "A Plan for the Liquidation of War Finances and the Financial Rehabilitation of Germany," now better known as, "The Dodge-Colm-Goldsmith Plan."

A currency reform had, of course, important political implications. According to the Potsdam Agreement, Germany was to be treated as a unit in economic matters, including currency reform. The well-known disagreement of the Western powers with the Russian government over German reparations and the control of German industry in the years from 1945 to 1947 delayed the reform until 1948. An earlier reform would have been beneficial for the German economy, but this could not be achieved. There was a genuine desire not to split Germany into currency areas but Russian policy with respect to Germany made this inevitable. In fact, the separate currency reforms in East Germany and in West Germany merely brought into the open an already manifest division of Germany. It is true, however, that the differences between the Soviet zone and the Western zones were less pronounced before the reforms, and it was relatively easy to go from one zone to the other. This situation changed radically after the currency reforms in West and East Germany. Since then, the two parts of Germany, belonging to two different economic systems, drifted rapidly apart. The likelihood of a peaceful reunification

---

1 Heinz Sauermann, "The Consequences of the Currency Reform in West Germany," *The Review of Politics*, 1950, p. 179. Heinz Sauermann, "Der amerikanische Plan für die Währungsreform," *Zeitschrift für die gesamte Staatswissenschaft*, 1955, Band. 3. Heft 2, p. 199. *Zur Vorgeschichte der Deutschen Mark*, Die Währungsreformpläne 1945–1948. Eine Dokumentation unter Mitwirkung von Wolfram Kunze. Herausgegeben und eingeleitet von Hans Möller (Basel: Kyklos Verlag, 1961).

has become very slim indeed. The separate currency reforms did have a high political price, but this fact was not immediately appreciated in 1948.

There was little disagreement as to the necessity of a currency reform in West Germany, but there were quite a few differences of opinion regarding the kind of currency reform that was desirable. Difficulties in the formulation of plans were aggravated by the lack of adequate statistical data on the West German economy. No one knew, even roughly, the amount of money in circulation, and national income could only be guessed. On the other hand, the planners of the reform had one advantage in that currency reforms in many other European countries had already occurred since the end of the war. These reforms were carefully analyzed and the information gained greatly assisted the planners of the West German currency reform in their task.[1]

The main problem connected with currency reform was an equitable distribution of war burdens. The burden which the war and postwar events had imposed on households and persons was, of course, very uneven. Some acceptable formula for an equitable distribution was necessary in order to avoid social unrest. In 1948, this was a completely unsolved problem. During the years of inflation between 1945 and 1948, not much could be done in this respect, and the whole matter had remained shelved.

It was evident that a currency reform would suddenly expose the inequitable distribution of the war burden. The German experts who assisted in preparing the reform continually pointed out how necessary it was to combine a currency reform law with an equalization of burden law. Unfortunately, the final version of the reform law did not provide for any equalization of burden.[2] The military governments believed that the problems involved were much too difficult for an acceptable solution to be found in a short time. The Allies requested the West German

---

1 Lloyd Metzler, "Recent Foreign Experiences with Monetary and Fiscal Reforms," Appendix O to Dodge-Colm-Goldsmith Plan.

2 *Deutschland Jahrbuch 1953*, p. 212 (Essen: Rheinisch Westfälisches Verlagskontor, 1953).

government to make a decision on this matter by the end of 1948. Before the end of that year, a preliminary measure, the so-called "Immediate Aid Levy" (Soforthilfe) was enacted by the West German government to provide aid for refugees. The "Law for Equalization of Burden" itself was not promulgated until 1952. Under it, 50% of all property existing at the time of the currency reform is to be redistributed over a 30 year period. The total amount involved is between 80 and 90 billion DM. Up to 1959, about 31 billion DM had been paid out.

The currency reform in 1948 was far from equitable because it did not simultaneously cope with the distribution of war burden. It was also inequitable in other respects. A few facts may be cited. According to the law, each person was entitled to receive a per capita quota amounting to 60 DM. Of this, 40 DM was to be paid immediately and 20 DM at a later date.[1] For these 40 DM the receiver had to pay 40 RM, or a ratio of 1/1. One week later, however, it was announced that the per capita allocation would be counted against deposits in banks—if there were any—when these were converted into DM. Thus, many small savers were not aware of the fact that they might liquidate their total savings in an initial spending spree. In fact, 30% of all deposits, mostly those of small savers, were wiped out through this provision. This was one of the worst features of the currency reform, and it caused great difficulties in later years when efforts were made to convince people with small incomes that saving in bank accounts was desirable.

In October, 1948, the Allied authorities were afraid that the initial inflationary pressure might become too large and declared 70% of the amounts in blocked RM accounts void. Deposits were thus converted in a ratio of about 1/16. This was a second blow.

The reform greatly favored those businessmen who had hoarded goods and those farmers who had built up their livestock herds instead of providing more meat for starving city

---

[1] Fritz Grotius, "Die Europäischen Geldreformen nach dem zweiten Weltkrieg," *Weltwirtschaftliches Archiv*, Band. 63, 1949, pp. 277–279.

populations.[1] Because the allies had engineered and implemented the reform, Germans could not blame each other for this.

So much for the equity aspects of the reform. These were mentioned first only because they had been of overriding importance in other western countries which had imposed currency reforms after the war.

Efficiency was another story. The reform substantially increased incentives, especially for business. Profits were high in the initial period after the reform and businessmen tried hard to become liquid again and to build up normal inventories. For workers, the situation was different. Wages remained fairly stable under the new DM and there was unemployment. Labor of many skills was, in 1948, the one abundant factor of production and its remuneration lagged sadly for a long time, however explicable this may be in economic terms.

To help business in overcoming the initial difficulties arising from the conversion of money and to enable firms to make wage payments, all firms with employees could, upon request, receive interim aid amounting to 60 DM per employee. This amount was later deducted when the converted DM balance kept on banks were claimed.

Public authorities received as a gift an initial allotment in DM equal to their average monthly revenues over a period of six months before the currency reform. All bank balances and cash kept by public authorities were, however, declared void. We may mention in this context that the large internal public debt created by, and enlarged during, the war was wiped out with a stroke of the pen.

The three military governments in the western zones of occupation received 770 million DM as deposits in the Bank Deutscher Länder (B.D.L.). The railway and postal services received 50% of their average monthly receipts in the form of deposits at the B.D.L.

---

1 Gains from hoarding seem to have approached 3 billion DM.

The amount of DM supplied by the currency reform through legal money creation was as follows:

TABLE 2

Money Supply—December 1948[1]

(In billions of DM)

| | |
|---|---|
| Per Capita Allocations | 2.850 |
| German public authorities | 2.360 |
| Business, railway, postal service | 0.810 |
| Military governments | 0.770 |
| Free accounts (including 20% released in October, 1948 from blocked accounts) | 5.500 |
| | 12.290[2] |

[1] F. A. Lutz, "The German Currency Reform and the Revival of the German Economy," *Economica*, 1949, pp. 122–142.

[2] According to B.D.L., "Report of the Bank Deutscher Länder for the Years 1948–1949," p. 15, up to December 1948, 12.8 bill. DM were created legally.

At the end of September 1948, the total money supply, including savings deposits was scarcely 10.5 billion DM. Releases from blocked accounts and rapidly increasing bank lending increased the money supply to 13.2 billion DM by December, 1948. This compares with the 122.4 billion RM presented for conversion.[1]

The excess supply of money caused by war financing was eliminated. However, new money was extremely tight.[2] The reform had greatly improved the position of those who possessed non-monetary assets but ruthlessly punished those with assets such as money, demand deposits, and savings deposits.[3] No other western country had been willing to submit to such a rigorous

[1] Walter F. Heller, "Tax and Monetary Reforms in Occupied Germany," *National Tax Journal*, 1949, p. 216.

[2] At the end of 1948 there was some inflationary pressure. Due to the special technique of the currency reform monetary authorities were unable to exert control over the money supply from the beginning. Early in 1949 this was, however, overcome.

[3] A survey immediately after the currency reform showed that low income groups suffered most and were rather more concerned about the future. Entrepreneurs were most optimistic. *Die Gegenwart*, Freiburg, Breisgau, 15 Sept. 1948, p. 15.

reform. If the West Germans had had their way, the reform would have been much more equitable. In fact, the Equalization of Burden Law later indemnified some of the losses suffered during the currency reform.

### g. *Doctrine of the "Social Market Economy"*

What was the economic philosophy in West Germany in 1948? For the understanding of the pursued economic policy, it is necessary to investigate the basic convictions of many influential government leaders.

West Germans very often call their economy a "Soziale Marktwirtschaft" (Social Market Economy).[1] To understand properly what this term means—no one has ever accurately defined the word "social"—it is necessary to look at its intellectual foundations. These can be found in the teachings of the neo-liberal "Freiburg School" which came into existence in the early 1930's. The leader of this school was Walter Eucken, who died in 1950. Prominent members are Franz Böhm, Alexander Rüstow, Wilhelm Röpke, Alfred Müller-Armack, Günter Schmölders and Otto Veit. Professor F. A. Hayek, who would probably not consider himself a member of the "Freiburg School," has also had some influence on the teachings of this group. Professor Ludwig Erhard, the present chancellor of the Federal Republic, should also be mentioned. He has, however, contributed relatively little to the school's theoretical writings but employs its general arguments and considers himself a member.[2] To belong to this school during the Nazi control of Germany took some courage.

The "Freiburg School" was founded in the early years of Nazism and its development is interesting from both the intellectual and historical points of view. During the years 1933–45, the traditionally strong influence of the state on economic matters greatly increased. The "Freiburg School" was, in a sense, a reaction to this. The trouble with reactions to an existing system

---

1 Alfred Müller-Armack, "Soziale Marktwirtschaft" in *Handwörterbuch der Sozialwissenschaften,* IX, 1956.
2 Henry M. Oliver Jr., "The German Neoliberalism," *The Quarterly Journal of Economics,* February, 1960.

is that very often the negative messages of the reaction are much stronger than the positive ones. This holds true, to a large extent, for the teachings of the "Freiburg School" and its offspring, the "Social Market Economy." What this school criticizes is obvious, but it is difficult to pinpoint the school's positive program.

The "Freiburg School" of economic thinking is thoroughly opposed to any excessive government interference in economic matters. As a reaction, it has designed a somewhat unrealistic model of a free-market economy. It assumes that in a market economy all markets are cleared through the smooth working of the forces of supply and demand. Vigorous competition is expected to reduce prices near to cost.[1] The markets must be protected against all forms of monopoly. Any interference with the price system will inevitably lead to distortions and presumably push the economy away from some sort of implied *Pareto optimum*. The solution which the price system provides is acceptable and a good one because preferences and cost patterns are in proper relationship.

From this basic conviction follow a number of very important ideas. The first contention is that given a properly working price system there can be no lack in aggregate demand. If unemployment occurs it is because wages are too high and out of step with productivity of labor. Keynesian methods to alleviate unemployment are largely useless because they lead only to price increases and cannot change the basic situation.

Most important for the proper working of the price system is price level stability. This assures that incentives will not be interfered with and that no arbitrary changes in income distribution will occur. In addition, price level stability will induce savings.

Savings are considered interest elastic. The interest rate itself is believed to have powerful influences as a cost element and will effectively select those projects where investments are most productive.

Fiscal policy should be "neutral"; that is, taxes should inter-

---

[1] Bruno Molitor, "Soziale Marktwirtschaft," *Hamburger Jahrbuch für Wirtschafts—und Gesellschaftspolitik,* Tübingen: J.C.B. Mohr, Paul Siebeck, 1958.

fere as little as possible with incentives or preference patterns. Balanced budgets would be desirable to avoid any interference with price level stability from the fiscal side. Discretionary compensatory fiscal policy to maintain full employment is not desirable. The government should not interfere in capital formation. This would ultimately distort the structure of production.

Roughly, these are the main ideas of the "Freiburg School" as far as "Marktwirtschaft" is concerned. If its teachings would be limited to the above statements, one could not help but feel that here is a sort of capitalistic Utopia, far removed from reality. To advocate that price and wage flexibility will always result in full employment in a world where big business confronts big labor and where big government is often the arbiter seems a doubtful thesis. To rely exclusively on vigorous competition to achieve optimum resource allocation seems somewhat of an illusion in a world where truly competitive markets are rare exceptions and monopolistic and oligopolistic situations are the rule.

While all of this reflects a "laissez-faire" attitude with the implicit notion that a free market economy is best for everyone, certain correctives are nevertheless desirable. Complete noninterference by the state is impossible because the working of a competitive market mechanism may lead to an income and property distribution which cannot be accepted on social grounds. In these cases, corrections through taxation are necessary, and the progressive income tax will avoid extreme differences in income. If some redistribution is necessary, care should be taken, however, that income taxes do not interfere with incentives.

The income distribution problem raises the question of what is socially acceptable.

Here, one must carefully distinguish between what is said and what is actually done. Strict adherents of the Free Market Doctrine would oppose any economic policy which might tend to create a welfare state. There would be an opposition—as there actually was during the last ten years—to rent ceilings, housing subsidies, and price supports to raise the income of lower income groups. (The argument is that the existing tax structure, which is believed to be strongly progressive, is sufficient. Complementing the tax structure are such government programs as Social Security and relief for hardship cases.) All of this presupposes that income inequality and security are considered less important than incentive, productivity, and progress. Though this attitude has had an influence in shaping West German economic policies, it should not be overrated. In practice, things were less extreme. Germany since the '80's has had a comprehensive Social Insurance System and the years since 1945 have seen many public policy measures geared to rehabilitate and aid the needy. Still, there can be no doubt that the premium was, and still is, on incentive. As yet there has been no great concern over income or even property distribution.

Members of the school acknowledge that state intervention is inevitable in a number of other cases. Certain goods and services cannot be provided by private business and must be furnished by the state. Further, the state has to assure that the general institutional and social framework of the market economy remains adequate. This involves a whole category of responsibilities—some of them very vaguely defined—and ranges from control of monopolies to family policy. Whatever the necessary interventions are, care must be taken in all cases that they do not disturb the market mechanism. The interventions must be "marktkonform,"[1] but opinions differ widely on what qualifies as a "marktkonform" intervention.

It would, of course, be wrong to assume that the actual economic policy pursued in West Germany after 1948 was exactly in line with the teaching of the "Freiburg School." The teachings served as a basic orientation for economic policy makers, although they frequently deviated from the course laid down by the School.

An area in which the recommendations of Free Market economists were largely ignored for a considerable time was capital

[1] Eva-Maria Dohrendorf, "Das Problem der Marktkonformität wirtschaftspolitischer Mittel," *Jahrbuch für Sozialwissenschaft,* III, 1952. E. Tuchtfeldt, *Zur Frage der Systemkonformität wirtschaftspolitischer Massnahmen* (Berlin: Duncker und Humblot, 1960). *Schriften des Vereins für Sozialpolitik,* NF Band 18, "Zur Grundlegung wirtschaftspolitischer Konzeptionen," p. 203.

formation. The continued strong influence of government in this field makes one doubt that investments will or can be allocated entirely by free market forces. In the area of capital formation, the neoliberals had to make great concessions, and the pursued policies departed widely from traditional principles. It is possible—but by no means certain—that past experiences will ultimately lead to some revisions in neoliberal teaching, bringing it a little more in line with the realities of our time.

### h. *Summary*

West German authorities had no significant influence on the course of economic events before the 1948 currency reform. Following the reform, when most of the responsibilities were again placed on their shoulders, they were confronted with a number of facts which they had little power to change. These were basic determinants for a future economic policy.

The first, and a very bitter one, was the division of the country, clearly revealed, but not caused by, the separate currency reforms. As a consequence of this, the break-up of a formerly well-integrated economy was made final. Some light industries now in East Germany were scarce or lacking entirely in West Germany. Most important, however, was the loss of the agricultural surplus areas beyond the Oder-Neisse line. West Germany had to increase substantially its own food production, and had to rely heavily on food imports.[1]

The second determinant was the change in the population. About seven million people had come to West Germany as refugees. They had to be absorbed by the economy and supplied with housing and other necessities.

A low level of industrial production was the third problem.

---

[1] It is occasionally argued that the break-up of Germany may have had some beneficial effects, at least economically. The argument is that labor was much less productive in the eastern agricultural area than it is now in West Germany, and that food can now be imported at lower prices from abroad than it could formerly from Eastern Germany. See for instance: Professor Charles P. Kindleberger's Statement in "Foreign Economic Policy," Joint Committee on the Economic Report, Congress of the United States, 84 Congress, p. 526, Washington, D.C., 1955.

This was due to the lack of incentives for both entrepreneurs and workers, plus missing raw materials. Industrial productive capacities were not fully used. In spite of some bottlenecks, production could have been substantially increased once incentives were created and badly needed raw materials were made available—as it actually was immediately after the currency reform.

The solution for the first and third problems depended greatly upon West Germany's ability to participate again in international trade and to become integrated in the world economy.

West Germany remained a capitalistic country. It had to rely on the abilities of its entrepreneurs for its economic revival. To make this possible, the necessary institutional framework for a well-functioning free-market mechanism had to be created. When this was accomplished, entrepreneurs were eager to work hard to regain their old economic and social positions which had been impaired during the war and postwar years. Motives were especially strong for those entrepreneurs who were refugees and had to start from scratch. Regaining their old position meant, in essence, the opportunity again to accumulate capital.

The 1948 currency reform designed by the occupying powers had wiped out the enormous excess money supply—a result of war financing. With it disappeared many illusions. The reform was designed to stimulate the economy. It created great incentives and favored owners of non-monetary assets. With the currency reform came the removal of most price controls, opening the way for the establishment of a free market system. Many influential West Germans, convinced by the arguments of the neoliberal "Freiburg School" of economics, believed in such a system.

In retrospect, one can say that a large number of factors and fortunate circumstances contributed to the solution of these problems.

One also finds, however, that the problem of capital formation was crucial to each situation. To overcome the disproportions in the industrial structure caused by the division of the country new productive facilities had to be built. Increases in agricultural production to provide part of the food imports formerly obtained from the east were possible only by modernization of equipment and costly land improvements. The integration of millions of refugees required large investments in new factories, businesses, and housing.

In international trade, so vital for the country's existence, West Germany had to expect stiff foreign competition and difficulty in recapturing markets. In the long run, West Germany could be competitive only if the export goods industries were highly efficient. This required modernization and expansion of existing facilities.

The export industries were not the only ones which needed investments. Much more important were industries such as mining, electricity production, and transportation. It was in these areas where bottlenecks in production soon appeared and seriously threatened the expansion of the economy. In all cases, new capital was necessary to increase efficiency and output.

Capital formation required savings, either voluntary or involuntary. The currency reform had set the keynote in a drive for efficiency and expansion. Subsequently, there was a very large capital formation, but the methods of financing were vastly different from those in earlier years. Strong internal financing by business and a heavy influence of public authorities on investable funds emerged as the dominant characteristics. These may have been necessary to achieve a high rate of economic growth, but they also resulted in inequitable distribution of property and income for which the country so far does not seem to have found a satisfactory solution.

Thus, capital formation was the necessary first step for West Germany's economic revival and growth. The following chapters will deal with this in more detail.

# II. Capital Formation, 1948–1960

CHAPTER I pointed out that capital formation was the key problem for West German economy in 1948. There was wide agreement that investments of all kinds were necessary. The problem was to find a way to obtain a sufficiently high rate of investment under the prevailing economic conditions.

Before investigating the various aspects of this capital formation as it occurred between 1948 and 1960, it is necessary to review a few well-known concepts and problems in capital formation and to indicate what will be discussed in the following chapters.

The capital concept as used in this study refers to capital goods which are tangible assets. These are, however, only a part of the total capital in an economy. In recent years, growing recognition has been given to the fact that a substantial part of a nation's capital consists of intangible assets such as the education people receive, their professional and entrepreneurial abilities, and their state of health. All of these are important to a country's economy but difficult to evaluate. The existence of this kind of capital was taken for granted by Western economists for many years. Suddenly, after World War II, when the focus of economists' interest shifted to underdeveloped countries with bad educational systems and poor health care, the significance of intangible assets was realized and its lack viewed as one of the great obstacles to economic development.

This study does not consider intangible capital. This is not because it was unimportant in West Germany. On the contrary, there existed a substantial amount of intangible capital. Education was generally of a high standard, professional abilities were abundant, and there was no lack of enterprising businessmen. These were the things in plentiful supply after World War II. Intangible capital did not constitute a bottleneck during the last ten years, and for this reason it is omitted in our discussion. It was tangible capital in the form of steel, brick, and stone which was lacking.

Experience teaches that long-term increases in productivity are generally possible only through capital formation. The latter has quantitative as well as qualitative aspects and it may be useful to say a few words about this in order to point out an advantage of West Germany over many other countries.

An existing capital stock may be thought of as a collection of capital goods, each embodying a specific level of technolgical knowledge. With technological progress, both reinvestments and net investments will change not only the quantity of the capital stock but also its quality. This fact is most important if there are rapid advances in technology. When this is the case, most of the "net" investment may actually be embodied in replacements and those who are able,—or forced—to replace old capital goods on a large scale may have a great advantage. Such replacement may perhaps net the same volume of capital goods, but the new capital stock may be vastly superior in the qualitative sense and be, therefore, much more productive.[1]

New capital goods in West Germany after 1948 were generally

---

[1] For a detailed analysis of the relationship between technical progress and capital formation see: Robert M. Solow, "Technical Change and the Aggregate Production Function," *Review of Economics and Statistics*, 39, August, 1957; Robert M. Solow, "Investment and Technical Progress," *Mathematical Methods in the Social Sciences*, Stanford University Press, 1960; Edmund S. Phelps, "The New View of Investment: A Neoclassical Analysis," *The Quarterly Journal of Economics*, November, 1962, and sources given in this article; and N. Kaldor and J. A. Mirrlees, "A New Model of Economic Growth," *The Review of Economic Studies*, June, 1962.

superior in quality because many old capital goods were prewar and often in bad repair. After the war, there were many technological improvements, but often there was little opportunity to take advantage of them because of wartime and postwar conditions. In 1948, there existed a backlog of innovations ready to be introduced. West Germany, which had to rebuild a large part of its capital stock after 1945, had, in this respect, an advantage which should not be underestimated. It is not possible to evaluate fully this qualitative aspect of the West German capital formation but it should be mentioned.

A well-known limitation on capital formation is the amount of savings—or non-consumption—a society is willing to generate. In Western countries, private and government consumption is roughly between 75% and 80% of aggregate income. Small changes in the total volume of consumption can therefore greatly affect the possible capital formation. If, with a given income, capital formation is to be increased, it is necessary to increase savings and to diminish consumption. How much will be consumed and saved is, however, not only a decision of consumers. Personal savings, the difference between personal disposable income and consumption, so important for capital formation in the past, are now only a relatively small part of total savings in Western economies. In modern times other important savers have evolved.

The first of these is business. A few decades ago, business relied much more heavily on external financing for its investments than at present. Today, the largest part of investable funds comes from depreciation charges and retained earnings.

Business, however, may not be the only strong saver. Governments may also save. In some Western economies, and especially in West Germany, government savings made possible through current revenues exceeding current expenditures have been very substantial and were of great importance for capital formation after the last war.

A third source of savings in modern economies is bank credit. Since there is no watertight compartmentalization between money markets and capital markets in countries with well-developed financial systems, changes in the money market will affect the amount of investable funds available. The desirability of credit creation by banks to obtain investable funds depends on the prevailing economic situation, and must be evaluated in the light of other policy objectives, such as full employment and price-level stability. If there is unemployment with stable, or even declining price levels, it might be advisable to resort to credit creation to finance investments.

Finally, a country may obtain resources from abroad. These could be used to augment domestic savings.

Total savings in an economy, therefore, depend little on the decision of the consumer to save or to consume. When, for example, his paycheck is received, he probably will have already contributed to the nation's total savings through taxation; when he spends his income, the prices which he pays in all likelihood contain business' savings. Decisions to save are now made in many different places in an economy, by different groups of people or different policy making units. Present-day decisions on savings not only involve personal time preferences but also such things as price policies, wage pressures by unions, tax policy, and the need for public expenditures.

Economic policy can favor any one of the above-mentioned sectors, and can thus change the composition of aggregate savings. If one of the sectors "saves" too much or too little the imbalance can be compensated by the savings of another. Shifts in the sectoral savings pattern will, however, usually interfere with the existing income and property distribution. If savings are largely made voluntarily as personal savings, the income brackets in which these savings are made may be quite different from those to which taxpayers belong who would be forced to save through taxation. Thus, policy-induced changes in the savings pattern are rarely neutral with respect to income distribution, a very important fact from a general welfare point of view.

Savings do not have to equal investments, for each of the above-mentioned groups or sectors in an economy.[1] Some sectors may

---

[1] The problem of the different concepts of government savings which arises in this context is discussed in Chapter III.

be creditors, other debtors. There will be a flow of funds between sectors, and the more developed the financial system the smoother the flow. It should be noted that in such a system banks not only channel investable funds, they also create them.

When it was stated that consumers have a relatively small influence on the total savings in a Western economy, this should not be misinterpreted. There may be shifts between the particular sectors which save, but the total amount of all sector savings is, under normal circumstance, a fairly stable percentage of aggregate income. This percentage varies for different countries, but a strong resistance occurs if aggregate consumption is reduced too far—a fact even the Soviet Union cannot quite ignore. Nevertheless, small reductions of consumption are possible in hugh consumption-level economies and may be necessary for economic growth. If this were the case, it would still be very important in what particular way the reductions were carried out and what sectors made the corresponding savings. Various problems which arose in this context in the West German economy will be given detailed discussion in Chapter III.

Another limitation to capital formation in market economies is the fact that the demand for capital goods is largely a derived demand and thus intimately related to the present and expected demand for consumer goods.[1] Investment decisions in market economies are made by entrepreneurs who are guided by profit expectations. The extent of profits depends strongly on aggregate demand and especially on its largest component, the demand for consumer goods. If consumer demand slackens, incentive to invest may drop. Investments may, in such cases, be postponed which may lead in turn to a further decline in aggregate demand and aggravation of the situation.

In a market economy, there should be a balance between consumption and investment. Consumption should be high enough to permit full use of existing capacities and it should grow fast enough to justify the building of new production facilities. Yet,

---

[1] For West Germany, export demand is of greatest importance, but this is not a "derived demand" in the normal sense.

consumption should be low enough so that sufficient savings are generated to finance the required investments.

Crucial in the balancing process are entrepreneurial expectations. These may be such that a stable pattern evolves, but they may also easily lead to wide fluctuations in economic activity. Such fluctuations may involve a considerable social cost in the form of unemployment and should be reduced to a minimum, if possible.

Since it is doubtful that a market economy can always achieve a desirable balance between investment and consumption and also maintain full employment with reasonable price stability, public authorities must be ready to take stabilizing measures. Through changes in public expenditures, they can increase or decrease aggregate demand. A decline in private spending can be compensated through an increase in public spending. On the other hand, if private demand is already very brisk, and the economy is using all available resources, it might be wise if the government abstained, at such time, from making additional purchases of goods and services. Through monetary and fiscal policy—the latter much stronger—governments are able to influence aggregate demand. This is the essence of modern business cycle theories which postulate a stabilizing interference by governments. The present concern over adequate economic growth has added still another consideration.

Assuring full use of resources at all times, as important as it is, is only part of the problem. It is not enough to achieve this regardless of the composition of the final output. An immediate problem may be temporarily solved by producing extravagant consumer goods leading to full use of resources. From the long-run point of view, however, it might be much better to base the solution on the production of capital goods to push back resource restraints on future levels of output. A country which cannot achieve full use of its present productive capacities may, of course, be much more concerned about this than about future production possibilities. Present full employment is one outcome, but lower future economic growth rates than potentially possible is the final result. The essential problem is assuring full resource use while at the same time producing an output mix which permits rapid economic growth. Compensatory policies by governments should thus have two objectives: to avoid waste of present resources, and to guarantee efficient use of future resources. If an income gap is to be closed, how much to produce should not be the only concern. An equally important consideration is *what* to produce.

The problem of aggregate demand in the West German economy, and the demand for capital goods in particular, will not be investigated in this book. This is not because there were no problems in this area or that the West German economy was in the '50's a case of a non-Keynesian economy par excellence, as is sometimes pretended. Large-scale unemployment existed in 1950 and 1951, and a high-level of aggregate demand was, in later years, maintained through a large rise in exports. Investigation of these developments properly would go beyond the scope of this book. The problem is mentioned here because at some future date lack in aggregate demand may become one of the most serious problems in the West German economy. This book will analyze only those problems of capital formation which will arise even if a high level of employment prevails. These problems are the volume and structure of savings, resource allocation, and equity aspects. This text investigates what contributions government made to find solutions to these problems. If the conclusion is that government contributions were vital for an economy in which aggregate demand was not the major concern, they must be that much more important when resources are not fully used.

Resource allocation in capital formation is the next problem. Most investments in Western countries are made by entrepreneurs. Given a reasonably well functioning price system, no great misallocations of resources are likely to occur. There are, however, well-known limitations to the efficient working of the mechanism of markets. One may be the result of monopolistic or oligopolistic market forms. Limitations may also occur because in vital sections of the economy the price system functions only inadequately, if at all. One reason is that there may be no market values for some of the goods and services produced. In these cases such goods and services must be provided publicly, if at all.

The domains of private and public investment have no clear-cut divisions in Western economies. Public sectors in Germany, as well as in other countries, have existed for centuries. They have experienced a relative growth, and in all likelihood may become even more important in the future. Their growth was the result of wars, trends in technology, and discontent with solutions the market system provided. The recent accent on economic growth has again stressed the importance of the public sector. Governments are now supposed to create conditions favorable to economic expansion. This task may involve heavy public investments to open up poorly developed areas in a country. It may mean giving support to industries critical to economic growth. In addition, substantial aid may be necessary for education and health care to develop and protect human resources. Many of these public measures require much economic insight and political skill. The task of public authorities in these areas is difficult in normal times. The responsibility of the public sector is greatly increased if there are serious disturbances in an economy, as is the case after a war. Under such extraordinary circumstances, governments may extend their field of influence far beyond the traditional range of economic activity to facilitate readjustments.

Investments in Western economies are made according to two principles. The first and most important is based upon decisions by entrepreneurs and reflects the working of the market system. These investments are based on profit expectations. The second principle is public investments which have to allow for the needs of the public and are largely independent of market solutions. Private and public investments are, however, often interdependent and in many cases complement each other. No general rules seem to exist to determine in what way a society should allocate its available resources for capital formation. There are many choices. The one finally adopted depends in essence on the prevailing economic doctrines, the aspirations and desires of the public, and tangible factors such as restraints on production through resource ceilings. The West German solutions will be discussed in Chapter IV.

Capital formation, especially when it is very rapid, invariably poses many equity problems. This will be the final problem in this book. That the distribution of newly formed capital is socially very important cannot be ignored. No democratic Western country, to be practical, would be willing to pay for a rapid economic growth with serious changes in income and property distributions in favor of the upper income brackets. A 19th century pattern of an extremely heavy concentration of property in the hands of a few and a large proletariat is considered intolerable nowadays. Still a controversial issue is the price, in terms of inequality, of a strong incentive growth process. This problem was and is a very important one in West Germany, though it has received only very casual treatment. The solution chosen during the last decade is indicated in Chapter V. The emphasis there will again be on the effects of public capital expenditures.

a. *Composition and Growth of Gross National Product*

To provide the reader with a proper background for the topics discussed in the following chapters, an overall picture of the growth and structure of West German Gross National Product and capital formation is useful. For this picture, national income data were primarily used, but other sources were drawn upon to help fill the information gaps.

Between 1950 and 1960, West Germany's total real G.N.P. doubled. In current prices it nearly tripled. In 1950, G.N.P. was 97.2 billion DM in current prices, and 113.1 billion DM in 1954 constant prices. This compares with 275.8 billion DM in current prices, and 233.8 billion DM in 1954 constant prices in 1960.[1] The country reached the 1938 level of total production by 1950. Per capita incomes did not quite double between 1950 and 1960. Real per capita G.N.P. in 1954 constant prices was 2,361 DM in 1950 and 4,378 DM in 1960. The level of per capita production in 1938 was reached in 1951–52.

The increases mentioned above imply growth rates for both

---

[1] *St. J.B.*, 1961, p. 544.

total and per capita G.N.P. which are rather high for a western country. For total G.N.P. they were in the neighborhood of 7.5% to 8%. For per capita G.N.P. they averaged 6.5%. Due to elimination of bottlenecks and time lags before investments became effective, the increases in G.N.P. were not evenly distributed. The highest growth rate after 1950 was achieved in 1955 with 11.5%. The lowest, in 1958, was 3.3%.

There were also price increases. During the '50's the country experienced some inflation as indicated by the implicit price trend in G.N.P. Between 1950 and 1960, prices for total G.N.P. rose by 37.3%.[1] A 16% increase occurred between 1950 and 1952 and was due to the Korean boom. After this, until 1954, there was no appreciable rise in prices. Since 1955, the year when the country reached full employment, rising prices have again become troublesome. In this respect, West Germany experienced very much the same difficulties as other Western countries having high levels of employment, though the continued refugee influx—until the Wall stopped it—somewhat eased the situation.

This analysis covers the short time of ten years, and even when reference is made to 1936, not more than 25 years are involved. Even in this period, some long-run changes in the structure of production can be observed which are typical results of economic growth. A look at the structure of the G.N.P. is revealing. Industry now contributes about 44% to G.N.P. in West Germany. It is followed by the services (including trade) with about 34%, construction and transportation 7% each, and agriculture 8%. Comparing these shares with those in 1936 one can observe significant shifts. Industry's share has stayed fairly constant, but there are indications that it will decline. Agriculture's share has, on the other hand, strongly decreased, and that of services increased. These developments are in accordance with an accepted theory of the evolution of the structure of production in growing economies. Typically, there is a relative decrease in the demand for

---

[1] This is considerably higher than the cost of living price index indicates. Between 1950 and 1960 the cost of living increased 23% for consumers in medium and 28% for consumers in lower income brackets. *St. J. B.,* 1961, p. 486.

## TABLE 3

### West German Gross National Product in Current and 1954 Constant Prices, Implicit Price Trend in G.N.P. and Growth Rates of G.N.P.[1]

| Year | G.N.P. in Current Prices Billions of DM. | G.N.P. in 1954 Constant Prices Billions of DM. | Indexes | | | | Growth Rates of Per Capita Real G.N.P. |
|---|---|---|---|---|---|---|---|
| | | | G.N.P. Current Prices 1950 = 100 | G.N.P. 1954 Constant Prices 1950 = 100 | Price Trend Implicit in Current G.N.P. | Growth Rates Real G.N.P.[3] | |
| 1948 2d half | 37.5 | n.a. | | | | | |
| 1949 | 79.8 | 87.5[2] | 82.1 | 77.4 | 106.0 | 29.3 | 27.1 |
| 1950 | 97.2 | 113.1 | 100.0 | 100.0 | 100.0 | 10.5 | 9.4 |
| 1951 | 118.6 | 125.0 | 122.0 | 110.5 | 110.4 | 8.3 | 7.6 |
| 1952 | 135.6 | 135.4 | 139.5 | 119.7 | 116.5 | 7.5 | 6.7 |
| 1953 | 145.5 | 145.6 | 149.7 | 128.7 | 116.4 | 7.4 | 6.1 |
| 1954 | 156.4 | 156.4 | 160.9 | 138.3 | 116.4 | 11.5 | 10.4 |
| 1955 | 178.3 | 174.4 | 183.4 | 154.2 | 118.9 | 6.9 | 5.6 |
| 1956 | 196.4 | 186.4 | 202.1 | 164.8 | 122.6 | 5.4 | 4.0 |
| 1957 | 213.6 | 196.5 | 219.8 | 173.7 | 126.5 | 3.3 | 2.1 |
| 1958 | 228.5 | 202.9 | 235.1 | 179.4 | 131.0 | 6.7 | 5.3 |
| 1959 | 247.9 | 216.5 | 255.0 | 191.4 | 133.3 | 8.0 | 6.8 |
| 1960 | 275.8 | 233.8 | 283.7 | 206.7 | 137.3 | | |

[1] St. J. B. 1952, p. 452; St. J. B. 1953, p. 544; St. J. B. 1961, p. 544.
[2] Own estimate.
[3] Calculated as: $\dfrac{Y_t - Y_{t-1}}{Y_{t-1}} \cdot 100$

raw materials largely produced by agriculture. Resources released in agriculture are absorbed in industry, where production is rapidly increasing. At the same time, many services are still performed in households. As personal incomes increase, some of these services are then sold in markets. Concomitant, there is often a shift in the demand pattern in the direction of higher quality services, and as a result, the service sector grows. These are long-run changes and can be observed in many countries. However, German prewar and postwar data should be compared with caution. The division of the country had a profound influence on production patterns and factor proportions. What might be considered a long-run growth phenomenon may, to some extent, be the consequence of structural adjustments due to far-reaching political changes.

As far as the distribution of income to factors of production is concerned, the National Income data indicates an interesting development. The often quoted 2/3:1/3 division of Net National Income between wages and salaries and capital income also holds roughly for West Germany.[1] The income share of labor was never quite as high as in some other Western countries. This was partly due to a somewhat different social structure, as is the case in the United States. The incomes of many independent artisans—people who would be in the labor force in the U.S. and their incomes included in wages and salaries—fall in the category of entrepreneurs in Germany. Still, even if an allowance is made for this, the wage share is relatively low. In 1928, during the Weimar Republic, this share was a little over 60% and, in 1931, 64.4%. During the Nazi era, when trade unions were wiped out, there began a rapid decline of the wage share. In 1938 it had reached an all time low of 54.9%, indicative of how social Hitler's regime was. In postwar years, the wage share rose, and in 1958 it was again 61.4%. A further strong increase in the near future is, however, not very likely.[2]

In the use of G.N.P. there occurred some changes which are also indicative of economic development in West Germany. We

---

[1] *St. J. B.*, 1961, p. 544.
[2] *St. J. B.*, 1958, p. 477; *St. J. B.*, 1961, p. 544.

## TABLE 4

### National Product by Industrial Origin

*Current Prices*[1]    *All Industries = 100%*

| Year | Agriculture Forestry Fishing | Industry[2] | Construction | Transport and Communication | Trade | All Others | All Others Inclusive Trade | Total |
|---|---|---|---|---|---|---|---|---|
| 1936 | 13.6 | 44.0 | 5.3 | 8.7 | 9.6 | 18.8 | 28.4 | 100 |
| 1950 | 12.1 | 40.0 | 6.4 | 7.3 | 13.5 | 20.7 | 34.2 | 100 |
| 1954 | 10.1 | 43.4 | 6.4 | 6.8 | 12.4 | 20.9 | 33.3 | 100 |
| 1956 | 8.9 | 44.0 | 6.8 | 6.9 | 12.7 | 20.7 | 34.4 | 100 |
| 1959 | 8.1 | 43.6 | 7.1 | 6.8 | 13.0 | 21.4 | 34.4 | 100 |

[1] Beitrag zum Netto Inlandsprodukt zu Faktorkosten.
For 1936 Half Year Averages, St. J. B. 1953, p. 548. For all other Years, St. J. B. 1961, p. 545.
[2] For 1936: Industry including artisans not employed in construction.

have explained that for many years capital formation was the limiting factor in the country's growth process. One would therefore expect that a high percentage of G.N.P. went into gross investment. This was actually the case. Between 1948 and 1960, gross investments were, in each year, substantially more than 20% of G.N.P. The lowest percentage was 21.4% in 1949, and the highest 26.5% in 1960. In addition, West Germany has had, since 1951, an export surplus which amounted in the last few years to between 2.5% to 4% of G.N.P. The country thus saved annually between 24% to 29% of G.N.P.[1] This percentage is very high for a Western country, and it necessitates an explanation.

The first reason for the high savings to income ratio is relatively low personal consumption. Compared with other Western countries personal consumption as a percentage of G.N.P. has always been very low. For instance, in 1936 it was only 62.1% of G.N.P. Due to pent-up consumer demand after the war, it rose temporarily to 65.8% in 1949. Since then, it has been falling and was down to 57.3% of G.N.P. in 1960. There are many reasons for this low personal consumption, and some of these will be discussed later. It will suffice to indicate at this point that it was partly a consequence of a deliberate government policy to repress consumption in favor of capital formation and partly due to the low wage share. Yet these two factors alone cannot furnish a complete explanation for such low personal consumption. The savings habits of the German people cannot be ignored. Thrift is still considered a basic virtue, though the experience of two hyperinflations in the lifetime of one generation made West Germans somewhat reluctant to save again after 1948. The rapid increase in the volume of savings in the form of savings deposits is an indication that deep-rooted savings habits are still very strong. One may also speculate to what degree the absence of a

[1] Gross capital formation as percentage of G.N.P. for the U.S. is estimated at 21.8% for the period 1939 to 1948 and 23.6% for 1946 to 1955. This includes public capital formation and increases in claims against foreigners. Simon Kuznets, "Capital in the American Economy," p. 95, Table 9. National Bureau of Economic Research, *Studies in Capital Formation and Financing, Vol. 9,* Princeton University Press, 1961.

## TABLE 5

### Percentage Distribution of Uses of G.N.P. 1949 to 1960. Current Prices.[1]

| Year | Private Consumption | Government Consumption | | Gross Domestic Investment | | Total = G.N.P. |
|---|---|---|---|---|---|---|
| | | Total | of which Defense | Total | Foreign Capital Formation | |
| 1949 | 65.8 | 16.0 | 5.6 | 21.4 | −3.3 | 100 |
| 1950 | 64.3 | 14.4 | 4.5 | 22.5 | −1.2 | 100 |
| 1951 | 61.1 | 14.7 | 5.1 | 22.3 | 1.9 | 100 |
| 1952 | 58.9 | 15.3 | 5.5 | 23.2 | 2.5 | 100 |
| 1953 | 60.2 | 14.5 | 4.3 | 21.6 | 3.7 | 100 |
| 1954 | 59.3 | 14.1 | 3.8 | 23.2 | 3.4 | 100 |
| 1955 | 58.0 | 13.3 | 3.4 | 26.3 | 2.4 | 100 |
| 1956 | 58.6 | 12.9 | 2.8 | 25.1 | 3.4 | 100 |
| 1957 | 58.8 | 12.8 | 2.5 | 24.3 | 4.1 | 100 |
| 1958 | 59.1 | 13.4 | 2.7 | 23.7 | 3.9 | 100 |
| 1959 | 58.1 | 13.6 | 3.2 | 24.9 | 3.4 | 100 |
| 1960 | 57.3 | 13.6 | 3.4 | 26.4 | 2.8 | 100 |

[1] Calculated from Table 6.

## TABLE 6

### Uses of Gross National Product 1949 to 1960. Bill. DM. Current Prices.[1]

| Year | Private Consumption | Government Consumption | | Gross Domestic Investment | | G.N.P. |
|------|------|------|------|------|------|------|
| | | Total | of which Defense | Total | Foreign Capital Formation | |
| 1949 | 52.5 | 12.8 | 4.5 | 17.1 | −2.6 | 79.8 |
| 1950 | 62.5 | 14.0 | 4.4 | 21.9 | −1.2 | 97.2 |
| 1951 | 72.5 | 17.4 | 6.1 | 26.4 | 2.3 | 118.6 |
| 1952 | 79.9 | 20.8 | 7.5 | 31.5 | 3.4 | 135.6 |
| 1953 | 87.6 | 21.1 | 6.3 | 31.4 | 5.4 | 145.5 |
| 1954 | 92.8 | 22.0 | 6.0 | 36.3 | 5.3 | 156.4 |
| 1955 | 103.4 | 23.8 | 6.1 | 47.0 | 4.2 | 178.4 |
| 1956 | 115.1 | 25.4 | 5.5 | 49.3 | 6.6 | 196.4 |
| 1957 | 125.6 | 27.3 | 5.4 | 52.0 | 8.7 | 213.6 |
| 1958 | 134.9 | 30.6 | 6.1 | 54.1 | 8.8 | 228.4 |
| 1959 | 144.1 | 33.7 | 7.9 | 61.7 | 8.5 | 247.9 |
| 1960 | 158.0 | 37.5 | 9.3 | 72.7 | 7.6 | 275.8 |

[1] St. J. B. 1961, p. 553; St. J. B. 1960, p. 550; St. J. B. 1953, p. 544; St. J. B. 1952, p. 452.
Details, due to rounding off, individual number may not add to indicated total.

## TABLE 7

### National Income Aggregates, 1948 2nd Half Year to 1960.
### Billions of DM. Current Prices.

| Year | G.N.P. (1) | Capital Consumption Allowance (2) | NNP. (3) | Indirect Taxes (4) | Subsidies (5) | National Income (6) |
|---|---|---|---|---|---|---|
| 1948 2.H.J. | 37.5 | 3.1 | 34.4 | n.a. | n.a. | n.a. |
| 1949 | 79.8 | 6.2 | 73.6 | n.a. | n.a. | n.a. |
| 1950 | 97.2 | 10.1 | 87.1 | 13.1 | 0.5 | 74.5 |
| 1951 | 118.6 | 12.0 | 106.7 | 17.2 | 0.8 | 90.3 |
| 1952 | 135.6 | 13.3 | 122.3 | 20.3 | 0.9 | 102.8 |
| 1953 | 145.5 | 13.4 | 132.1 | 21.8 | 0.3 | 110.6 |
| 1954 | 156.4 | 13.6 | 142.8 | 23.3 | 0.1 | 119.7 |
| 1955 | 178.3 | 14.8 | 163.5 | 26.3 | 0.2 | 137.5 |
| 1956 | 196.4 | 16.6 | 179.9 | 28.7 | 0.9 | 152.1 |
| 1957 | 213.6 | 18.3 | 195.3 | 30.9 | 1.4 | 165.8 |
| 1958 | 228.5 | 19.9 | 208.6 | 32.5 | 1.4 | 177.5 |
| 1959 | 247.9 | 20.8 | 227.1 | 36.1 | 1.2 | 192.2 |
| 1960 | 275.8 | 23.0 | 252.8 | | | 214.7 |

Sources: St. J. B. 1952, p. 454.
   St. J. B. 1953, p. 544.
   St. J. B. 1961, p. 544.
   St. J. B. 1960, p. 542.
Details, due to rounding off, individual number may not add to indicated total.

full-fledged consumer credit system has tended to keep down personal consumption.

Another factor which permitted high-level capital formation was West Germany's low defense expenditures. In 1935–36, at a time when the armament program under the Nazi regime had just started, about 7% of G.N.P. was used for defense expenditures.[1] During the first years of the '50's, West Germany contributed to the cost of occupation, which may be considered a contribution to the defense expenditures of the Western world. This amounted to 5.4% of G.N.P. in 1948, but soon decreased. In 1956, defense expenditures amounted to only 2.8% of G.N.P., and as late as 1960 to 3.4%. This is very different from the heavy defense burdens other countries such as France and the United Kingdom had to bear, especially during the Korean crisis when defense expenditures were more than 8% of G.N.P. The U.S. had to allocate, in each year of the '50's, more than 10% of G.N.P. for defense purposes.

A low defense burden in West Germany released resources which could be used for capital formation. It facilitated large direct public investments and the transfer of public funds to finance investments in the private sector. A small defense burden contributed greatly to the country's ability to grow—something which should be kept in mind when comparisons of the West German economic performance are made with other Western countries.

During the '50's, government expenditures for uses other than defense amounted to about 10% of G.N.P. This is somewhat higher than in most other European countries, with the exception of the United Kingdom which has reached this level in the last years.[2] Aid given to the Social Security System and transfer payments to victims of the war are mainly responsible for these large expenditures.[3]

---

[1] Fiscal year, refers to area of former Reich. *Die deutsche Industrie im Kriege, 1939–1945, op. cit.,* p. 17.

[2] *St. J. B.,* 1958, p. 166;* *St. J. B.,* 1961, p. 147.*

[3] Victims of war entitled to government aid totaled 4.3 million persons in 1954. After World War I, the number was 1.5 million. Transfers to these people amounted, in 1954, to 2.9 billion DM, in 1956 to 4.1 billion DM. *Allgemeine Vorbemerkungen zum Bundeshaushaltsplan,* 1956, p. 266.

Another large part of government expenditures went into capital formation. This occurred in the form of direct investments made by public authorities, or through subsidies and loans to private investors. In 1949, 4.4% of G.N.P. was used for direct government investments, but since then this share has risen. It amounted to 6.5% in 1958. At present, there is little indication that the government's role in the nation's capital formation will diminish. The percentage of public expenditures used for capital formation in Germany has never been as high as at the end of the '50's.[1] As late at 1958, 30% of all gross investments were financed by public authorities. Most of these investments were net investments. In many years, more than 40% of all net investments were financed by the government.

The last use of G.N.P. is capital formation on foreign accounts.[2] There, West Germany has been so successful that many people have wondered whether or not something was wrong. The story of the West German capital formation on foreign account is, in essence, that of the country's exports. In the first years after 1948, import surpluses prevailed, financed to a large extent through Marshall Plan funds. In 1950, total exports amounted to 11.9 billion DM and imports to 13.1 billion DM. Since then, there have been strong increases in both exports and imports. In 1960, exports were 70.5 billion DM and imports 63.2 billion DM. A year before this West Germany had surpassed the United Kingdom's share of world exports. Export surpluses have occurred during all years since 1951. In some years, they were nearly as high as $2 billion, or 4% of G.N.P. They were so recurrent that they were referred to as a genuine disequilibrium in the balance of payments. As a result, claims against foreigners increased rapidly. Never before in history, not even in the days before 1914, did Germany, as a whole, possess such large foreign exchange reserves as were held by the F.R. in 1960.

A large number of factors contributed to this foreign trade

---

[1] *Bundesbank M.R.*, August 1959, p. 12, Table I.

[2] Capital formation on foreign accounts is defined here as the difference between exports and imports and is not identical with the increase in claims against foreigners which includes income transfers, debt settlement, and some reparation payments, e.g., those to Israel.

success. Changes in world demand for exports, inflationary trends abroad, and, in West Germany, productivity changes and maladjustments in existing exchange rates could be given as reasons for expanding foreign trade. Some of these will be discussed in greater detail.

b. *Developments in Gross Domestic Capital Formation:*
   *An Aggregate Picture*

Since West Germany's currency reform in 1948, an average of more than 22% of G.N.P. has been used each year for gross domestic capital formation. As G.N.P. increased rapidly, so did the absolute volume of gross domestic investment. It would be advantageous if an analysis of this capital formation could be in real terms. With the existing West German data on investments this is not possible. Before describing the various components of capital formation, it should therefore be pointed out what the price increases in capital formation were.

In current prices, total gross domestic investments amounted to 21.9 billion DM in 1950, and 72.7 billion DM in 1960. In constant 1954 prices, investments were 25.5 billion DM in 1950, compared with 61.2 billion DM in 1960. The price trend in investment was approximately the same as that for total G.N.P. Prices for investment goods and construction, on the average, increased by 3.5% annually. Again, as with total G.N.P., a large part of the price increase was due to the Korean boom. Since 1955 prices have risen 2% annually for investment goods and more than 6% for residential construction. For the various investment goods industries, prices rose at different speeds. They increased between 1950 and 1960 as follows: machine building, 46%; steel construction, 81%; electrotechnical industry, 17%. It is not known what accounted for these differences. A possible explanation is rising labor cost, the impact of which depends on how labor-intensive an industry is. Another may be that technological innovations and a resulting higher efficiency in some industries kept unit cost down. A final reason may be the demand situation with which the various industries were confronted.

## TABLE 8

### Price Indexes to Capital Formation in West Germany 1949 to 1960. 1950 = 100

| Year | Gross Domestic Capital Formation[1] | Investment Goods Industry Total[2] | Machine Building[2] | Steel Construction[2] | Electrical Equipment[3] | Residential Construction[4] |
|---|---|---|---|---|---|---|
| 1949 | n.a. | n.a. | 104 | 103 | 111 | 105 |
| 1950 | 100 | 100 | 100 | 100 | 100 | 100 |
| 1951 | 114.2 | 117 | 117 | 120 | 122 | 116 |
| 1952 | 121.4 | 127 | 127 | 148 | 121 | 123 |
| 1953 | 118.2 | 125 | 127 | 156 | 115 | 119 |
| 1954 | 116.0 | 122 | 126 | 150 | 111 | 120 |
| 1955 | 119.8 | 124 | 129 | 154 | 113 | 126 |
| 1956 | 123.7 | 128 | 135 | 162 | 117 | 130 |
| 1957 | 127.5 | 132 | 141 | 171 | 116 | 134 |
| 1958 | 129.9 | 134 | 144 | 178 | 116 | 138 |
| 1959 | 132.5 | 133 | 142 | 177 | 116 | 146 |
| 1960 | 137.8 | 136 | 146 | 181 | 117 | 157 |

[1] Calculated from St. J. B. 1961, p. 553.
[2] St. J. B. 1958, p. 398; St. J. B. 1961, p. 462; St. J. B. 1953, p. 470.
[3] Includes electricity generation and distribution. St. J. B. 1960, p. 463; St. J. B. 1958, p. 400.
[4] St. J. B. 1961, p. 484.

Inelastic demand for housing, for instance, seems to have been one of the main reasons for steep price increases in construction.

West Germany's postwar capital formation occurred in a climate of slowly rising prices. Whether this has favored capital formation or acted as a deterrent is a difficult question and no definite answer can be given. The rapidity of growth suggests that, on balance, this was not too serious a deterrent.

A first problem which arises in discussing the aggregates of West German capital formation is the distinction between gross and net investment. Some economists have pointed to net investment—defined as gross investment minus depreciation—as the crucial factor for economic expansion. The depreciation charges are supposedly used for reinvestment to keep the capital stock intact. Here the difficulties begin. As technological progress occurs, new capital goods are usually of a higher quality than those replaced. Thus a good deal of all "net" investment may be contained in replacements, a fact which is very important for capital formation in countries with a large but relatively old capital stock.[1] It is in these cases that "quality" matters more than "quantity." One may expect that in such countries capital consumption allowances, and their supposed counterpart in the form of replacements, constitute a high percentage of gross capital formation.

In West Germany there occurred a strong accumulation in the quantitative sense. However, underestimating the importance of the rejuvenation of West Germany's capital stock must be avoided. Immediately after the last war this capital stock had a rather unfavorable age structure.[2] This was true for both equipment and residential construction. Equipment had been used to

---

[1] The importance of fast replacement of obsolete plant and equipment in order to obtain the full benefit from improvements in technical knowledge is now widely recognized in the U.S. See: *Money and Credit,* The Report of the Commission on Money and Credit (Englewood Cliffs, N.J.: Prentice-Hall, 1961), p. 36.

[2] Rolf Krengel, Die Finanzierung der industriellen Expansion in der Bundesrepublik während der Jahre des Wiederaufbaus, p. 74 (Deutsches Institut für Wirtschaftsforschung, Sonderhefte No. 49, Berlin: Duncker und Humblot, 1960).

the utmost during the war, and there had been no great improvement in housing since the building boom in the '20's. In addition there were war losses. Total industrial capacities were still substantial at the time of the currency reform in 1948, but there existed severe gaps and bottlenecks, which became very restraining with higher levels of production. Reinvestment, under these circumstances, did a lot to improve productive facilities. Qualitative factors in capital formation, though difficult to judge, were of great importance to West Germany.

Since it is not easy to define net investment in a satisfactory way we shall therefore use the concept of gross investment for our analysis. This facilitates our task because West German statistics on investments in different industries, as well as on particular categories of investments (equipment, construction, etc.) usually refer to gross investment.[1]

At this point, a few capital output ratios for the total economy and for industry may be shown. The ratios, as given in Table 9, are marginal capital output ratios. Increases in production are assumed to be the result of investments made one year earlier. This is, of course, an oversimplification which ignores many important structural changes in capital stock, such as different gestation periods and introduction of new methods of production. Therefore it is necessary to look at the ratios with some reservations in mind. Still, these values appear indicative of an underlying trend in the West German economy. What they reveal is that future increases in the country's production will necessitate strong increases in investments. In the past, West Germany relied upon a high rate of capital formation, and apparently will have to follow this trend into the future. The low ratios for the initial years should not be deceiving. The years shortly after 1949 show that large increases in production were possible with relatively small investments, and that expansion

---

[1] For these subgroups consisting of equipment, residential construction, other construction, and inventory changes, no net investment figures are available. Capital consumption allowances are given in West German National Income Data as global values. Depreciation is broken down by business and government.

was largely due to an increased employment as idle labor was drawn into the production process. This was a period of readjustment. Later on, after about 1954, expansion became possible only through heavy investments. To raise resource ceilings, many basic investments were needed which very often did not immediately lead to large increases in production. During this second period output increases required much larger investments than before—a trend expected to continue. There are good reasons to believe that, if the present high rate of growth is to be sustained, an increasing part of the national product must be devoted to capital formation. With growing defense expenditures and consumers dreaming of a larger share of the total product, this problem has no easy answer.

TABLE 9

Marginal Capital Output Ratios for
West German Economy and Industry 1950 to 1960[1]

| Year | Gross Ratio[2] | Net Ratio inclusive changes in Inventories[3] | Net Ratio exclusive changes in Inventories[4] | Gross Ratio for Industry[5] |
|---|---|---|---|---|
| 1950 | 0.8 | 0.7 | 0.4 | 0.6 |
| 1951 | 2.1 | 1.8 | 0.8 | 0.8 |
| 1952 | 2.5 | 2.2 | 1.0 | 1.6 |
| 1953 | 3.0 | 2.5 | 1.2 | 1.4 |
| 1954 | 2.9 | 2.8 | 1.5 | 1.4 |
| 1955 | 2.0 | 1.9 | 1.1 | 0.8 |
| 1956 | 3.8 | 3.6 | 2.3 | 2.4 |
| 1957 | 4.6 | 4.7 | 3.0 | 2.5 |
| 1958 | 7.4 | 8.1 | 5.0 | n.a. |
| 1959 | 3.6 | 3.5 | 2.1 | n.a. |
| 1960 | 3.1 | 3.2 | 2.0 | n.a. |

[1] Calculated with 1954 constant prices. Investment is one period lagged.
[2] Annual increases in Gross National Product divided by Gross Domestic Investment of previous year.
[3] Annual increases in Net National Product divided by Net Domestic Investment, inclusive changes in inventories, of previous year.
[4] Annual increases in Net National Product divided by Net Domestic Investment, without inventories, of previous year.
[5] Industry without mining and electricity production. Annual increases in Production divided by Gross Investment in fixed assets of previous years. Investment figures according to an estimate by the Deutsches Institut für Wirtschaftsforschung Berlin, deflated to 1954 prices.

In what way were investments made between 1948 and 1960; what was the share going into equipment and into construction? Of total gross domestic investment, about 46% was in equipment of all kinds. The bulk of this went to business and only a small fraction to government.[1] By eliminating government purchases, investments in equipment made by West German business can be compared with those purchases made by business in the United States. Table 12 shows that West Germany has devoted a larger share of its gross private domestic investment to equipment than has the United States. The Germans in some years used more than 50% of all investable private funds for purchasing equipment. Information is not available on the sectors in which these investments were made, but it can be safely assumed that a large share went into highly competitive export goods industries.

Gross investment in construction amounted to 40% to 43% of gross domestic investment. Roughly one quarter of these construction investments were made by the government. From 1949 to 1956, it is known that 19% of gross domestic investment—not quite 50% of all construction—was residential construction. That this percentage did not change very much in later years is a safe assumption.

There remains for discussion, as part of gross domestic investment, changes in inventories. These have varied over the years depending on changes in business conditions. After the 1948 currency reform, business strongly desired normal inventories. Investments in these were high—well over 15% of gross domestic capital formation up to 1952. The Korean War caused additional stockpiling and, in 1951, increases in inventories reached an all-time high, 19.1% of gross domestic capital formation. Since then, this percentage has fallen considerably. It was 7% in 1958 and 7.3% in 1959. So far, there has been no year where changes in inventories were negative. West Germany not only rebuilt its physical plant, but today has at hand a sufficiently large stock of

---

[1] About 1% of gross domestic investment. Equipment bought by government is defined as "Beschaffung von beweglichem Vermögen."

TABLE 10

Structure of Gross Domestic Capital Formation,
1948 2d Half Year to 1960, Current Prices
Gross Domestic Capital Formation = 100[1]

*Gross Domestic Capital Formation*
*of which*

| Year | Total | Equip- ment | Resi- dential Construc- tion[2] | Other Construc- tion | Total Construc- tion 3 + 4 | Changes in Inven- tories |
|---|---|---|---|---|---|---|
| | (1) | (2) | (3) | (4) | (5) | (6) |
| 1948[2] 2.H.J. | 100 | n.a. | n.a. | n.a. | n.a. | 17.0 |
| 1949 | 100 | n.a. | 14.6 | n.a. | n.a. | 11.7 |
| 1950 | 100 | 42.9 | 16.4 | 24.2 | 40.6 | 16.9 |
| 1951 | 100 | 45.8 | 17.8 | 21.6 | 39.4 | 14.8 |
| 1952 | 100 | 45.1 | 17.5 | 19.7 | 37.2 | 17.8 |
| 1953 | 100 | 49.0 | 22.3 | 22.3 | 44.6 | 6.4 |
| 1954 | 100 | 48.2 | 22.6 | 20.1 | 42.7 | 9.4 |
| 1955 | 100 | 46.6 | 19.4 | 21.3 | 40.7 | 12.8 |
| 1956 | 100 | 48.1 | 20.1 | 23.1 | 43.2 | 8.7 |
| 1957 | 100 | 46.6 | n.a. | n.a. | 43.3 | 10.1 |
| 1958 | 100 | 47.7 | n.a. | n.a. | 45.3 | 7.0 |
| 1959 | 100 | 45.9 | n.a. | n.a. | 46.7 | 7.5 |
| 1960 | 100 | 45.8 | n.a. | n.a. | 45.7 | 8.5 |

[1] Calculated from Table 11.
[2] Calculated from "Investitionen und ERP Finanzierung," p. 119, Egon R. Baumgart,

raw materials, semi-finished, and finished products necessary for the smooth working of an expanding economy.

Domestic capital formation is not the total capital formation in an open economy such as West Germany's. Included in the total is capital formation on foreign account previously mentioned. This type of capital, arising from an excess of exports over imports, takes the form of claims against foreigners and must be viewed somewhat differently than domestic capital formation. Like domestic investments it requires domestic savings, but it does not directly increase production at home. How-

TABLE 10 (*cont.*)

| | Capital Consumption Allowance | | | Net Domestic Capital Formation | | |
|---|---|---|---|---|---|---|
| | Total 8 + 9 | by Business | by Gov't. | Total (1 − 7) | Assumed 20% of all Business depreciation to be Net Inv. | Assumed 40% of all business depreciation to be Net Inv. |
| | (7) | (8) | (9) | (10) | (11) | (12) |
| 1948[2] 2.H.J. | 35.2 | 31.8 | 3.4 | 64.8 | 71.1 | 77.5 |
| 1949 | 36.2 | 33.9 | 2.3 | 63.8 | 70.6 | 77.4 |
| 1950 | 46.1 | 44.3 | 1.8 | 53.9 | 62.7 | 71.5 |
| 1951 | 45.4 | 43.6 | 1.8 | 54.6 | 63.4 | 72.2 |
| 1952 | 42.2 | 40.3 | 1.9 | 57.8 | 65.8 | 73.8 |
| 1953 | 42.7 | 40.8 | 1.9 | 57.3 | 65.3 | 73.3 |
| 1954 | 37.5 | 35.8 | 1.7 | 62.5 | 69.7 | 76.9 |
| 1955 | 31.5 | 30.0 | 1.5 | 68.5 | 74.8 | 81.1 |
| 1956 | 33.7 | 32.3 | 1.4 | 66.3 | 72.8 | 79.3 |
| 1957 | 35.2 | 33.7 | 1.5 | 64.8 | 71.6 | 78.4 |
| 1958 | 36.8 | 35.3 | 1.5 | 63.2 | 70.2 | 77.2 |
| 1959 | 33.7 | 32.3 | 1.4 | 66.3 | 73.1 | 79.9 |
| 1960 | 31.6 | 30.3 | 1.3 | 68.4 | 74.7 | 81.0 |

Deutsches Institut für Wirtschaftsforschung Sonderhefte Nr. 56, Duncker und Humblot, Berlin 1961.

ever, it may make exports possible if these are based on credit, and thus there may be an indirect effect on domestic capital formation.

West Germany, as stated before, has had large export surpluses since 1951. During some years, these amounted to nearly $2 billion. The capital formation on foreign account, understood as an increase in claims against foreigners, was not quite as high as the export surpluses because West Germany made restitution payments to other countries and had to settle prewar debts. For instance, when West Germany had an export surplus of 8.7 bil-

TABLE 11

Components of Gross Domestic Capital Formation.
2nd Half Year 1948 to 1960. Current Prices. Billions of DM.[1]

| Year | Gross Domestic Capital Formation | Equipment | Residential Construction | Other Construction | Total Construction | Changes in Inventories | Capital Consumption Allowance | | | Net Domestic Capital Formation |
|---|---|---|---|---|---|---|---|---|---|---|
| | | | | | | | Total | by Gov't | by Business | |
| 1948 2.H.Y. | 8.8 | n.a. | n.a. | n.a. | n.a. | 1.5 | 3.1 | 0.3 | 2.8 | 5.7 |
| 1949 | 17.1 | n.a. | 2.5 | n.a. | n.a. | 2.0 | 6.2 | 0.4 | 5.8 | 10.9 |
| 1950 | 21.9 | 9.4 | 3.6 | 5.3 | 8.9 | 3.7 | 10.1 | 0.4 | 9.7 | 11.8 |
| 1951 | 26.4 | 12.1 | 4.7 | 5.7 | 10.4 | 3.9 | 12.0 | 0.5 | 11.5 | 14.4 |
| 1952 | 31.5 | 14.2 | 5.5 | 6.2 | 11.7 | 5.6 | 13.3 | 0.6 | 12.7 | 18.2 |
| 1953 | 31.4 | 15.4 | 7.0 | 7.0 | 14.0 | 2.0 | 13.4 | 0.6 | 12.8 | 18.0 |
| 1954 | 36.3 | 17.5 | 8.2 | 7.3 | 15.5 | 3.4 | 13.6 | 0.6 | 13.0 | 22.7 |
| 1955 | 47.0 | 21.9 | 9.1 | 10.0 | 19.1 | 6.0 | 14.8 | 0.7 | 14.1 | 32.2 |
| 1956 | 49.3 | 23.7 | 9.9 | 11.4 | 21.3 | 4.3 | 16.6 | 0.7 | 15.9 | 32.7 |
| 1957 | 52.0 | 24.2 | n.a. | n.a. | 22.5 | 5.3 | 18.3 | 0.8 | 17.5 | 33.7 |
| 1958 | 54.1 | 25.8 | n.a. | n.a. | 24.5 | 3.8 | 19.9 | 0.8 | 19.1 | 34.6 |
| 1959 | 61.7 | 28.3 | n.a. | n.a. | 28.8 | 4.6 | 20.8 | 0.9 | 19.9 | 40.9 |
| 1960 | 72.7 | 33.3 | n.a. | n.a. | 33.2 | 6.2 | 23.0 | 1.0 | 22.0 | 49.7 |

[1] St. J. B. 1952, p. 454.
St. J. B. 1953, p. 546.
St. J. B. 1960, p. 550.
St. J. B. 1961, p. 553.

TABLE 12

Gross Investment in Equipment as % of
Private Gross Domestic Investment in
West Germany and United States

| Year | West Germany[1] | U.S.A.[2] |
|------|-----------------|-----------|
| 1950 | 46.2 | 37.8 |
| 1953 | 54.2 | 44.4 |
| 1955 | 51.2 | 36.2 |
| 1958 | 51.7 | 32.4 |

[1] Business equipment as % of gross private domestic investment.
[2] Producers durable equipment as % of gross private domestic investment. United States Department of Commerce, *U.S. Income and Output 1957*, p. 119. *St. J. B.*, 1961, p. 147.

lion DM in 1957, transfers to other countries and to West Berlin amounted to 2.9 billion DM.[1] Thus, the increases in claims against foreigners was only 5.8 billion DM. Between 1950 and 1959, total net claims against foreigners rose by 37.2 billion DM, of which 2.8 billion DM were against West Berlin. West Germany has today substantial foreign exchange reserves which can contribute greatly to its own economic stability as well as to that of other countries.

The foregoing is an outline of West Germany's capital formation from 1948–1960. By world-wide standards, West German achievements present an impressive record. The next chapter will investigate what made this outstanding accumulation of capital possible.

---

[1] West Berlin is treated like a foreign country in West German statistics concerning capital formation.

# III. Sources of Savings for Capital Formation

CAPITAL FORMATION requires savings. From this basic fact there is no escape. A society can consume what it produces, precluding any capital formation and more efficient production. On the other hand, a country can consume less than it produces, leaving some resources for investments. These released resources constitute savings. The choice open to a society is between present consumption and capital formation. Capital formation in itself is, however, not an ultimate purpose. The expectation is that it will make possible greater future consumption. Therefore, the decision to save or not to save is, in essence, a question of consuming now or in the future. Since capital formation in developed countries is an essential vehicle for economic growth, a desire to enjoy high-level present consumption may therefore mean limited increases in future output and eventually lead to a stationary economy. On the other hand, a diversion of resources from consumption into investment may mean austerity at present but a rapid future growth.

The previous chapter indicated the great scope and significance of West Germany's capital formation. The question at hand is: from where did the necessary savings come; how were they obtained? To provide an overall picture, aggregate savings by economic sectors will be first discussed. Thanks to the pioneering work of Dr. H. Schlesinger and his collaborators of the

Deutsche Bundesbank in Frankfurt, it is now known what the different sectors of the economy—persons, business, government, and the social-security system—contributed to total savings. Many important insights can be gained from these sector savings, and they may be used as a starting point for this analysis. There are, of course, limitations. These aggregates, like those in National Income Accounts, are ex-post accounting values. As such they cannot reveal underlying causal relationships which are of greatest interest from the political, economic, and sociological point of view.

Gross and Net savings by economic sectors are shown in Table 13. To evaluate the aggregates, the sectors must be defined, and overlaps indicated.

The first sector comprises the savings of individuals but includes only the change in financial assets. Savings necessary for investments in tangible assets are excluded here. The largest item omitted is residential construction, but all other savings necessary for the acquisition of consumer durables are also missing. Tangible capital formed by individuals is included in the business sector. As a result, the net savings shown for individuals are too low, and those of business too high. Also, no depreciation allowances are made for assets owned by individuals. Capital consumption allowances for residential real estate are imputed to business. The division between the business sector and individual sector is thus not clearly defined. This causes considerable difficulties if, for instance, an item such as non-corporate retained earnings is to be classified. Whether these are business savings or individual savings is a matter of judgment.

The next sector contains the savings of the Social Security System. Included are sickness, unemployment, accident, and old age insurances. In addition, such special insurances as those for railroad employees are accounted for in this sector. The savings of the insurance system are defined as current receipts over current expenditures. Inter-insurance payments are eliminated. In this sector no adjustments are necessary to estimate savings.

The government sector includes the federal, state, and local government levels of West Germany, and the Equalization of

## TABLE 13

### Gross Investment and Gross Savings; 1948 2nd Half Year to 1960; Billions of DM.; Current Prices

| Year | Net Domestic Investment plus increase in claims against foreigners and West Berlin[1] (1) | Capital Consumption Allowance[2] (2) | Gross Capital Formation Total Economy (3) | Individual Net Savings[3] (4) | Social Security System Net Savings (5) |
|---|---|---|---|---|---|
| 1948 2.H.Y. | 5.7 | 3.1 | 8.8 | 2.0 | 0.1 |
| 1949 | 10.9 | 6.2 | 17.1 | 2.4 | 0.5 |
| 1950 | 12.0 | 10.1 | 22.1 | 2.0 | 1.2 |
| 1951 | 17.2 | 12.0 | 29.2 | 2.3 | 1.8 |
| 1952 | 21.0 | 13.3 | 34.3 | 4.3 | 1.7 |
| 1953 | 22.0 | 13.4 | 35.4 | 5.4 | 2.4 |
| 1954 | 26.3 | 13.6 | 39.9 | 6.7 | 2.8 |
| 1955 | 34.5 | 14.8 | 49.3 | 6.9 | 3.3 |
| 1956 | 37.2 | 16.6 | 53.8 | 7.0 | 3.7 |
| 1957 | 39.5 | 18.3 | 57.8 | 11.1 | 2.7 |
| 1958 | 40.2 | 19.9 | 60.1 | 12.8 | 2.1 |
| 1959 | 45.6 | 20.8 | 66.4 | 14.1 | 2.3 |
| 1960 | 53.6 | 23.0 | 76.6 | 14.8 | 3.3 |

[1] For 1948 and 1949 own estimate, for 1950 to 1957 Bundesbank, M. R. July 1960. p. 54; for 1958 to 1960 Bundesbank, M. B. June 1961. Due to rounding off, individual numbers may not add to total.
[2] See table 7, column 2.
[3] Net savings without transfers received, includes savings due to special tax-exemptions.

## TABLE 13 (cont.)

| Year | Government | | | Business | | | | | Gross Savings Total Economy |
|---|---|---|---|---|---|---|---|---|---|
| | Net Savings[4] | Depreciation[5] | Gross Savings | Corporate Retained Earnings[6] | Non Corporate Retained Earnings[8] | Total Net Savings | Depreciation[9] | Gross Savings[10] | |
| | (6) | (7) | (8) | (9) | (10) | (11) | (12) | (13) | (14) |
| 1948 2.H.Y. | 1.7 | 0.3 | 2.0 | n.a. | n.a. | 1.9 | 2.8 | 4.7 | 8.8 |
| 1949 | 3.3 | 0.4 | 3.7 | n.a. | n.a. | 4.7 | 5.8 | 10.5 | 17.1 |
| 1950 | 4.1 | 0.4 | 4.5 | 1.5 | 3.3 | 4.7 | 9.7 | 14.4 | 22.1 |
| 1951 | 5.5 | 0.5 | 6.0 | 1.1 | 6.3 | 7.5 | 11.5 | 19.0 | 29.2 |
| 1952 | 6.5 | 0.6 | 7.1 | 2.5 | 5.7 | 8.4 | 12.7 | 21.1 | 34.2 |
| 1953 | 8.3 | 0.6 | 8.9 | 2.6 | 3.0 | 5.8 | 12.8 | 18.6 | 35.4 |
| 1954 | 9.0 | 0.6 | 9.6 | 2.5 | 5.2 | 7.8 | 13.0 | 20.8 | 39.9 |
| 1955 | 10.7 | 0.7 | 11.4 | 3.9 | 9.6 | 13.6 | 14.1 | 27.7 | 49.3 |
| 1956 | 11.7 | 0.7 | 12.4 | 3.8 | 10.7 | 14.7 | 15.9 | 30.6 | 53.8 |
| 1957 | 11.8 | 0.8 | 12.6 | 4.1 | 9.8 | 14.0 | 17.5 | 31.5 | 57.8 |
| 1958 | 10.7 | 0.8 | 11.5 | 4.7 | 9.8 | 14.6 | 19.1 | 33.7 | 60.1 |
| 1959 | 13.6 | 0.9 | 14.5 | 5.2[7] | 9.9[7] | 15.6 | 19.9 | 35.5 | 66.4 |
| 1960 | 18.1 | 1.0 | 19.1 | n.a. | n.a. | 17.4 | 22.0 | 39.4 | 76.6 |

[4] Includes capital transfers to other countries and West Berlin.
[5] Wi. und Stat. Oct. 1960; St. J. B. 1961. p. 541.
[6] Corporate retained earnings after taxes, Wi. und Stat. October, 1960, p. 606.
[7] Preliminary value.
[8] Wi. and Stat. October, 1960, p. 606.
[9] Found as residual, includes depreciation of residential real estate. See also: St. J. B. 1961, p. 541.
[10] Includes savings due to special tax-exemptions.

Burden Fund. Receipts and expenditures at these four levels are consolidated, eliminating transfers between the various levels, which, under the German system of equalization of finances (Finanzausgleich), are quite large. Government savings are defined as an excess of current receipts over current expenditures. Included in government savings are a few smaller transfer items, such as funds for the acquisition of land, which should have been left out. Public enterprises and the state owned railway and postal systems are not included in the government sector. This is a shortcoming from the standpoint of this study because the government owns about 14% of all West German corporations.[1] There seems to be no reason why the savings of two large government-owned enterprises such as the railroad and postal systems are included in the business sector. Also included in the government sector are capital transfers to or from foreigners. When West Germany received foreign aid this augmented the savings of the government. When it transferred capital to other countries as reparation payments or in settlement of debt, savings decreased. As far as the indicated capital consumption allowances allocated to the government sector are concerned, they seem low. Official budget figures show reinvestment in fixed assets about 50% higher than those shown in Table 14.[2]

As a last aggregate, there remains the business sector. Considering the above discussion, savings of this sector are too large. This sector includes some savings made by both individuals and the government. Total business savings in the system of accounts developed by the Bundesbank were ascertained as a residual and are considered the least reliable. This is especially true for the savings of non-incorporated business.

Whatever the shortcomings of these four categories, they are not too serious for an analysis of private and public savings. If the business and individual sectors are consolidated as a private

---

[1] Gross investments of government enterprises were 1.35 billion DM in 1959. Since the currency reform, 8.24 billion DM have been invested. Bundesminister für Wirtschaftlichen Besitz des Bundes, "Der Bund als Unternehmer," p. 12, Bad Godesberg, 1960.

[2] *St. B. R. D.* Band 59, p. 39.

sector, part of the overlapping disappears. The Social Security System can be consolidated with the government sector as a public sector. Deducting one-half a billion DM from the values of gross savings for the early years in the private sector, and one billion DM in gross savings from the values for later years, and adding them to the public sector results in a fairly accurate estimate of where the savings originated.

Arranging data in this manner creates an interesting dichotomy between private and public contributions to West German capital formation. Since the currency reform in 1948, it appears that public authorities have directly supplied between one-third and one-half of all net savings, and between one-quarter and one-third of total gross savings. This, however, demands closer investigation.

First, how did it happen that such a large part of all investable funds were supplied by public authorities? Another equally important question is: will this public share remain constant, decline, or increase? Last, did the large part of investable funds supplied by public authorities facilitate or accelerate economic growth? This chapter is limited to answering the first question, postponing the others until later in this book. Since there were many different government influences, both direct and indirect on the supply of investable funds, it will be useful to examine each source of savings separately. We shall start with those savings which the West Germans would like to total the largest amount, namely individual savings.

a. *Individual Savings*

West German data on individual savings between 1950 and 1960 refers only to monetary savings. This data substantially underestimates total individual savings since the time span covers ten years in which households made large investments in durables and housing. Very little is known about this consumer capital formation in tangible assets. Therefore, the analysis must be limited to monetary savings, indicating what resources were made available by individuals for investments in other sectors of the economy.

## TABLE 14

### Components of Net Capital Formation: 1948 2nd Half Year to 1960; Billions of DM.; Current Prices

| Year | Net Domestic Capital Formation (1) | Capital Consumption Allowance | | | Gross Domestic Capital Formation | | | |
|---|---|---|---|---|---|---|---|---|
| | | Total[1] 3 + 4 (2) | of which by government[2] (3) | of which by business[3] (4) | Total 6 + 7 + 8 (5) | Equipment (6) | Building (7) | Change in Inventories (8) |
| 1948 2.H.J. | 5.7 | 3.1 | 0.3 | 2.8 | 8.8 | n.a. | n.a. | 1.5 |
| 1949 | 10.9 | 6.2 | 0.4 | 5.8 | 17.1 | n.a. | n.a. | 2.0 |
| 1950 | 11.8 | 10.1 | 0.4 | 9.7 | 21.9 | 9.4 | 8.9 | 3.7 |
| 1951 | 14.4 | 12.0 | 0.5 | 11.5 | 26.4 | 12.1 | 10.4 | 3.9 |
| 1952 | 18.2 | 13.3 | 0.6 | 12.7 | 31.5 | 14.2 | 11.7 | 5.6 |
| 1953 | 18.0 | 13.4 | 0.6 | 12.8 | 31.4 | 15.4 | 14.0 | 2.0 |
| 1954 | 22.7 | 13.6 | 0.6 | 13.0 | 36.3 | 17.5 | 15.5 | 3.4 |
| 1955 | 32.2 | 14.8 | 0.7 | 14.1 | 47.0 | 21.9 | 19.1 | 6.0 |
| 1956 | 32.7 | 16.6 | 0.7 | 15.9 | 49.3 | 23.7 | 21.3 | 4.3 |
| 1957 | 33.7 | 18.3 | 0.8 | 17.5 | 52.0 | 24.2 | 22.5 | 5.3 |
| 1958 | 34.2 | 19.9 | 0.8 | 19.1 | 54.1 | 25.8 | 24.5 | 3.8 |
| 1959 | 40.9 | 20.8 | 0.9 | 19.9 | 61.7 | 28.3 | 28.8 | 4.6 |
| 1960 | 49.7 | 23.0 | 1.0 | 22.0 | 72.7 | 33.3 | 33.2 | 6.2 |

[1] St. J. B., 1952 p. 454; St. J. B., 1953 p. 546; St. J. B., 1960 p. 542; St. J. B., 1961 p. 544.
[2] For 1948, 1949 and 1960 own estimate, for other years Wi. und Stat. October 1960; Wi. und Stat. October 1961. The values given seem to be on the low side.
[3] Found as residual, includes residential construction.

## TABLE 14 (*cont.*)

| Year | Balance on Foreign Account—exports minus imports[4] | Transfer to foreigners and West Berlin[5] | Increase in claims against foreigners and West Berlin | Total Gross Capital Formation = Gross Savings $5+9$ | Total Net Capital Formation[6] $=1+11$ |
|---|---|---|---|---|---|
| | (9) | (10) | (11) | (12) | (13) |
| 1948 2.H.J. | -1.2 | n.a. | n.a. | 7.6 | 5.7[7] |
| 1949 | -2.6 | n.a. | n.a. | 14.5 | 10.9[7] |
| 1950 | -1.2 | 1.5 | 0.3 | 20.7 | 12.1 |
| 1951 | 2.3 | 0.8 | 3.1 | 28.7 | 17.5 |
| 1952 | 3.4 | -0.6 | 2.8 | 34.9 | 21.0 |
| 1953 | 5.5 | -1.5 | 4.0 | 36.9 | 22.0 |
| 1954 | 5.3 | -1.7 | 3.6 | 41.6 | 26.3 |
| 1955 | 4.2 | -1.9 | 2.3 | 51.2 | 34.5 |
| 1956 | 6.6 | -2.2 | 4.4 | 55.9 | 37.1 |
| 1957 | 8.7 | -2.8 | 5.9 | 60.7 | 39.6 |
| 1958 | 8.8 | -2.9 | 5.9 | 62.9 | 40.1 |
| 1959 | 8.5 | -3.6 | 4.9 | 70.2 | 45.8 |
| 1960 | 7.4 | -3.5 | 3.9 | 80.1 | 53.6 |

[4] For 1948 own estimate, for 1949 estimated from St. J. B. 1953, p. 550/555. For other years, St. J. B. 1960, p. 551, St. J. B. 1961, p. 554.

[5] For 1948 and 1949 assumed that there were no transfers. For other years, see Bundesbank M. R. November 1957, June 1958. All values given here were found as residual. Minus sign indicates a net transfer to foreigners and West Berlin.

[6] These values agree with those given by the Bundesbank M. R. July 1960 and June 1961. The only difference seems to lie in the estimate for changes in inventory; for 1951 the Bundesbank gives these as 3.6 billion DM. whereas the Statistische Bundesamt shows 3.9 Billion DM.

[7] Assumes complete offset of foreign trade balance by transfers to West Germany.

There seems to be a long-run trend towards a relative decline in individual savings as a source of investments. This is observed in the German economy as well as in many Western economies, and a number of reasons can be given for this. Some explanations are of a behavioristic nature, others institutional.

Disposable personal incomes in developed Western economies have generally risen strongly during the last decades, and there should have been greater savings. Higher incomes should have meant a greater ability to save; but there was also a desire for a higher level of consumption, thus reducing the potential for individual savings. Also, during this period some traditionally strong incentives for individual savings diminished. The emergence of a comprehensive Social Security System and of pension funds, to which employees as well as employers contributed, partly eliminated the need to save for old age. Other insurances, such as sickness, accident, and fire decreased the need for personal savings to meet emergencies. There were still other influences causing changes. A few decades ago most purchases were made with cash. Today, credit facilities make it possible to acquire consumer durables and real estate with relatively small initial savings.

Taxation should also be mentioned in this context. Higher income groups, which had always been strong savers, because of income taxes, now often prefer to accumulate capital in the form of corporate retained earnings and unrealized capital gains instead of other forms of savings. Finally, inflationary trends prevailing in many economies during the last decades, may have acted as a deterrent to large monetary savings by the individual.

West Germany experienced very much the same development in individual savings as other countries. Between 1936 and 1938, individual savings accounted for 42.5% of all net savings.[1] After the 1948 currency reform, this figure had dropped by 1951 to a record low of 13.4%. In addition to the general long-run factors enumerated above, there were a few very specific factors which strongly tended to decrease individual savings.

Germany had a hyperinflation in 1923 which wiped out most

---

[1] Wi. und Stat., 1952, p. 401, 402.

monetary savings. This left bitter memories. Another harsh currency reform came in 1948 which severely—and one may say, unnecessarily—punished savers, especially small savers. These experiences caused many people to believe that the riskiest assets were monetary, an important psychological factor influencing savings behavior.

Low real income in the first years after the 1948 currency reform was most responsible for the small amount of savings.[1] Added to this was a need to replenish household implements, following a period of ten years when this was nearly impossible. As a result, the personal savings volume was far from sufficient and could not be relied upon for the huge amount of capital formation needed. Later on, due to rising incomes after 1956, individual savings increased both absolutely and relative to other sources of savings. In 1958, individual savings amounted to more than 31% of total net savings, but they dropped in 1960 to 27.7%. This was still well below the prewar level.

Monetary savings by individuals in West Germany essentially took four forms: first, savings in banks; second, payments made to building associations; third, premiums paid to insurances; and fourth, the acquisition of securities. Since 1950 there had been large shifts between these categories because of changes in individual preferences over the form in which to hold financial assets.

Initially, the bulk of all individual savings after 1948 was held in the form of bank deposits. In later years, these increased absolutely but declined relative to other forms of savings. There were increases in the relative shares of savings in building associations and in purchases of securities. Savings in insurance companies, however, remained relatively constant.

Two tentative conclusions can be drawn from these developments. One is that individual savers in West Germany increasingly preferred to save for a purpose. The other is that, with the broadening of West Germany's security markets and the ready availability of all sorts of financial assets tailored for small in-

[1] B. Gleitze, "Die Lohnpolitische Situation" article in *Konjunkturpolitik,* 1957, p. 10.

TABLE 15

Components of Individual Savings.
1948. 2nd Half Year 1960. Billions of DM.[1]

| Year | Savings[2] in Banks Net | Payments[3] to Building Associations | Insurance[4] Premiums | Purchase of Securities | Total[5] |
|---|---|---|---|---|---|
|  | (1) | (2) | (3) | (4) | (5) |
| 1948 2.H.Y. | n.a. | n.a. | n.a. | n.a. | 2.0 |
| 1949 | n.a. | n.a. | n.a. | n.a. | 2.4 |
| 1950 | 1.1 | 0.4 | 0.5 | .0 | 2.0 |
| 1951 | 1.4 | 0.3 | 0.6 | .0 | 2.3 |
| 1952 | 3.2 | 0.5 | 0.7 | 0.2 | 4.4 |
| 1953 | 4.2 | 0.9 | 0.8 | 0.3 | 6.1 |
| 1954 | 5.0 | 1.3 | 1.0 | 0.7 | 8.0 |
| 1955 | 3.9 | 1.6 | 1.2 | 0.7 | 7.4 |
| 1956 | 3.4 | 2.0 | 1.3 | 0.7 | 7.4 |
| 1957 | 6.2 | 2.6 | 1.5 | 1.2 | 11.4 |
| 1958 | 7.1 | 3.1 | 1.6 | 1.8 | 13.5 |
| 1959 | 6.8 | 3.8 | 2.2 | 2.3 | 15.2 |
| 1960 | 7.2 | 4.6 | 2.4 | 2.5 | 16.7 |

[1] Bundesbank, M. R. July 1960, p. 64. June 1961, Rounded values. For 1948 and 1949, own estimate.
[2] Includes demand deposits, time deposits, and other credits to banks. Deducted are credits from banks and consumer credits.
[3] Deposits in Bausparkassen, include from 1953 on, premiums paid by government. M. R. Bundesbank, August 1960, p. 6.
[4] Includes pension funds.
[5] Includes transfers. Values shown are therefore higher than those in Table 13, Column 4.

vestors, individual savers preferred to buy bonds or shares. The general trend during the last decade has been into less liquid but higher yield assets.

The bulk of all deposits held by individuals in banks consisted of savings deposits. Annual increases in these ranged from 1 billion DM in 1950 to nearly 7.0 billion DM in 1959. For a large part of the population—especially for low and medium income brackets[1]—the traditional form of savings is in savings accounts.

[1] Heinz Osthues, *Einkommensverhältnisse und private Geldkapitalbildung in Westdeutschland, 1925–1953* (Berlin: Duncker und Humblot, 1957), p. 112. W. D. Becker, "Das Kontensparen im Spiegel der sozialen Stellung," *Sparkasse*, 15, November 1961, p. 347.

Nowadays business and public authorities also keep some funds in savings accounts.

There is no information available concerning the income brackets to which owners of savings deposits belong. The average amount saved per account has always been relatively low. In 1930, the average was 645 RM but it was only 294 DM in 1952.[1] Since then the amount has risen to 940 DM in 1959. In the same year 57% of all savers were employees.

Various kinds of banks receive savings depsoits, but the largest share goes to the savings banks (Sparkassen). These belong to a national system which has its own clearing houses and maintains a dense network of offices throughout West Germany. Savings banks in West Germany—unlike savings and loan associations in the United States—do the same kind of business as commercial banks, though their asset structure is somewhat different from the latter. Traditionally, savings banks have supplied funds for local needs, and their preferred field here has been residential real estate. Savings deposits in West Germany are the main source for long-term loans by banks. For some time monetary authorities in West Germany were concerned with the possibility that a concentration of individual savings in savings banks might interfere with an efficient use of investable funds because of the trend in the past toward local lending. Authorities wanted, rather, to see a larger flow of these savings into security markets. For a long time, the established savings behavior and, to some extent, the vested interest of savings banks were against this policy.

The catastrophic housing situation after World War II and the need for financing large scale residential construction accounts for the boom of the building associations (Bausparkassen). These received a mere 73 million RM as in-payments in 1938, but increases were rapid after the war: in 1953, 991 million DM; in 1957, 2.6 billion DM; and in 1960, 4.6 billion DM were listed by the Bundesbank as contributions to these associations.[2] Between

[1] Osthues, *op. cit.*, p. 147. It is not clear whether this refers to the area of the F.R. or to the Reich.

[2] M. R., August 1960, p. 6.

1950 and 1960, 21.1 billion DM were saved in this way, and a large part of the new residential construction was financed with these funds.

Savings in insurances have risen from 1 billion DM in 1950 to nearly 2.5 billion DM in 1960. A large part of these savings are made through life insurance premiums. Life insurance seems to have become more accepted in Germany, though rather slowly. Only 1 person in 1000 had life insurance in 1850; in 1952, in the F.R., the figure was 1 in 568.[1] One of the reasons that life insurance as savings for old age has remained relatively unimportant is probably because social insurance is more comprehensive in West Germany than in many other Western countries. In the '50s, about 84.3% of the salaried employees and 99.6% of the workers were covered under obligatory old-age programs. Life insurance is usually purchased only by high-income salaried employees or self-employed persons not obligated to join the Social Security System. To indicate the income brackets to which persons belong who buy life insurance is difficult. Since 1930, the purchases of life insurance by workers (in West Germany the lower income bracket) did increase somewhat.[2]

The last form of individual savings is purchases of securities. Such savings were negligible until 1951 but they increased later on. In 1957, sales of securities to individuals passed the 1 billion DM level, and in 1960 they reached 2.5 billion DM. Still, securities purchases by private persons constitute only a small fraction of the total security sales. The amount of fixed interest securities sold in 1959 was 10 billion DM. Another 1.3 billion DM was sold in shares. Of this, the largest part, more than 8.4 billion DM, was bought by credit institutes and public authorities. It is true that part of the securities were resold and may have ended up in the portfolios of individuals. However, the share of private purchases, direct and indirect, has probably not exceeded 22% of all securities sold.

All of this is indicative of profound changes in the pattern of

---

1 Osthues, *op. cit.*, p. 133.
2 For developments since 1948, see M. R. Bundesbank, June 1958, p. 53.

investment financing during the last decades. There have been considerable shifts between the groups supplying funds for the security markets in Germany, as well as in other Western countries. A few figures may be cited. In 1913, 83.6% of all securities were owned by individual investors. This declined somewhat after World War I. Yet, 70% was still possessed by individuals in 1932.[1] On the average, from 1926 to 1928 more than 35% of all monetary savings took the form of purchases of securities and the percentage was not very much lower shortly before World War II.[2] Things changed drastically after 1948. In the early 1950's, security purchases were only a fraction of total monetary savings. They amounted to 4.5% of all personal savings in 1952, but climbed to 15.1% in 1959. It can be safely concluded that individual investors as suppliers of funds for security markets have lost their former importance in West Germany. Their place has been taken by institutional investors and public authorities, and there will probably be no comeback.

b. *Public Policy Measures and Individual Savings*

During the last decade, the bulk of all savings for capital formation in West Germany was accumulated by business and government, with individuals contributing only about 20%. This pattern of financing was viewed by West German officials as inevitable under the prevailing conditions, but they were never happy about it. There was a fear that this could lead to strong concentrations of economic power in business and government. It was felt that such concentration could easily become a reason for political efforts to redistribute income and property.[3] Concern over the low percentage in individual savings brought to the foreground the question of equable participation in the West

---

[1] Heinrich Strathuis, "Die Kapitalmarktpolitik gestern und heute," *Volkswirt*, Sonderheft "Wertpapier und Sparer," n.d., p. 4.

[2] This figure is taken from a paper by the Kreditanstalt für Wiederaufbau, "Kapitalmarkt und Investitionsfinanzierung in der Bundesrepublik," Dec. 28, 1953, Frankfurt, Table 2. 43.3% are shown for 1926/28 and 39.7% for 1936/38.

[3] Der Bundesminister für Wirtschaft, *Sonderhefte zum Bericht über die wirtschaftliche Lage in der Bundesrepublik*, Heft 3, Bonn, Feb., 1957.

German capital formation. This important problem will be discussed in detail later, but the attention of the reader should be drawn to it at this time since recognition of this situation helps to explain why public authorities tried to boost individual savings.

Measures designed to increase individual savings varied. They can be classified in two broad groups: measures to increase willingness to save; and measures to increase the ability to save. The majority of all measures belonged to the first group. West German policy makers devoted much more attention to the question of how a given income would be divided between consumption and savings than to how the height of income influences the ability to save. Only recently have there been timid legislative measures acknowledging the importance of income for savings, and, more specifically, the inadequate income of employees.[1]

An opinion widely held in West Germany is that high incentives generate savings. From what has been written on this subject, it is necessary to infer that savings were believed to be determined mainly by the rate of interest—though it is difficult to detect to which degree savings were supposed to be interest elastic. Many policy measures geared to induce savings aimed at increases—in the rate of interest—that is, the effective rate of interest, not necessarily the nominal one.

Before discussing this, another factor bearing on savings incentives should be mentioned. Constant emphasis on a high degree of price level stability was considered an absolute requirement if personal savings were to be forthcoming. The argument was that the catastrophic experience of the two hyperinflations within 25 years had made Germans very suspicious of even slight inflationary trends which could erode the real value of savings. A monetary policy aimed primarily at price level stability would make an outstanding contribution to capital formation by strengthening the confidence of savers, thus inducing larger savings. Examining the facts, one begins to doubt the validity of this assertion. There is no doubt that hyperinflations, such as Ger-

---

1 "Gesetz zur Förderung der Vermögensbildung der Arbeitnehmer," vom 12 Juli, 1961, *Bundesgesetzblatt*, July 18, 1961.

many experienced after two World Wars, are thoroughly disruptive to any kind of savings. Confusing such major disasters with the price increases most countries, including West Germany, experienced during the 1950's is, however, unrealistic. The record shows that personal savings have, since 1949, risen rapidly with increases in disposable personal income. People saved when their incomes were high enough to permit it. At the same time, there is no evidence that price increases during the last decade inhibited personal savings. Between 1950 and 1952, price levels rose by about 16.5%.[1] Total annual personal savings rose in the same time from 2.0 billion DM to 4.4 billion DM. During the years 1952 to 1954, years in which prices remained nearly constant, savings increased to 8.0 billion DM annually. Since 1955, the price level has again risen by 3% to 4% annually but savings continued to increase between 1.5 billion DM to 4.0 billion DM annually, amounting to 16.7 billion DM in 1960. This is far from suggesting that price increases actually induced personal savings, but it seems reasonable to point out that the West German saver did not pay too much attention to "creeping inflation." Price increases or no price increases, he saved. What contribution the pursued monetary policy actually made in maintaining price level stability and inducing a high level of personal savings during the last decade is indeed very difficult to assess.

High interest rates can normally be expected when investable funds are scarce. A look at the nominal interest rates paid on savings deposits in West Germany between September 1948, and July 1954, reveals, however, that this was not the case. Nominal interest rates were between 3% and 4%, which cannot be considered exceptionally high. Banks would have been willing to pay higher nominal rates on savings deposits, but under the West German law they were not free to do so. Since banks were faced with a brisk demand for investable funds, and could charge 10% to 14% on loans, they welcomed any new savings. Therefore, to induce savings efforts were made to raise the effective rate of interest—effective rate understood here as the rate of interest after taxes.

---

[1] This refers to the price index implicit in G.N.P.

A question may be asked at this point. If it is believed that a higher effective interest rate would have actually generated a larger amount of savings, why not raise the nominal interest rate? There were a number of reasons for not doing this after 1948, most of them related to the problem of the cost of long-term investable funds and in particular those available in the capital market.

Savings deposits are part of the capital market, but in West Germany, for institutional reasons, they have always been separated. In referring to the capital market what are usually talked about are the security markets. There were close relationships between savings deposits and certain types of securities. In many cases these two financial assets were substitutes, though not perfect ones. In West Germany nominal interests paid on savings deposits and securities were tightly, though not rigidly, linked through a law dating back to the '30's, the so-called "Habenzinsabkommen" (agreement on interest to be paid on deposits).[1] Thus savings deposits competed to a considerable extent with securities, and savings banks kept an eye on the interest rates paid on securities. They made sure that the rates of return compared favorably. Interest on savings deposits depended greatly on the rates prevailing in security markets, which makes it necessary to investigate developments in the latter area.

In the early years after the currency reform the supply of long-term investable funds for security markets was highly inadequate. This was partly due to low savings and partly also to a failure of financial intermediaries with various opportunities for highly lucrative loans to channel available long-term funds into these markets. The capital market funds were rationed. To prevent too many demands for the few funds available, a special committee was set up which decided how many and what types of securities should be offered.[2] This was in accordance with a pro-

---

[1] *Reichs-Anzeiger* No. 126, May 29, 1943, and No. 299, December 22, 1936. This agreement originally intended to avoid ruinous competition between banks for deposits. Lately it has been considered a severe obstacle to efforts broadening the money and capital market.

[2] Kapitalverkehrs-Gesetz, November 2, 1949.

vision of the Marshall Plan which requested that capital market funds be used only for approved purposes. Distribution of funds was especially managed as far as sectors of the economy were concerned where investments were vital but where there was no possibility of obtaining investable funds from other sources, or where the particular sectors were unable to pay high credit cost. Such sectors were residential construction, the Federal Railway, and some basic industries.

The nominal interest rates in security markets were 6% to 6.5% in 1948–49. Low capital market rates—and they were low compared with bank rates—were a result of an attempt by the government to supply some crucial sectors of the economy with low cost investable funds. Consequently, a gap appeared in the interest rate structure. Low rates in the capital market existed simultaneously with high bank rates. Some funds were available at low capital market rates. These were savings deposits which were made irrespective of the level of the rate of interest, and public funds available for security purchases. Banks profited from the first, and a few interest-sensitive sectors got the benefit of the latter. Artificially low interest rates in security markets contributed, however, to the absence of large private investable funds. With the existing income tax rates, after-tax yields of securities were too low and out of line with the return of capital in business. To overcome this handicap, effective security yields had to rise, but the authorities did not wish to raise the low nominal rates. In this situation the government resorted to tax incentives.

Paragraph 10 of the German personal income tax law allowed for certain deductions for savings made by individuals in the form of payments to insurances and building associations.[1] These were considered socially desirable and received preferred tax treatment. The categories of tax exempt savings after 1949 were considerably broadened and, among others, tax-free savings deposits were introduced. Anyone wishing to make use of the

---

[1] Deductions for insurance payments were permitted in the German Income Tax Law of 1925. Deductions for contributions to building associations have been permitted since 1934.

exemption provision could make a contract with an institutional investor stipulated for this purpose—in most cases commercial or savings banks. It should be mentioned, however, that under German law only natural citizens could benefit from this. An individual would promise to pay at once, or in intervals, certain amounts into blocked savings accounts. The amounts saved were tax deductible. This same privilege was granted when stipulated kinds of fixed interest securities were bought.[1] Some limitations were, however, placed on the amount of savings, either savings deposits, contributions to insurances and building associations, or purchases of securities which would be tax-free.[2] Between 1951 and 1954, these limits were 800 DM for a husband and 400 DM for his wife and each child. In addition, an amount not exceeding 15% of total income could be claimed as a special tax-free exemption if any of the aforementioned types of savings were made. A married man with two children and 100,000 DM income could thus place 17,000 DM in tax-deductible savings. These amounts were strongly reduced beginning with 1955, and the same man could then only claim 3750 DM as tax-deductible. The exact provisions were very complicated. They took into account the age of the saver and the time intervals within which payments were to be made. Banks published small booklets in which experts explained the tax saving possibilities under this particular paragraph of the income tax law.[3]

No precise information exists concerning the amounts deducted for various kinds of tax-free savings. A total of 669 million DM was deducted by persons liable under the personal income tax in 1950.[4] Not included in this amount are deductions made by persons paying the wage tax (Lohnsteuer) who were also entitled to use these tax-saving possibilities. The total

---

1 The essential legal provisions for these tax favored capital accumulation agreements can be found in: *E. St. G.* para. 10 Abs. 1, No. 2 d. (1951–1954); *E. St. G.* para. 10 Abs. 1, No. 4 (1955–58); *E. St. G.* 52 (1956–58); and *E. St. D. V.* 25 (1951–54).

2 Property taxes, church taxes, interest, and rents paid could also be deducted under the same paragraph.

3 Rhein-Main-Bank, "Steuerersparnis durch steuerbegünstigtes Sparen," 1952, 1953 (paperbound, place of publication not indicated).

4 *St. B. R. D.*, Band 125, p. 39, Table 21.

amount deducted under the personal income tax as well as wage tax was estimated as 800 million DM to 1 billion DM in 1950. Tax-free savings deposits amounted in that year to 188.3 million DM. Total payments to building associations amounted to 400 million DM and payments to insurance companies totaled 500 million DM. It is not known what tax deductions were claimed for these two categories of tax-favored savings. Security purchases and tax deductions for these were negligible and probably not higher than 20 million DM.[1] Total deductions have risen in later years, and though no direct data on this are available estimates indicate that between 1.5 billion DM and 1.7 billion DM were deducted annually after 1954.

It is not known to what income brackets these savers belonged. The available distributions[2] by income brackets of tax exemptions under the aforementioned paragraph of the tax law covers persons liable under the personal income tax only. Also included here are tax exemptions for paid property taxes, church taxes, and other items. Still, there is a clue as to which income brackets benefited from these tax exemptions.

About 15% of all deductions were made by taxpayers with less than 3,000 DM annual income in 1950. On the other hand, taxpayers in income brackets over 25,000 DM accounted for 22.2%. On the average, 735 DM were deducted. The average amounts deducted in each bracket were, however, vastly different. In the bracket under 1,500 DM income, deductions were a mere 298 DM, whereas for income over 100,000 DM, deductions reached 17,356 DM.

Little direct information is available about the budget losses caused through these deductions. The Bundesfinanzmisterium in Bonn has made an estimate for budget losses through deductions for payments to building associations, which is shown in Table 17. Rough estimates can be made from this table on the total budget losses. These must have been about 350 million DM in 1950, 550 million DM in 1954, and perhaps 700 million DM in 1957.

[1] See Table 15.
[2] *St. B. R. D.,* Band 125, p. 38, Table 20; *St. J. B.,* 1958, p. 385.

# TABLE 16

## Tax-Favored Savings Deposits, Fixed Interest Securities, and Premiums for Savings in Building Associations 1949 to 1960, millions of DM

| Year | Total[1] Savings Deposits | Increase In — In Savings[1] Banks | Increase In — Tax Exempt[2] Savings Deposits | Increase In — Savings[2] Deposits with Premiums | Tax Exempt Securities — Total[2] |
|---|---|---|---|---|---|
| | (1) | (2) | (3) | (4) | (5) |
| 1949 | 1500 | 900 | 89 | — | n.a. |
| 1950 | 1000 | 700 | 188 | — | n.a. |
| 1951 | 1000 | 600 | 331 | — | n.a. |
| 1952 | 2500 | 1500 | 355 | — | n.a. |
| 1953 | 3900 | 2400 | 550 | — | 2435 |
| 1954 | 5700 | 3400 | 771 | — | 3358 |
| 1955 | 4200 | 2900 | 206 | — | 354 |
| 1956 | 2900 | 2000 | 392 | — | 18 |
| 1957 | 5000 | 3100 | 868 | — | 1 |
| 1958 | 6800 | 4200 | 871 | — | n.a. |
| 1959 | 8100 | 5100 | −112 | 557 | — |
| 1960 | 7800 | 5700 | −835 | 848 | — |

[1] St. H.B. BDL., p. 128; Bundesbank, M.R. June 1961.
[2] BDL. M.R. and Bundesbank M.R. various numbers.

TABLE 16 (cont.)

| Year | Tax Exempt Securities | Tax Favored Securities | | Savings in Building Associations | |
|---|---|---|---|---|---|
| | Estimated[3] amount purchased by Persons | Total[2] | Estimated[3] amount Purchased by Persons | Total[4] | Of which: Premiums Paid[5] to Savers in Building Associations |
| | (6) | (7) | (8) | (9) | (10) |
| 1949 | n.a. | n.a. | n.a. | n.a. | — |
| 1950 | n.a. | n.a. | n.a. | 400 | — |
| 1951 | n.a. | n.a. | n.a. | 300 | — |
| 1952 | n.a. | n.a. | n.a. | 500 | — |
| 1953 | 244 | 466 | 47 | 900 | 27 |
| 1954 | 235 | 1332 | 93 | 1300 | 66 |
| 1955 | 14 | 647 | 27 | 1600 | 129 |
| 1956 | 2 | 10 | 1 | 2000 | 183 |
| 1957 | — | 8 | 1 | 2600 | 225 |
| 1958 | — | n.a. | — | 3100 | 283 |
| 1959 | — | — | — | 3800 | 307 |
| 1960 | — | — | — | 4600 | n.a. |

[3] Estimate based on total security purchases by individuals. St. H.B. BDL., p. 234.
[4] See Table 15. Column 2.
[5] Finanzbericht 1961, p. 116, Bundesministerium der Finanzen; Bonn. M.R. Bundesbank, August 1960, p. 6.

There have been extended discussions in West Germany over the desirability of tax exemptions to increase personal savings.[1] How effective were tax exemptions and what were their shortcomings? To evaluate this, the purpose for which deductions were granted has to be studied. What was needed was a larger supply of long-term investable funds obtained through a voluntary reduction of consumption. Given this, the first question which arises is whether tax exemptions should have been granted for funds obtained through a liquidation or reshuffling of existing assets.[2] Possibly the second should have been excluded, because asset transfers do not increase resources available for investments. There may have been some fear that such transfers could lead to increased consumption or non-essential investments. To prevent this, a price had to be paid. If, on the other hand, it was reasonably safe to assume that these results would not have occurred, it was a waste of public means to exempt from taxes "savings" made with such funds. Experience shows that in many cases savers did obtain tax benefits through asset transfers, e.g., by shifting funds from a normal savings account to a tax-favored account. There was little or no control over this. The law makers were evidently aware of abuses and tried to forestall those which were excessive. For example, it was forbidden to take a bank loan in order to open a tax-exempt savings account or to buy tax-exempt securities.[3] This provision was very difficult to enforce and perhaps it was not even necessary. To take out a loan in order to increase tax exempt savings could have been, with the prevailing high bank rates, lucrative only for upper income brackets. For the latter it was possible, however, to make much larger tax savings in other ways. Still there was the opportunity—and it was made use of in some cases—to make a handsome profit

---

1 *Jahresbericht 1954*, Deutscher Sparkassen und Giroverband, e. V., Bonn, p. 9; *Sparkasse*, Heft 22, Deutscher Sparkassen und Giroverband, e. V., Bonn, 1957, "Förderung der freien Kapitalbildung durch den Staat"; *Handelsblatt* 12, 1957, No. 2, p. 5, "Im Wirwarr von Zinsen und Steuern"; *Industriekurier*, 10, 1957, No. 192, p. 2, "Problematik des Steuerbegünstigten Sparens."

2 In West Germany, tax exemptions were granted for both.

3 Except for the time from January 1, 1955 to June 10, 1956.

by claiming tax exemptions for savings and deducting the interest on bank loans as a business cost.

### TABLE 17

Tax Deductions by Persons under Capital Accumulation Agreements. Estimated Budget Losses through Deductions by Savers in Building Associations 1949 to 1959. Millions of DM.

| Year | Deductions | | Budget Losses | |
|---|---|---|---|---|
| | for Tax-exempt[1] Savings Deposits | Total[2] | through deductions made by Savers in Building Associations[3] | Total[4] |
| | (1) | (2) | (3) | (4) |
| 1949 | 89 | 500 | 90 | 200 |
| 1950 | 188 | 800 | 165 | 280 |
| 1951 | 331 | 940 | 145 | 250 |
| 1952 | 355 | 1160 | 175 | 300 |
| 1953 | 550 | 1250 | 215 | 320 |
| 1954 | 771 | 1500 | 250 | 370 |
| 1955 | 206 | 1500 | 270 | 370 |
| 1956 | 392 | 1700 | 275 | 400 |
| 1957 | 868 | 1500 | 320 | 420 |
| 1958 | 371 | | 285 | |
| 1959 | | | 345 | |
| Total 1949–1957 | 3750 | 10850 | 1905 | 2910 |

[1] M.R. BDL. and M.R. Bundesbank, various numbers.
[2] Estimate by experts of Bundesfinanzministerium, Bonn.
[3] Finanzbericht 1961, p. 116 Bundesminister der Finanzen, Bonn.
[4] Own estimate.

This leads us now to the crucial question. What additional savings were actually generated through the tax measures? The answer will be found by investigating the different kinds of individual savings.

Two categories were, in all likelihood, very little influenced by these tax benefits: savings in insurance companies and building associations. The people who made these kinds of savings were induced to do so by considerations such as the desirability to secure a family's future through life insurance or to own a home. These in themselves were strong incentives to save. For these kinds of savings the effects of tax measures to generate additional savings were probably only marginal.

A third category of individual savings took the form of security purchases. As stated previously the volume of securities sold to individuals after the last war was very small. The bulk of all security purchases was made by credit institutions and the government. Given a general disinclination of private investors to buy securities, it seems unlikely that tax exemptions did much to increase sales to individuals. These tax measures certainly could not and did not end the chronic shortage of investable funds in security markets.[1] It should be noted that, beginning with 1955, personal deductions in the West German income tax law were sharply curtailed. Investors in higher income brackets who held fixed interest securities could take extensive advantage of tax exemptions under paragraph 10 only until the end of 1954. Large increases in security purchases by individuals occurred, however, only after 1955. The obvious reason for this is that personal incomes had not risen enough to make these purchases possible until after 1955.

Whether tax exemptions induced people to make additional savings in savings accounts is difficult to say. There are sound reasons for doubting this. Between 60% and 70% of all savings deposits were made in savings banks. The majority of the savers in these banks were employees and belonged to lower income brackets with low marginal income tax rates. Tax exemptions had no great interest for such people, but they were attractive for recipients of higher incomes. Though no data is available concerning the income brackets of holders of savings deposits, who the depositors were can be guessed at from the kind of banks where tax exempt savings were made. Usually customers of the so-called "Big Banks" (large commercial banks) and the private banks do not belong to low income brackets. In these banks, 40% of all savings deposits were tax-exempt. In savings banks where

---

[1] Much more effective were other tax incentives which were of interest to banks as the main buyers of securities. These incentives were created in 1952 with the "Law to Favor the Capital Market."

the German in the lower income brackets deposited his savings, 91% of all deposits were made without the benefit of tax incentives.[1]

The reason that higher income brackets became strongly interested in these tax-exempt savings is easy to find. As an example, let us assume that an investor compared after-tax yields for both taxable investment as well as tax exempt savings. If he was a married man in 1949 with one child and in the 10,000 DM taxable income bracket, the marginal income tax rate was 26.2%. If he put 100 DM into a tax exempt savings account, he could immediately deduct 26.2 DM from his tax bill. Although the savings were blocked for three years, it was possible to withdraw them earlier. (In that case he had to post-pay the taxes deducted.) The nominal interest rate on tax exempt savings was 4.5%. At the end of the third year, the investor would have readily available 110.30 DM.[2] Had he not chosen tax-exempt savings, but a taxable investment, what rate of interest would have been necessary to leave him at the end of the three years with 110.30 DM? With tax-free interest, the rate would have had to be at least 17.4%; if interest were taxable, 20.4%. Such high nominal interest rates were difficult to obtain in taxable investments.

There was a good reason, then, for higher income brackets to invest in tax-exempt savings. As is well known, these income brackets are by tradition strong savers. If they received tax benefits they most likely received them largely for savings which they would have made anyway. In most cases, these savings were

---

[1] That workers did not benefit too much from these tax exemptions is corroborated in another way. A savings bank in the city of Gelsenkirchen in the Ruhr analyzed new accounts for tax favored savings in 1953. It was found that merchants and salaried employees had made most of the deposits. The workers of the county of Gelsenkirchen, who were certainly among the best paid workers in West Germany, and who accounted for 72.6% of all employed, had made only 6.8% of all tax favored deposits. *Geschäftsbericht für 1953 der Stadtsparkasse Gelsenkirchen*, p. 18; H. Osthues, *op. cit.*, p. 109.

[2] Interests could have been put back into tax-exempt savings accounts, but this complicates the problem. We assume here that the investor withdrew the interest and put it into another taxable account carrying a 4.5% rate of interest.

not the result of a cut in consumption.[1] Savings would have been made without tax incentives, though perhaps not in the form of long-term savings deposits.

A special effort to increase the supply of long-term investable funds may be mentioned in this context. The West German government faced difficulties in financing the desired amount of construction for the social housing program in 1956. Under the so-called "Lex Preusker" program, high tax incentives were granted for new savings and the acquisition of bank bonds.[2] Up to 6,000 DM could be deducted from taxes if twice that amount was paid into a savings account and blocked for three years. This law was in effect between December, 1956, and March, 1957. In this time, 108,630 savings agreements were signed and 709.8 million DM were raised.[3] It was estimated that additional savings accounted for only 20% of the total funds received. The remainder was obtained through a reshuffling or transfer of funds.[4] Budget losses under the "Lex Preusker" were estimated as higher than the additional savings obtained.

Given other existing strong saving incentives and deep rooted savings habits, it must be concluded that personal savings through tax exemptions did little to increase the supply of investable funds and were rather costly in terms of revenue losses.[5] A distinct disadvantage was inevitable inequities in the distribution of tax benefits. Administratively, satisfactory control to pre-

[1] This has never been claimed in West Germany, not even by the strongest proponents of tax-exempt savings. Though there is no data on the consumption of higher income brackets available, many observers felt that it was right from 1948 on at a high level and in many instances ostentatious.

Professor Erhard himself evidently believed that consumption could be decreased only through government measures. Speech in Bundestag 126. Sitzung, 14, März, 1961.

[2] *B. G. Bl.*, Dec. 1956, p. 918. Further: Rhein-Main Bank, "10 Fragen und Antworten zum steuerbegünstigten Sparen," Dec. 1956 (paperbound, no place of publication indicated).

[3] *Bundesbank, M. R.*, April 1957, p. 12; May 1957, p. 11.

[4] Berliner Bank, *Die Börse 1957*, Berlin, p. 23. Further: Bundesminister für Wirtschaft, *Sonderheft*, Heft 3, Bonn, February 1957, p. 7.

[5] Bundesminister für Wirtschaft, *Sonderhefte zum Bericht über die wirtschaftliche Lage in der Bundesrepublik*, Heft 3, February 1957, p. 5.

vent abuses was very difficult. In the first phase of their use, between 1949 and 1955, tax exemptions were of low efficiency in generating additional investable funds. Yet they contributed strongly to the capital formation of people with high incomes.

To date, West Germany has not been completely willing to give up savings incentives by the individual, but there have been some important changes. The tax-exempt amounts which could be saved have become more and more restricted, but the limits on savings are still wide enough to permit small savers all the tax-favored savings they can make. On the other hand, the limitations make it impossible for persons in income brackets with high marginal income tax rates to use or abuse tax exemptions extensively. There was considerable criticism of these tax incentives, and after ten years they were partly abolished. Tax-exempt savings in savings accounts were outlawed in 1962, but will continue to exist for savings in insurances and building associations.[1]

To avoid some of the inequitable features of tax exempt savings, the government resorted to premium payments on savings deposits (Sparprämie) in the late '50's. Analogous to a similar existing provision for small savers in building associations (Bausparprämie),[2] this was another attempt to induce additional savings. The improvement was that the benefits also accrued to income recipients in lower income brackets. After years of controversy the law on premium savings became effective in 1959.[3] It stipulated that a saver entered into an agreement with a credit institution to keep savings in a blocked account for at least five years. He received the usual rate of interest on these savings, but after five years the government added 20% of the originally deposited amount. Premiums were paid even for very small annual savings (60 DM). If a 3.5% nominal interest rate is assumed, the

---

[1] Savers in building associations had an option either to deduct within legal limits, savings from taxable income or request payment of a premium. Members of higher income groups generally used the former, those of lower ones the latter. *Sparkasse,* Heft 20, p. 339, Bonn, October 1954. For premiums paid out, see Table 16; for tax deductions, Table 17.

[2] Werner Lehman, *Bauspar ABC,* Bonn: Domus Verlag, 1958, p. 101; *Deutscher Bundestag I, Wahlperiode, Drucksache 3625.*

[3] Deutscher Sparkassen and Giroverband e.V., *Jahresbericht 1958,* p. 20.

payment of 20% of the original amount deposited at the end of
the period brought the effective interest rate into the neighborhood of 6.5%. Special provisions for installment savings existed,
but the blocking period became, in this case, somewhat longer.
Savings banks, which have always received about 50% of all tax
exempt savings, reported rapid increases in contracts for this
kind of savings. Their number was 1.33 million in 1960. In the
same year, total premium savings in all credit institutions
amounted to 848 million DM of which 596 million was in savings
banks.[1] Premiums on savings, like tax exemptions, are not expected substantially to increase the total savings volume. They
are, however, more equitable and they further government efforts
to increase capital formation in lower income brackets.

c. *Business Savings*

In West Germany after 1948 nearly 35% of all funds for net
capital formation were supplied by the business sector. This was
the largest source of net savings until 1952, when the government
sector (including the Social Security System) surpassed it. Since
the business sector has had to earn more than 90% of all depreciation charges each year it has always been the largest supplier of
gross savings. After 1948, business savings were influenced by a
great number of factors, some of them of a long-run nature; other
factors were linked to the specific economic conditions in postwar
West Germany. Fiscal policy in particular greatly influenced
business savings. Before beginning a discussion on public policy
measures designed to increase business savings, a few general
remarks about the latter are in order.

A business firm is a complex institution owning both real and
financial assets. Real assets take the form of equipment, buildings, and land. Financial assets are usually claims against other
members of the domestic economy, but they may also be claims
against foreigners. Increases in both kinds of assets must be financed either internally or externally.

Internal financing refers to funds which are available in the
firm for acquisition of assets. These may be used to augment

---

[1] Deutscher Sparkassen und Giroverband e. V., *Jahresbericht 1960*, p. 19.

financial assets or to finance net additions to existing real assets and replace those used up in the process of production. To assure that replacements can be made, a firm will include depreciation charges in the price for its products. If the market is willing to pay for depreciation, funds will accumulate in the firm at first as financial assets. One day these funds will be used to replace the worn-out plant or equipment. Depreciation charges are thus the first important source for internal financing.

The other source of internal funds is retained earnings. These are profits after taxes which firms decide to retain. Only the owners of a business have a right to decide on the use of internally available funds.

About 35% of all increases in business assets were financed through depreciation charges in West Germany. Retained earnings accounted for another 25%. As the corporate sub-sector is less important in West Germany than in the United States, only about one-third of all retained earnings were corporate. Detailed information on this internal financing can be found in Tables 18 to 20.

External financing refers to funds which a business obtains from other units in the economy in order to increase its assets. Such funds may be obtained through the sale of equity or through the issue of fixed-interest securities. In the simplest case, a firm may just receive a loan. Some of the funds may be obtained directly from other members or sectors in an economy which happen to have a surplus of funds. Other investable funds may reach business through financial intermediaries, such as banks, insurance companies, or savings associations. External funds can be both long-term and short-term. If a firm decides to finance externally, the freedom of decision-making of the original owners usually decreases. To what extent this will occur depends on the specific way in which funds are obtained. When equity is sold, there are new ownership rights; if fixed interest securities are floated, there is a debt service involved; and if a loan is obtained, the lenders may closely watch the performance of the business. A firm which finances externally generally has to pass a much harder test in the market than a business which finances internally. Such a firm first has to earn enough profits, which is true for any business; but in addition it is exposed to the scrutiny of critical lenders.

TABLE 18

Increase in Assets in Business Sector
1948 2d Half Year to 1960. Billions of DM. Current Prices[1]

| Year | Gross Investment in Real Assets[2] | *Increase in Financial Assets* | | Total Increase in Assets |
|---|---|---|---|---|
| | | Total[3] | Short-term[4] | |
| 1948 2.H.Y. | n.a. | n.a. | n.a. | n.a. |
| 1949 | n.a. | n.a. | n.a. | n.a. |
| 1950 | 19.4 | 5.8 | 2.8 | 25.2 |
| 1951 | 23.2 | 4.4 | 2.4 | 27.6 |
| 1952 | 28.0 | 4.6 | 1.4 | 32.6 |
| 1953 | 27.3 | 4.7 | 1.2 | 32.0 |
| 1954 | 32.0 | 3.5 | 2.4 | 35.5 |
| 1955 | 41.5 | 4.9 | 1.5 | 46.6 |
| 1956 | 43.3 | 5.2 | 1.7 | 48.5 |
| 1957 | 45.7 | 7.3 | 2.7 | 53.0 |
| 1958 | 47.2 | 7.5 | 4.1 | 54.7 |
| 1959 | 52.9 | 9.0 | 4.1 | 61.9 |
| 1960 | 63.0 | 8.6 | 2.4 | 71.6 |

[1] Includes residential construction, government owned corporations, the postal system and the federal railroad.
[2] Consists of net investments in tangible assets plus re-investments which were assumed to be equal to depreciation charges.
[3] Bundesbank, M.R. July 1960, M.R. June 1961.
[4] Consists of increases of demand deposits, and other claims of a short-term nature. Included are also increases in cash (currency) balances. Bundesbank, M.R. July 1960, M.R. June 1961.

Business in West Germany has drawn for its external financing mainly on eight different sources which are listed in Table 19. Bank lending supplied 22% of all available funds between 1950 and 1958. Of these 6.4% were—on the average—short-term funds, but immediately after the currency reform this share became much larger. Many long-term investments were at that time probably financed with short-term bank loans. The volume of medium and long-term bank loans to business has fluctuated between roughly 12% and 18% of all asset increases. The increase in medium and long-term loans was very large in absolute terms.

This increase was 3.9 billion DM in 1950. In 1959 it surpassed 10.5 billion DM.

Besides the banks, suppliers of long-term funds were building associations and insurance companies, which gained rapidly in importance. These two institutions provided 0.7 billion DM in 1950. Their loans to business had increased, however, to 5.5 billion DM in 1960 which indicates that in West Germany non-bank lenders are also becoming very important.

Government, too, has supplied business with credits. In addition to the direct government credits shown in Table 19, business has received government credits indirectly. These will be discussed in greater detail in Chapter 4.

Some funds for business financing came from abroad. Foreigners and West Berlin supplied, on the average, 1.2%. These were partly long-term capital imports, partly short-term funds. The amounts fluctuated greatly, especially for short-term funds. Sometimes these fluctuations were influenced by speculative capital movements and prepayment of exports, especially when adjustments in the DM exchange rate were expected.

Security markets are mentioned as the last source of funds. The sale of securities, though rapidly increasing, did not furnish large amounts of funds. Between 1950 and 1958, business obtained only 3.5% of its total funds in security markets. Of this, 1.9% was obtained through the sale of fixed interest securities and 1.6% through the sale of shares. The best year for the issue of securities so far was 1958, when a volume of 7 billion DM was sold. Security markets in West Germany are still of relatively small importance for business financing. Until now there has been no year in which more than 18% of all external funds could be raised through the security market.

There is no way of detecting which business funds were used for what asset acquisitions. Depreciation allowances may have had a counterpart in short-term financial assets. Short-term financial loans may have been used to finance long-term investments. It is also impossible to trace the use of external or internal funds. An analysis of internal business financing is necessarily

TABLE 19

Financing of Increase in Business Assets[1] 1948 2d Half Year to 1960
Billions of DM. Current Prices

| Year | Total Internal[2] Funds = Gross Savings of Business | Bank Credit | | Credit from | | | |
|---|---|---|---|---|---|---|---|
| | | Short-Term[3] Bank Credit | Medium and[3] Long Bank Credit | Building[3] Associations | Insurance[3] Companies | Government[4] | Foreign and West Berlin |
| | (1) | (2) | (3) | (4) | (5) | (6) | (7) |
| 1948 2.H.Y. | 4.7 | n.a. | n.a. | n.a. | n.a. | n.a. | n.a. |
| 1949 | 10.5 | n.a. | n.a. | n.a. | n.a. | n.a. | n.a. |
| 1950 | 14.5 | 4.2 | 4.4 | 0.4 | 0.3 | 1.1 | — |
| 1951 | 18.9 | 2.5 | 3.9 | 0.3 | 0.4 | 1.3 | — |
| 1952 | 20.9 | 3.1 | 3.9 | 0.4 | 0.5 | 2.7 | 0.6 |
| 1953 | 18.4 | 2.8 | 5.8 | 0.6 | 0.6 | 3.1 | -0.1 |
| 1954 | 20.7 | 3.4 | 6.6 | 1.0 | 0.8 | 2.0 | -0.2 |
| 1955 | 27.6 | 2.7 | 8.6 | 1.4 | 0.9 | 3.1 | 0.3 |
| 1956 | 30.4 | 1.4 | 7.6 | 1.9 | 1.1 | 3.0 | 1.0 |
| 1957 | 31.4 | 2.2 | 6.1 | 2.3 | 1.1 | 4.6 | 2.0 |
| 1958 | 33.6 | 0.2 | 8.2 | 2.6 | 1.2 | 3.0 | 0.5 |
| 1959 | 35.5 | 2.1 | 10.5 | 3.2 | 1.5 | 5.3 | 0.6 |
| 1960 | 39.4 | 4.9 | 9.5 | 4.2 | 1.6 | 3.9 | 3.9 |

[1] Includes residential construction, government owned corporations, the postal system, and the Federal railroad.
[2] For breakdown into corporate retained earnings, non-corporate retained earnings, and depreciation changes see Table 13.
[3] Bundesbank, M.R. July 1960; M.R. June 1961.
[4] Direct credits by government.

**TABLE 19** (cont.)

| Year | Sale of Securities Fixed Interest (8) | Shares (9) | Total External Funds (10) | Internal plus External Funds (11) | Unexplained difference between total increase in assets and available funds.[5] (12) |
|---|---|---|---|---|---|
| 1948 2.H.Y. | n.a. | n.a. | n.a. | n.a. | |
| 1949 | n.a. | n.a. | n.a. | n.a. | |
| 1950 | 0.3 | .0 | 10.7 | 25.2 | 0.0 |
| 1951 | 0.1 | 0.1 | 8.6 | 27.6 | 0.0 |
| 1952 | 0.1 | 0.2 | 11.5 | 32.6 | 0.0 |
| 1953 | 0.4 | 0.2 | 13.4 | 32.0 | 0.0 |
| 1954 | 0.8 | 0.3 | 14.7 | 35.5 | 0.0 |
| 1955 | 0.6 | 1.2 | 18.8 | 46.4 | 0.0 |
| 1956 | 0.5 | 1.6 | 18.1 | 48.7 | 0.2 |
| 1957 | 1.0 | 1.4 | 20.7 | 52.3 | 0.7 |
| 1958 | 2.9 | 0.8 | 19.4 | 53.1 | 0.4 |
| 1959 | 1.1 | 1.5 | 25.8 | 61.3 | 0.6 |
| 1960 | 0.2 | 3.8 | 32.0 | 71.4 | 0.2 |

[5] Difference between column 4 Table 18 and column 11.

## TABLE 20

### Financing of Increase in Business Assets, Percentage Distribution of Sources of Funds. 1950 to 1960. Current Prices.[1]

| Year | Depreciation Charges | Retained Earnings by Corporations | Retained Earnings by Non-Corporate Business | Total Internal Funds = Gross Savings of Business | Bank Credit Short term | Bank Credit Medium and long term | Credit From Building Associations |
|---|---|---|---|---|---|---|---|
| 1950 | 38.5 | 5.9 | 13.0 | 57.5 | 16.7 | 17.5 | 1.6 |
| 1951 | 41.8 | 4.0 | 22.9 | 68.7 | 9.1 | 14.2 | 1.1 |
| 1952 | 39.1 | 7.7 | 17.5 | 64.3 | 9.5 | 12.0 | 1.2 |
| 1953 | 40.3 | 8.2 | 9.4 | 57.8 | 8.8 | 18.2 | 1.9 |
| 1954 | 36.7 | 7.1 | 14.7 | 58.5 | 9.6 | 18.6 | 2.8 |
| 1955 | 30.4 | 8.4 | 20.7 | 59.5 | 5.8 | 18.5 | 3.0 |
| 1956 | 32.8 | 7.8 | 22.1 | 62.7 | 2.9 | 15.7 | 3.9 |
| 1957 | 33.6 | 7.9 | 18.8 | 60.3 | 4.2 | 11.7 | 4.4 |
| 1958 | 36.0 | 8.9 | 18.5 | 63.4 | 0.4 | 15.5 | 4.9 |
| 1959 | 32.5 | 8.5 | n.a. | 57.9 | 3.4 | 17.1 | 5.2 |
| 1960 | 30.8 | n.a. | n.a. | 55.2 | 6.9 | 13.3 | 5.9 |
| 1950 to 1958 | 35.8 | 7.6 | 18.0 | 61.4 | 6.4 | 15.6 | 3.1 |

[1] Calculated from tables 13 and 19.

**TABLE 20** (*cont.*)

| Year | Credit From | | | Sale of Securities | | Total External Funds | Internal plus External Funds |
| --- | --- | --- | --- | --- | --- | --- | --- |
| | Insurance Companies | Government (Direct Credits) | Foreign and West Berlin | Fixed Interest | Shares | | |
| 1950 | 1.2 | 4.4 | — | 1.2 | .0 | 42.5 | 100 |
| 1951 | 1.4 | 4.7 | — | 0.4 | 0.4 | 31.3 | 100 |
| 1952 | 1.5 | 8.3 | 1.8 | 0.3 | 0.6 | 35.7 | 100 |
| 1953 | 1.9 | 9.7 | −0.3 | 1.3 | 0.6 | 42.1 | 100 |
| 1954 | 2.3 | 5.6 | −0.6 | 2.2 | 0.8 | 41.5 | 100 |
| 1955 | 1.9 | 6.7 | 0.6 | 1.3 | 2.6 | 40.5 | 100 |
| 1956 | 2.3 | 6.2 | 2.1 | 1.0 | 3.3 | 37.3 | 100 |
| 1957 | 2.1 | 8.8 | 3.8 | 1.9 | 2.7 | 39.7 | 100 |
| 1958 | 2.3 | 5.7 | 0.9 | 5.5 | 1.5 | 36.6 | 100 |
| 1959 | 2.4 | 8.6 | 1.0 | 1.8 | 2.4 | 42.1 | 100 |
| 1960 | 2.2 | 5.5 | 5.5 | 0.3 | 5.3 | 44.8 | 100 |
| 1950 to 1958 | 2.0 | 6.8 | 1.2 | 1.9 | 1.6 | 38.6 | 100 |

linked with that of external financing and the acquisition of real and financial assets. No separation is possible.

That the business sector was the most important supplier of gross savings has already been established. Capital formation was very large in this sector. Observers visiting West Germany after 1948 and witnessing the renaissance of business, with its mushrooming buildings and large-scale investment in equipment, guessed this long before data on the extent of business capital formation were available. What explanations did the West Germans themselves, however, give when asked about this large business capital formation? Usually it was argued that it was possible because of high prices in seller markets. Also often cited was a non-aggressive wage policy by trade unions after 1948 which kept wages and cost low.[1] High profits led to rapid capital formation. Although the pursued price and wage policy is often stressed, the important influence of government on business savings is rarely mentioned and generally little understood. Occasionally encountered is the opinion that the high rate of business saving was not astonishing since a long-run trend caused the increase.

From what is known about the pattern of business financing, there is actually a general long-run trend towards a larger share of internal financing. This share seems to have risen especially between the two World Wars in Germany, but more research is needed to know the exact extent of these increases.[2] For the United States more information is available. In this country the share of internal financing has slowly increased in the business sector and especially in the corporate sub-sector over the last 80 years. The increase was 5% for the first and 6% for the second.[3]

---

[1] Foreign observers concurred with this. Professor Henry C. Wallich, who analyzed the growth of the West Germany economy up to 1954, observed in this context: "It is true that West Germany's past progress has been achieved at the expense of a rapidly increasing inequality in the distribution of wealth. By enabling business to earn high profits and reinvest them, labor has in effect helped entrepreneurs to accumulate great wealth with extraordinary speed." Henry C. Wallich, *Mainsprings of the German Revival*, New Haven, Yale University Press, 1955, p. 304.

[2] *Wi. und Stat.* 1956, p. 554, table 6.

[3] Kuznets, *op. cit.*, p. 10.

Developments in Germany may have been similar. Internal financing in West Germany would in all likelihood have played a larger role after 1948 than in the '20's, even if an additional boost through fiscal policy had not been received. Long-run changes in the pattern of business finances should not, however, be overestimated. As shown in Kuznets' study they evidently occur very slowly.

A comparison of total business gross capital formation and its financing in West Germany in the postwar period with that of the United States is not possible.[1] Such a comparison can, however, be made for the financing of corporations. The results are presented in Table 21. On the asset side, a striking difference exists for the period before 1950. West German corporations at that time were still trying to overcome the consequences of the currency reform of 1948. They were in a rather illiquid position and had accumulated mainly financial assets. As conditions became more normal, formation of real assets increased. Though no data are available on corporate financing for the years after 1955, it can be assumed that the pattern was not much different from that for United States corporations. An analysis of the various sources of business funds reveals that between 1948 and 1955, internal financing supplied 58.1% of all funds in West German corporations. This includes the years 1948 and 1949, in which internal financing was exceptionally low. The United States average from 1946 and 1956 was 57.8%. During the first period, 1946–49, the United States had a very high average of 62.5%. Considering these differences, there is no doubt that West German corporations, during the first part of the last decade, financed a larger part of all increases in assets internally than did U.S. corporations.

Another important difference between the two countries is in the use of depreciation charges as a source of internal financing. These have been considerably higher in West German than in the United States corporations. There are two reasons for this.

---

[1] The reason for this is that West German data on business capital formation includes government enterprises and residential construction. It is not known exactly what sectors financed the latter.

## TABLE 21

### Comparison of Corporate Financing in West Germany and United States. Percentage Distribution of Increases in Assets and Sources of Financing. Current Prices.

#### WEST GERMANY[1]

| | 1948/49 | 1950 | 1951 | 1953 | 1954 | 1955 | 1948/55 |
|---|---|---|---|---|---|---|---|
| *Increase in Assets:* | | | | | | | |
| Real Assets: | 47.5 | 49.7 | 74.2 | 69.5 | 68.7 | 72.1 | 66.0 |
| Financial Assets | 52.1 | 50.3 | 25.8 | 30.5 | 31.3 | 27.9 | 34.0 |
| of which short-term claims | 52.4 | 48.8 | 22.5 | 19.7 | 21.1 | 20.3 | 27.4 |
| Total | 100.0 | 100.0 | 100.0 | 100.0 | 100.0 | 100.0 | 100.0 |
| *Financing of Assets Increase:* | | | | | | | |
| Internal Funds: | 39.2 | 52.7 | 54.6 | 61.0 | 66.7 | 62.0 | 58.1 |
| of which Depreciation Charges | 25.8 | 33.3 | 25.9 | 46.1 | 48.3 | 39.6 | 38.3 |
| External Funds: | 60.8 | 47.3 | 45.4 | 39.0 | 33.3 | 38.0 | 41.9 |
| of which short-term Obligations | 59.3 | 40.2 | 37.5 | 13.1 | 10.4 | 21.3 | 26.4 |
| Total | 100.0 | 100.0 | 100.0 | 100.0 | 100.0 | 100.0 | 100.0 |

#### UNITED STATES[2]

| | 1946/49 | 1950/56 | 1946/56 |
|---|---|---|---|
| *Increase in Assets:* | | | |
| Real Assets: | 83.0 | 75.5 | 78.0 |
| Financial Assets: | 17.0 | 24.5 | 22.0 |
| Total | 100.0 | 100.0 | 100.0 |
| *Financing of Assets Increase:* | | | |
| Internal Funds: | 62.5 | 55.6 | 57.8 |
| of which Depreciation Charges | 23.0 | 32.7 | 30.0 |
| External Funds: | 37.5 | 44.4 | 42.2 |
| Total: | 100.0 | 100.0 | 100.0 |

[1] Corporations in industry. Egon Baumgart, Rolf Krengel und Werner Moritz, "Die Finanzierung der industriellen Expansion in der Bundesrepublik während der Jahre des Wiederaufbaus," Duncker und Humblot p. 32, 35. Berlin, 1960.
[2] Nonfinancial corporations. Department of Commerce estimates. Simon Kuznets, "Capital in the American Economy" (Princeton, New Jersey, Princeton University Press, 1961), p. 248. Table 39.

The most important is that from 1949 to 1954, internal financing was strongly tax-favored in West Germany, a policy partly implemented by granting generous depreciation allowances. The other is that up to 1954 it was nearly impossible to finance externally. Long-term funds were very difficult to obtain in security markets, an area where the government enjoyed strong privileges. Also, due to a tight monetary policy, short-term funds were scarce and rather costly. All of this changed significantly after 1955.

A question arising at this point is whether the pattern of capital formation and its financing in the West German corporations can be considered as indicative of the whole business sector. In West Germany it has always been argued that corporations have easier access to security markets than non-corporate business; therefore, their share of external financing should be larger. Calculations for the period 1950 to 1958 indicate that the total business sector financed about 61.4% of all increases in assets with internal funds. Corporations financed 58.1% internally between 1948 and 1955. Non-corporate business did actually rely more on internal financing in the aggregate.

However, it should be pointed out that there may have been considerable differences in the financing of large non-incorporated industrial enterprises, farms, and small artisans which are all included in the non-corporate sub-sector. Capital formation in these sub-sectors is a subject about which little is known.

### d. *Public Policy, Tax Incentives and Business Savings*

The pattern of business investment and financing can be strongly influenced by public policy. Through fiscal policy measures, such as lower tax rates for retained earnings or accelerated depreciation which may permit quicker recovery of capital, firms may be induced to finance internally. If internal financing does not seem desirable, other incentives or penalties may make them inclined to seek outside funds. Low-cost public funds may be made available for new investments in some cases, or higher tax rates may be imposed on retained earnings. Monetary policy also has its influence on business financing. Firms may be more inclined to borrow if credit is readily available. Under tight money conditions, on the other hand, firms may have to use for current transactions internal funds which were originally put aside for the financing of investment in plant and equipment. Investments may be postponed in other cases because of difficulties in obtaining funds in security markets.

The West German government, in one way or another, had an influence on all sources of business financing mentioned in the preceding section. Fiscal policy directly affected depreciation charges, retained earnings, and the issuing of securities. Through savings incentives, fiscal policy affected funds obtainable from banks, building associations, and insurance companies, as was shown in Chapter II. Monetary policy had its impact on the cost and availability of bank funds and, to some extent, on funds from abroad.

Attempts to induce business savings through tax incentives started at the end of 1948, even before a West German government was formed. The background for these measures can be found in the difference of opinion between West Germans and the Allied Occupation authorities concerning what the income tax rates should be.

The Allies, in 1946, had substantially increased taxes in an effort to siphon off excess money. In that year, income tax rates were the highest Germany had ever seen. Before the war, in 1939, the marginal tax rate of a married taxpayer with one child in the 5,000 RM income bracket was 5.5%. This rose to 11.7% in 1946. The same man in the 20,000 RM income bracket had a marginal tax rate of 15.5% in 1939 and 54.3% in 1946! This was of little concern to many Germans as long as black market conditions existed between 1945 and 1948; but when the currency reform was planned objections to these tax rates became very strong.

When plans were made for the currency reform, West Germans favored a combined currency reform and tax reform, arguing that the prevailing high tax rates would weaken incentives and lead to all kinds of tax dishonesty.[1] They felt that the personal income tax rates should be reduced by 50% and that the corpo-

---

[1] *Wirtschaftsrat des Vereinigten Wirtschaftsgebietes, Drucksache 806.*

rate income tax should be changed from a graduated tax ranging from 35% to 65% to a flat rate tax of 50%. The tobacco tax was to be cut by 65%, the property tax by 60%, and the inheritance tax by 40%.[1] The Allies disagreed strongly with the West Germans on this tax-cut program. Allied concern was at that time mainly with stability of the new DM currency. They did not wish to see it endangered through possible budgetary deficits financed with credits by the Central Bank. High tax receipts were considered desirable, especially in view of expected large public expenditures.

The opinion of the Allied authorities seems to have been that increases in economic activity after the currency reform would automatically result through the large amount of new investments necessary. High tax rates were not considered a serious obstacle, and they refused to agree completely with the West German proposition.

Taxes were cut in 1948, but not as much as had been hoped. Income taxes were substantially decreased for lower income brackets, but for medium and higher brackets they were still much higher than before the war.[2] In 1949 the West Germans did not yet have the right to change income tax rates under Allied control, but they soon invented other methods to avoid the imposed taxation.[3] One simple method was to reduce taxable income by granting special tax exemptions for capital formation. For example, if part of income was used say, for investment purposes, it could be deducted as non-taxable or was in some cases taxable only after a certain length of time.

The hope was that granting tax exemptions for capital formation by business would act as a strong incentive to invest. That this would mean budgetary losses was acknowledged. The in-

---

[1] Walter W. Heller, "Tax and Monetary Reform in Occupied Germany," *National Tax Journal*, No. 3, 1949.

[2] If one allows for the fact that prices had risen substantially since 1938, the real tax burden for low income brackets in 1948 was higher than before the war.

[3] *Wirtschaftsrat des Vereinigten Wirtschaftsgebietes, Drucksachen, 785, 806, 892, 974.*

crease in capital formation and the resulting increase in total income and taxes, however, were expected to offset, or more than offset, revenue decreases.[1] These tax measures also gave public authorities the potential to influence capital formation selectively. To what extent this was accomplished is discussed below.

*Accelerated Depreciation in Business*
One of the tax incentives used to stimulate investment was accelerated depreciation. German income tax law provides, in paragraph 7, for depreciation and the loss and depletion in substance (in mining, for instance) which are deductible from taxable income. Additions were made to that paragraph after 1949, paragraphs 7a to 7f, through which fiscal authorities exerted a strong indirect influence on capital formation. Paragraphs 7a referred to accelerated depreciation of equipment and paragraph 7e to that of buildings for productive purposes. Both became part of the income tax law late in 1948. Accelerated depreciation was also permitted in the framework of the Investment Aid Law for a limited time in 1952.[2]

Paragraph 7a, introduced in 1949, granted accelerated depreciation for capital goods which were bought after the first of January, 1949. In the first two years after the acquisition, the buyer could deduct up to 50% of the purchase price as depreciation. The upper limit was 100,000 DM. Favored at that time was new equipment, irrespective of its purpose. Later, accelerated depreciation was permitted only if the new capital good fulfilled a similar purpose to that which was replaced. Replacements for all capital goods becoming useless after 1938 were eligible for special tax treatment. In 1951, it was decided to limit the benefit of paragraph 7a to a small circle of persons who had suffered persecution (Verfolgte) under the Nazis. Refugees were also included in this category. Paragraph 7a has remained in the income tax law, but there have been additional modifications

---

[1] Speech by Representative Blücher in *Wörtlicher Bericht über die 33. Vollversammlung des Wirtschaftsrates des Vereinigten Wirtschaftsgebietes,* Frankfurt am Main, n.d.
[2] Paragraph 36, *Investitions Hilfe Gesetz.*

limiting those who can benefit. Also, time limits on the purchase of capital goods were introduced.

Provisions for accelerated depreciation of buildings changed in a similar way. Under paragraph 7e special tax benefits were generally permitted between 1949 and 1952 for plants which were built after June, 1948. In the year of construction and the year following, 10% of the cost of the buildings could be deducted. After that, normal depreciation rates applied. After 1952, this paragraph could be used only by the same selective group of persons entitled to benefits under paragraph 7a.

To overcome bottlenecks in the structure of production, the West German government introduced in 1952 the so-called Investment Aid Law. This law was made to force business in general into providing 1 billion DM for investments in basic industries, such as mining, iron and steel, and electricity production. These external funds were to be augmented by internal funds. Benefitting industries were permitted to depreciate new equipment up to 50% and buildings up to 30% within three years. The condition was that depreciation funds be immediately reinvested in the industry concerned. All new investments had to increase the output of coal, steel, and electricity. This special accelerated depreciation provision ended in 1956.

After 1956, accelerated depreciation was allowed for all equipment with a lifetime of more than 10 years. For a capital good with a lifetime of exactly 10 years, 28.3% of the remaining book value could be deducted as depreciation in each year. This percentage was considered too high and was later reduced to 25%. After 1958 capital goods with a lifetime of less than 10 years were also allowed accelerated depreciation.

A special law which had indirect effects similar to accelerated depreciation is worth mention at this point. Connected with the currency reform in 1948 was the problem of a new DM opening balance sheet for firms. The balance sheet continuity was broken with the introduction of the currency reform, and new asset values, within certain limits set by the law, could be chosen.[1]

---

[1] "Gesetz über die Eröffnungsbilanz in DM und die Kapitalneufestsetzung," *Wirtschaftsgesetz Blatt,* 21.8, 1949, p. 279.

This reevaluation of assets was seen from two points of view by businessmen. One group argued that reevaluating assets to as high a level as possible would provide firms with better depreciation possibilities in the future—in particular for assets with a short lifetime. The other group argued that, with a capital levy under the Equalization of Burden Law impending, a high reevaluation would mean a future excessive tax burden because assessments would be based on the DM values of the reevaluated assets at the day of the currency reform. Most firms decided on high evaluation of assets in DM values to take advantage of higher depreciation in following years. Uncertainties as to what the Equalization of Burden Law would provide, and the feeling that once this law was passed it would be effective for a very long period resulting in relatively low annual burdens, may have been decisive. It also seems that most people felt that tax rates would be cut when the German government again had the power to decide tax matters. If tax rates could be expected to fall, any delay in paying taxes would mean a definite gain.

Germans distinguish between fixed assets (unbewegliches Anlagevermögen) and equipment (bewegliches Anlagevermögen). The law concerning the reevaluation of assets provided that, in general, for the first category of assets (fixed assets) the "Einheitswert," with a value basis of 1935, should be the upper limit of reevaluation, except for a few special cases. The reevaluation of land and buildings for business and residential purposes was thus limited by an historical value as an upper ceiling. The annual depreciation allowance for this category of assets was low, and businessmen were not eager to give a high reevaluation, even had that been possible. The depreciation of land and buildings could not supply firms with large amounts of additional funds. Too high a valuation would mean the disadvantage of paying more under the Equalization of Burden Law.[1]

Equipment was valued quite differently. The law stated that the new value in DM should be determined with the aid of two

---

[1] W. Reiss, *Steuerersparnis als Leitgedanke für die DM Umstellung*, Köln: Finanzwissenschaftliches Forschungsinstitut, Universität Köln, 1952.

ratios: that of the DM purchase value to the old RM historical cost price; and the book value of an asset on the day before the currency reform to the historical RM cost price. With the aid of these ratios, upper limits were found to which equipment could be reevaluated. The implication was that the more an asset was depreciated at the day of the currency reform, the higher the reevaluation could be. The case could, of course, arise in which there was no book value left. When this happened, the DM purchase value of the asset was the upper limit for the reevaluation, and there was no longer any relationship between the old RM balance sheet and the new DM balance sheet. This meant that the asset could once more be depreciated in later balance sheets in DM value.

Firms generally used this reevaluation possibility extensively. Available data for 21 corporations show that on the average the DM values for equipment were 3 to 4 times the RM values before the currency reform.[1]

New DM capital of corporations in West Germany was very high after the reevaluation compared with what it had been in previous RM values. According to calculations of the Statistische Bundesamt, 2,241 corporations had, up to August 31, 1951, made the RM/DM conversion of their capital in a ratio of 10 to 8.4. The ratio was 10 to 4.7 for West Berlin where war losses had been much higher.[2] The law on the reevaluation of assets permitted firms to boost the DM values of their assets substantially. High asset values meant that future depreciations could be high. This temporarily reduced tax liabilities, an essential factor for business financing.

Accelerated depreciation of one kind or the other thus played an important role for West German capital formation in the postwar period. Little is known about the extent of increases in depreciation charges through initial asset reevaluation and later general accelerated depreciation after 1955. A few estimates exist

---

[1] Karl Heinz Förster, "Finanzierung durch Abschreibungen," Tables pp. 39, 42, Stuttgart: C. H. Poeschel, 1953.
[2] *Die Börse 1951*, p. 10 to 13, Berliner Bank, Berlin, quoted from Wirtschaft und Statistik, n.d.

## TABLE 22

### Deductions under Various Paragraphs for Accelerated Depreciation by Business.
### Budget Losses through Paragraph 7b. E.St.G. 1949 to 1959.
### Millions of DM. Current Prices

| Year | 7a. E.St.G.[1] Depreciation of Equipment | 7b. E.St.G.[1] Depreciation of Housing | 7e. E.St.G.[1] Depreciation of Factory Buildings | 36. Investment Aid[1] Law. Depreciation of Plant and Equipment | Total Deductions | Budget Loss[2] Through Paragraph 7b. E.St.G. |
|---|---|---|---|---|---|---|
| | (1) | (2) | (3) | (4) | (5) | (6) |
| 1949 | 450.4 | 38.2 | 46.8 | – | 535.4 | 20 |
| 1950 | 428.9 | 79.4 | 77.8 | – | 586.1 | 40 |
| 1951 | 35.0 | 150.0 | 10.0 | – | 195.0 | 50 |
| 1952 | 50.0 | 250.0 | 10.0 | 600.0 | 910.0 | 70 |
| 1953 | 55.0 | 350.0 | 10.0 | 750.0 | 1165.0 | 100 |
| 1954 | 64.7 | 446.0 | 10.0 | 855.7 | 1376.4 | 140 |
| 1955 | 70.0 | 600.0 | 10.0 | 600.0 | 1280.0 | 180 |
| 1956 | 70.0 | 750.0 | 10.0 | 400.0 | 1230.0 | 250 |
| 1957 | 101.8 | 1163.5 | 10.2 | – | 1275.5 | 345 |
| 1958 | – | 1350.0 | – | – | | 400 |
| 1959 | – | 1350.0 | – | – | | 450 |
| 1949 to 1957 | 1325.8 | 3827.1 | 194.8 | 3205.7 | 8553.4 | 1195.0 |
| 1949 to 1959 | | 6527.1 | | | | 2045.0 |

[1] For 1949 and 1950: Wi. and Stat. 1953. pp. 157, 373; St. B.R.D. Band 125, p. 57; for 1954: information by Statistische Bundesamt; for 1957: St. JB. 1961, p. 446; for other years: estimate by experts of Bundesfinanzministerium Bonn.
[2] Finanzbericht 1961, p. 116 and 117. Bundesministerium der Finanzen, Bonn, no date. These are budget losses in the years shown, which is not equal to the ultimate loss.

on the amounts deducted under paragraphs 7a, 7b, 7e, E. St. G. and 36a of the Investment Aid Law. It is estimated that between 1949 and 1957, 1.3 billion DM was deducted under paragraph 7a, about 195 million DM under paragraph 7e, and 3.2 billion DM under paragraph 36 of the Investment Aid Law. These are aggregate values. No information is available concerning what amounts were deducted by various industries.

*Accelerated Depreciation in Housing*
The West German income tax law which provided accelerated depreciation for housing stimulated investment in residential construction.[1] Paragraph 7b of the income tax law, introduced January 1, 1949, permitted a 10 per cent depreciation of the cost of a house in the year of construction and the year following. After this, the rate dropped to 3 percent. In 12 years, 50 percent of the value of a new house could be deducted as depreciation.

To prohibit accelerated depreciation being used for non-residential construction, especially when the accelerated depreciation under paragraph 7e for plants became restricted, it was stipulated that a building had to be used at least 80% (later 66%) for residential purposes. Since 1950, there have been slight changes in this paragraph; for instance, accelerated depreciation was granted for purchases of old houses or separate apartments.

With the rapid growth of the house-building program after 1949, the amounts deducted under this paragraph rose from 38.2 million DM in 1949 to 1,163.5 million DM in 1957. The estimated total deductions under this paragraph between 1949 and 1957 were more than 3.8 billion DM.

*Loans as Capital Incentives*
Besides accelerated depreciation, tax-deductible loans were also used to stimulate capital formation. The intention was to in-

---

[1] Part of the benefits derived accrued to individuals, and they might have been discussed under personal savings. It was decided, however, to include this under business savings because residential construction is, in West German statistics, included in this sector. In addition, a large number of persons claiming deductions under this paragraph received income from business or had rental income. It can be safely assumed that the business sector benefited substantially from paragraph 7b, *E. St. G.*

crease the supply of funds for investments in bottleneck sectors, particularly in residential construction and shipbuilding. Loans for residential construction were tax-favored after 1949 under paragraph 7c of the income tax law, and shipbuilding loans under paragraph 7d. Loans made to these sectors could be deducted as business costs in the year in which they were granted. These loans were interest-free and repaid in installments within a stipulated period. Repaid amounts were reported as taxable income. These paragraphs had a particular appeal to higher income brackets since they permitted reduction of the tax burden in years when there were high profits. The tax burden could then be spread over a number of years with installment payments—an important feature when tax rates began to fall.

A disadvantage was that such loans deprived the creditor of liquid funds. In many cases, this was probably circumnavigated by taking bank credit. To borrow for the purpose of making a tax-deductible loan was illegal, but this was difficult to control, especially where large firms were concerned. Businessmen simply compared the taxes saved with the interest charged by banks to see if the manipulation was worthwhile. Both corporations and individual income tax-payers used the two paragraphs in the tax law for savings. In 1950, the majority of all deductions were made by persons who received income from business, and the average deduction was high—10,542 DM. Some corporations had a strong interest in loans for shipbuilding. In 1950, 55 corporations granted 21.4 million DM in loans, which meant that on the average they deducted about 400,000 DM from their taxable income.

To prevent excessive use and abuse of these deduction provisions, the government soon imposed restrictions. Only specially designated credit institutions such as building associations and certain banks were entitled to receive these funds.[1] In the case of loans for residential construction the amount loaned for each apartment could not exceed 7,000 DM. Later it was ordered that the total loan could not be more than 50% of total profits of the

---

[1] *Bundes-Gesetz Blatt,* 1950, p. 97, per April 29, 1950.

firm. Originally, the whole amount of the loan was deductible from taxable income, but after 1955 the figure dropped to 25%. Similar restraints were imposed on loans for shipbuilding.

Under these two paragraphs, 318 million DM were deducted in 1950 and 859 million in 1954. It is estimated that a total of 4.2 billion DM was deducted between 1949 and 1957.

In addition to tax exempt loans under the two paragraphs, it was also possible to deduct amounts which were prepaid to the Equalization of Burden Fund. During 1953 and 1954 when this provision was in effect the total amount deducted was about 148 million DM.

*Tax Exemptions on Retained Earnings*
Another incentive for capital formation found in the West German income tax law was the granting of tax exemptions for retained earnings. These exemptions could be claimed in two ways. Under paragraph 10 E. St. G., 15% of the total profit or half of the retained profit could be deducted from taxable income.[1] All firms were entitled to use this paragraph until 1950; in later years, it was reserved for special groups of persons such as the politically persecuted and refugees. Deductions were therefore especially high for the years 1949 and 1950. They amounted to 332.3 million DM in 1949 and 500.3 million DM in 1950. Total deductions under this paragraph between 1949 and 1957 are estimated at 1.25 billion DM.

The alternate method for claiming tax exemptions for retained earnings appeared in paragraph 32a of the income tax law, also effective in 1949 and 1950. If yearly income before taxes was larger than 30,000 DM the income recipient could apply for a flat tax rate of 50%. Applications were granted if not more than 15,000 DM was withdrawn from the business. This tax exemption had a distinct advantage for higher income brackets. A married man with one child and a taxable income of 100,000 DM had a marginal tax rate of 75.7%. If he did not take advantage of

---

[1] Up to 1950: paragraph 10 abs. II, Ziffer 3, *E. St. G.*, after that paragraph 10a.

any of the tax-saving possibilities outlined so far he would certainly welcome this flat tax rate. This paragraph made the top marginal tax rate practically equal to 50%.[1] The total amount deducted under paragraph 32a in 1949 was 362.9 million DM, and it was probably 100 million DM in 1950. The benefit which accrued to the higher income bracket is evident from the average amounts deducted. These ranged from 36,000 DM for the bracket between 20,000 to 50,000 DM, to 242,000 DM for the bracket over 100,000 DM.

*Taxes and the Capital Market*
The catalogue of tax exemptions for capital formation in West Germany is long, and no attempt will be made to enumerate all exemptions. Those discussed so far were the most important in allowing business to reduce or delay tax payments. Nevertheless, mention should be made of the efforts to increase the flow of investable funds into security markets.

These markets suffered during the first half of the '50's from an insufficient supply of funds. Security purchases were tax exempt when persons bought them, but this advantage had not perceptibly increased the supply of funds. To provide a stimulus to other taxpaying investors, especially banks, the Law for the Encouragement of the Capital Market was passed in 1952.[2] This law stipulated that the interest on certain fixed interest securities was tax-free, which resulted in a substantial increase in the effective yield of securities. The law was in effect between 1952 and 1954, during which time the annual sale of fixed interest securities rose from 1.5 billion DM to 4.6 billion DM. Deductions under this paragraph are estimated to have been 90 million DM in 1953 and between 150 million DM and 160 DM annually until 1957. Most of the tax benefits accrued to institutional investors. In 1953 alone budget losses through deductions of inter-

---

1 It is interesting to note that in the 1958 income tax law the top marginal tax rate was near 50%. West Germans evidently believe that the government should never take more than half a man's income, however high it may be.
2 *Deutscher Bundestag, 1; Wahlperiode: Drucksachen 3143, 3773, 3596, 2. Wahlperiode Drucksache 565.*

TABLE 23

Deductions by Business under Various Paragraphs for Tax-exempt Loans,
Retained Earnings, Export Aids, and Interest on Tax-Favored Securities.
1949 to 1957. Millions of DM. Current Prices

| Year | 7c E.St.G. Credits for Housing[1] | 7d E.St.G. Credits for Ship-building[1] | 7f E.St.G. Prepay-ment of Equaliza-tion of Burden[1] | 10a E.St.G. Retained Profits in Firms[1] | 32 or E.St.G. Flat-Rate 50% for Income Tax[1] | Law to favor exports | | Law to favor Capital Markets Para 3a E.St.G. Tax Free Security Yields[4] | Total 1 to 8 |
| | | | | | | Para 3 Forma-tion of Reserves[1] | Para 4 Lower Profits | | |
| | (1) | (2) | (3) | (4) | (5) | (6) | (7) | (8) | (9) |
| 1949 | 147.6 | 10.8 | — | 332.3 | 362.9 | — | — | — | 853.6 |
| 1950 | 270.3 | 47.9 | — | 500.3 | 100.0 | — | — | — | 918.5 |
| 1951 | 350.0 | 275.0 | — | 30.0 | — | 100.0 | 150.0 | — | 905.0 |
| 1952 | 400.0 | 300.0 | — | 40.0 | — | 125.0 | 200.0 | — | 1065.0 |
| 1953 | 400.0 | 325.0 | 83.4[3] | 50.0 | — | 150.0 | 225.0 | 90.0 | 1323.4 |
| 1954 | 589.9 | 319.0 | 65.1 | 60.1 | — | 188.5 | 274.6 | 160.0 | 1607.2 |
| 1955 | 287.0[2] | 100.0 | — | 70.0 | — | — | 200.0 | 165.0 | 822.0 |
| 1956 | 190.0[2] | 100.0 | — | 80.0 | — | — | — | 155.0 | 525.0 |
| 1957 | 65.0[2] | 75.4 | — | 90.0 | — | — | — | 150.0 | 380.4 |
| Total 1949 to 1957: | 2649.8 | 1553.1 | 148.5 | 1252.7 | 462.9 | 563.5 | 1049.6 | 720.0 | 8400.1 |

[1] For 1949 and 1950, Wi. und Stat. 1953, p. 157; Horst Jecht in "Einkommensbildung und Einkommensverteilung," p. 152. Schriften des Vereins für Sozialpolitik, Berlin 1957, St.B.R.D. Band 125, p. 57. For 1954 information by Statistische Bundesamt. For 1957, St.J.B. 1961, p. 446. For other years, estimates by experts of Bundes Finanzministerium Bonn.
[2] Estimated from budget losses as shown in: "Finanzbericht 1961" op. cit., p. 116.
[3] Lastenausgleichsamt, L.A. IV. 3, LA 2116, LA 2953, Bar F/K.
[4] Estimated according to volume of tax favored securities outstanding.

est paid on tax-favored securities issued for the financing of housing were estimated by West German tax authorities at 45 million DM. The estimate was 100 million DM in 1958 and 1959.

### Taxes and Exports

After the last war West Germany had to regain its place in international trade and in 1951 the government passed the Law to Favor Exports.[1] This law enabled exporters to create a tax-free reserve to accumulate the necessary capital for export business. Such a reserve was to be liquidated and included in taxable income in equal installments over a period of ten years. Exporters could also take tax-free deductions on the profits made in the export business. Both tax aids to exporting firms ceased in 1956. Total tax deductions made under the tax law were near 1.6 billion DM.

An additional subsidy to exports in the form of guarantees was given by the government.[2] For a number of years the government guaranteed 2 billion DM, and sometimes more, of exports.[3] It is not possible to quantify this insurance, but it certainly was a substantial indirect aid to the export business.

At this point, we should also mention the aid which export businesses received through monetary policy. To promote exports, export drafts were discounted at the rate which prevailed in countries to which exports were made whenever the rate there was lower than in West Germany. German interest rates in the early '50's in many cases were higher than in foreign countries. This also was a considerable help to exporters, especially for those who possessed drafts on the United States and Switzerland. This was a sort of hidden export subsidy, and it is believed that the average margin may have been around 3%, but this figure cannot be checked. Preferential discounting started in 1951, and it had practically ended in 1958. On the average, 2.0 billion DM

---

1 *Deutscher Bundestag, 1, Wahlperiode Drucksachen No. 2061, 4242.*

2 It may seem surprising that this is referred to as a subsidy. Private insurance would have cost something.

3 *Deutscher Bundestag, 3, Wahlperiode, Anlage zur Drucksache 300, p. 262.*

in export drafts received annual preferential discounting.[1] Assuming a 2% margin, at least 40 million DM in additional funds were probably made available each year to export business. It should be noted that preferential discounting of export drafts was one of the few instances where monetary policy in West Germany was used selectively.

Data on the various tax exemptions discussed may be found in Tables 22 to 24. As may be seen, total deductions—indicating the amount of funds on which government had an influence—and budget losses were substantial. In West Germany it is sometimes argued that tax incentives increase aggregate business savings. Proof of this is not available, but we may say a few words about the likelihood of such an increase.

A large part of all tax exemptions was used by non-corporate business which consists, with some exceptions, of a multitude of small and medium sized firms in West Germany. Many of these firms struggled to become liquid after the currency reform and to build up reasonable inventories. Firm owners were generally very eager to accumulate capital and little inclined to withdraw funds excessively. There may have been cases where additional savings were made; for instance, under paragraph 32 E. St. G. which stated that not more than 15,000 DM could be withdrawn from a firm. Yet these cases may have been compensated for by other owners who felt that they could withdraw more funds from business because tax reductions had made them more liquid.[2] Overall, there were probably very few additional savings induced in the non-corporate sector.

We may now have a look at the corporations. It is sometimes argued that granting accelerated depreciation, or any other tax exemption which increases the cost of running a business as shown in the balance sheet, will tend to increase total internal funds of corporations. The reason for this is that dividends are believed to be a function of profits. With accelerated deprecia-

---

[1] *BDL Annual Report,* 1957, p. 86.
[2] Inquiries at West German firms elicited that both cases occurred.

## TABLE 24

### Total Deductions Made by Business and Resulting Budget Losses. 1949 to 1957. Millions of DM. Current Prices

| Year | Deductions due to Accelerated Depreciation[1] (1) | All Other Deductions[2] (2) | Total Deductions by Business (3) | Average Tax Rates[3] | | Budget Losses[4] | |
|---|---|---|---|---|---|---|---|
| | | | | Tax payers who used Paragraph 7b (4) | Tax payers who used Paragraph 7c (5) | Estimate I (6) | Estimate II (7) |
| 1949 | 535.4 | 853.6 | 1389.0 | 52.0 | 71.0 | 722 | 986 |
| 1950 | 586.1 | 918.5 | 1504.6 | 50.0 | 59.0 | 752 | 888 |
| 1951 | 195.0 | 905.0 | 1100.0 | 33.3 | 51.0 | 366 | 561 |
| 1952 | 910.0 | 1065.0 | 1975.0 | 33.3 | 50.0 | 658 | 988 |
| 1953 | 1165.0 | 1323.4 | 2488.4 | 31.0 | 50.0 | 771 | 1244 |
| 1954 | 1376.0 | 1607.2 | 2983.2 | 31.0 | 42.0 | 925 | 1253 |
| 1955 | 1280.0 | 822.0 | 2102.0 | 30.0 | 42.0 | 630 | 883 |
| 1956 | 1230.0 | 525.0 | 1755.0 | 30.0 | 42.0 | 527 | 737 |
| 1957 | 1275.5 | 380.4 | 1655.9 | 29.6 | 38.5 | 490 | 638 |
| Total 1949 to 1957 | 8553.0 | 8400.1 | 16953.1 | | | 5841 | 8178 |

[1] Table 22, Column 5.
[2] Table 23, Column 9.
[3] These tax rates are implied in an estimate by experts of Bundesfinanzministerium in "Finanzbericht 1961" p. 116, 117. For some years own estimates. Rates shown refer to individuals and corporations.
[4] Estimate I is made with tax rates as shown in Column 4, Estimate II with those shown in Column 5.

tion, dividends might be lower because the management of a corporation convinced shareholders that earnings were low. Lower dividends would indicate that tax incentives did actually lead to increased business savings.

When corporations in West Germany used tax exemptions extensively between 1949 and 1954, dividends were very low.[1] It would, however, be too simple to infer that this was solely the result of tax factors. The West Germans always insisted that the alleged "double taxation" of dividends under the corporate as well as personal income tax made it forbidding to pay these out.[2] For tax reasons, investors, especially large ones, preferred to keep profits in firms. Occasionally, this was pointedly referred to as "tax-favored saving in shares."[3] Also mentioned was the danger that corporations would lose too much liquidity through dividend payments—losses which at that time could not be recovered through issuance of new shares.[4] The level of profits was evidently not a decisive factor in the payment of dividends. With profits at the same level dividends were much higher in the prewar than in the immediate postwar period.[5]

In view of these different factors bearing on the payment of dividends, it is impossible to determine the actual effect of tax exemptions on corporate savings. Tax exemptions may have caused some decline in dividend payments, but if this is true, the drop can have been only marginal.

In our opinion, tax exemptions for capital formation in West Germany did little to increase the aggregate volume of savings above the level they would otherwise have reached. Exemptions were, in essence, equal to outright government subsidies and, in

---

[1] *St. J. B.*, 1961, p. 201.

[2] That the corporate income tax may have been to a large extent shifted, was mentioned, but considered unlikely.

[3] Berliner Bank, A. G., *Wirtschaftsberichte*, Heft 2/57, p. 7; Franz Blücher, Überlegungen zur Frage der Sanierung des deutschen Kapitalmarktes," p. 20, Bad Godesberg, 1957, typewritten; Kreditanstalt für Wiederaufbau, "Kapitalmarkt und Investitions-Finanzierung in der Bundesrepublik," Frankfurt 28, Dec. 1953, typewritten.

[4] Shares, unlike some fixed interest securities, were not tax-favored.

[5] *Wi. und Stat.*, Nov. 1956, Heft II, p. 551.

some cases, to interest-free loans. As such, they were not very effective in inducing additional savings.

### e. *Government Savings*

One of the most remarkable features of West German capital formation was the contributions which government made. What kind and how large these were can be learned only by an analysis of the tangled budget figures for the different fiscal levels. For this, a necessary first step is a review of the institutional set-up of the West German fiscal system and the budgetary picture between 1948 and 1957.

West Germany has four fiscal levels: federal, state (Länder), local governments and, as a special addition since 1949, the Equalization of Burden Fund. Each level receives specific taxes. The federal government has as the main source of its revenue the yields from the turnover tax, customs, and the tobacco, coffee, sugar, alcohol, and other indirect taxes. Besides this, it is entitled to receive a certain percentage of the personal and corporate income taxes.[1] There are a number of other smaller taxes which also go to the federal government. The bulk of the revenue of the federal government comes from indirect taxes. The Länder receive income taxes, inheritance taxes, the beer tax, the automobile tax, and other smaller items. The local level has the "Grundsteuer" (real estate tax) and the "Gewerbesteuer" (a sort of business activity tax) as the main sources of revenue. The fourth level, Equalization of Burden Fund, receives payments made under the Equalization of Burden Law—a form of capital levy.

Shares of the different government levels in total tax receipts have changed over the years. Since 1955, approximately 55% has gone to the federal government, 27% to the Länder, 13.5% to the local governments, and 4.5% to the Equalization of Burden Fund. Vertical as well as horizontal connections exist between all of these levels. The Länder may receive funds from the federal

---

[1] The division between taxes of the federal government and the Länder is regulated in the West German constitution. In 1958, the federal government received 35% of the income taxes.

government and vice versa. Among the Länder there is the traditional "Finanzausgleich" (Equalization of Finances). Because tax yields in the different Länder vary considerably—income differentials rather than differences in tax rates and tax structure cause the differences in total tax yields—the richer states such as North-Rhine Westfalia have to support the poorer Länder such as Schleswig Holstein. Communities likewise receive funds from and pay to the Länder. There is also a sort of equalization of finances existing on the local level which helps financially weaker communities. This equalization is done according to a carefully developed set of rules which are complicated and differ slightly from state to state. The Equalization of Burden Fund is linked with all other fiscal levels, receiving funds from various levels and transferring back certain amounts.

Consolidated administrative budgets are available for the four levels. Total receipts and expenditures are shown including the transfer between the different levels. Included in total receipts are borrowing and funds obtained through the sale of assets. Information on cash budgets has become available lately for the federal and state level, but there is no consolidated cash budget for all levels.

Before investigating government savings it is important to state what these are. There are two widely used definitions. The first is government savings defined as an excess of current receipts over current expenditures; the second is government savings in a National Income sense.[1] These two concepts must be sharply distinguished. To avoid any confusion they will be treated separately.

The concept of government savings as excess of current receipts over current expenditures is set in terms of a full employment equilibrium and fits into the theoretical framework of a classical system. Since aggregate savings must be equal to aggregate in-

---

[1] For a discussion of the meaning of a "surplus" and a "deficit" in West German official statistics see: Wilhelmine Dreissig, "Die Abschlussergebnisse des Bundeshaushalts für die Rechnungsjahre 1949/50 bis 1954/55," *Finanzarchiv*, N.F. 16, Heft 3, p. 381–98; Willi Albers, "Der Umfang der staatlichen Tätigkeit und ihre wirtschaftlichen Wirkungen," *Weltwirtschaftliches Archiv*, Band 77, 1956, p. 176.

vestment, the role of government savings in such a system can be easily described.

If:

T are taxes and all other current receipts

$E_c$ are current expenditures

$E_k$ are capital expenditures

$S_p$ are public credits to private sector

$S_g$ are savings by government

then:

$$T - E_c - E_k = S_p$$
$$T - E_c = S_g$$

or:

$$S_p = S_g - E_k$$

$S_p$ can of course be negative which means that the government borrows from the private sector.

If government saves as much as it invests, no transfer of savings to the private sector is necessary since private savings will equal private investment. If the government saves in excess of its own investment, there will be a savings gap in the private sector which could be filled by a transfer of public investable funds. If the government should refuse to transfer funds, the savings gap would have to be closed in other ways or the price level would fall. A Central Bank which might wish to keep the price level stable could, in this case, expand credit far enough to offset government hoarding. Other factors which could contribute to bridge the savings gap are an increased velocity of money and dishoarding. In this classical framework, employment and the level of aggregate demand would be invariant to government saving.

As the West German economy has had near full employment since 1954, this savings concept may have its merits. Because budget policy and Central Bank policy were, however, not perfectly synchronized there may occasionally have been strong effects on aggregate demand even in this period.

How large were total government savings when defined as an excess of current receipts over current expenditures? On this no direct data are available. For a number of years estimates of such government savings have been made, however, by the Bundesbank in Frankfort.[1] For the sake of comparison, we have derived from available West German budget data two independent estimates. In one case, government savings were calculated as the difference between current receipts and current expenditures; in the other, as the sum of all government gross investments plus loans and subsidies granted to non-government investors plus increases in financial assets, minus borrowing and depreciation. Both estimates (shown in Table 25) differ somewhat from that of the Bundesbank. Values derived in the first estimate are, on the average, higher, and those in the second, lower, than the Bundesbank's.

The reason for the different average level of savings is that the Bundesbank, having better information on the composition of different budget items, has eliminated some items which are listed under investments but which are actually current expenditures. Differences in the savings for each year are due to the fact that the Bundesbank estimate refers to the calendar year and our calculations to the fiscal year. There is no doubt that the Bundesbank estimate is of the right order of magnitude.

Government savings may also be defined as part of the National Income. This allows us to bring income and employment effects of the pursued budget policy into sharper focus.

During the early years after 1948, when the country experienced some unemployment, the budget certainly had a great effect on aggregate demand. This effect could have been analysed with the aid of a government income and product transactions account in which government surpluses and deficits have an income leverage and offset private savings and investment. Government savings in such an account are defined in a Keynesian, not in a classical sense.

No official data for the government sector reflecting surpluses or deficits in the sense of the National Income accounts is avail-

---

[1] For a recent attempt on this side of the Atlantic to estimate the surpluses and deficits of the West German Federal Government see: Andrew H. Gantt II, "Central Governments: Cash Deficits and Surpluses," *The Review of Economics and Statistics,* February, 1963, p. 43.

TABLE 25

Alternative Estimates of Government Net Savings
1948 to 1957
Billions of DM

| Year | Estimate[1] I | Estimate[2] II | Bundesbank[3] Estimate |
|---|---|---|---|
| 1948 2.H.Y. | 2.4 | 1.8 | n.a. |
| 1949 | 3.9 | 3.5 | n.a. |
| 1950 | 3.4 | 4.1 | 4.1 |
| 1951 | 5.0 | 5.5 | 5.5 |
| 1952 | 7.8 | 5.6 | 6.5 |
| 1953 | 9.4 | 7.5 | 8.3 |
| 1954 | 10.8 | 9.6 | 9.0 |
| 1955 | 13.6 | 8.7 | 10.7 |
| 1956 | 11.9 | 10.7 | 11.7 |
| 1957 | 10.7 | 10.8 | 11.8 |

[1] Federal, State and Local Government, and Equalization of Burden Fund. Determined as: excess of current receipts over current expenditures. Data from *St.B.R.D.*, Band 227, p. 18.
[2] Federal, State and Local Government, and Equalization of Burden Fund. Determined as: total gross investment by government, plus loans, subsidies and participations as shown in column 9, table 27, plus change in reserves (Rücklagen) minus borrowing and depreciation charges. Data from: *St.B.R.D.*, Band 227, p. 18.
[3] See table 13.

able for West Germany. Nevertheless, we have made an estimate of such a balance from rather unsatisfactory budget sources. This estimate was then combined with the sources and uses of savings in the private sector as shown in Table 13. The discrepancies were found to be small, which suggests that the estimate must be reasonably correct. The results are shown in Table 26. From this table, two important conclusions may be drawn: one with respect to compensatory fiscal policy, the other concerning government influence on capital formation.

The West German economy went through a period of unemployment from 1948 to 1954, and after that it had full, or nearly full, employment. According to economic theory, one would have expected that in the first period the government would have run a deficit on its income and product transaction account and that in the second period, with full employment, the fiscal authorities would have tried to achieve surpluses to aid the monetary authorities in their attempts to keep prices from rising. There was no sign of any such compensatory fiscal policy in West Germany. In the income and product transaction account which we were able to construct, and which is certainly not perfect owing to lack of data, the government has always had a surplus, with or without unemployment.

Before 1954 no attempt was made to increase aggregate demand and decrease unemployment by running a large government deficit.[1] The reason for this was the belief that unemployment was a structural problem and that efforts to cure it through government deficits would only be inflationary. Inflation was considered the worst thing which could happen and something to be avoided at all cost. The insistence of the Allies on a balanced budget, which was written into the "basic law," greatly strengthened this conviction.[2]

Surpluses have, in later years, inadvertently helped the monetary authorities prevent a rapid inflation. Between 1953 and 1956, the government decided to save for future defense outlays, and accumulated large amounts of funds—the famous "Julius Tower."[3] Whatever the wisdom of this accumulation, it came in handy for the monetary authorities, who at that time faced a difficult situation. The influx of foreign exchange, due to rising export surpluses, caused strong domestic inflationary pressures. Through its monetary accounts, the treasury exerted a strong restrictive influence on bank reserves and effectively reduced monetary expansion. If this had not been the case, West Germany might have seen substantial price increases between 1953 and 1956.

---

[1] In 1950, a small public works program was started but without much success. *BDL. Annual Report,* 1950, p. 29.

[2] *Grundgesetz für die Bundesrepublik Deutschland,* München, Berlin, 1952 Artikel 110, 112, 115. What "balanced budget" is here referred to is not quite clear. It seems that the term was used differently as, for instance, in the United States or England.

[3] This accumulation of public funds is, in West Germany, referred to as the "Julius Tower." The latter is a tower in the fortress of Spandau in Berlin and was used in Imperial Germany after 1870 to store the war treasure.

TABLE 26

Estimate of the Influence of Surpluses and Deficits on Income and Products Transaction Account of Government on Sources and Uses for Gross Private Investment 1949 to 1957 Billions of DM. Current Prices

| | 1949 | 1950 | 1951 | 1952 | 1953 | 1954 | 1955 | 1956 | 1957 |
|---|---|---|---|---|---|---|---|---|---|
| 1 Gross Private Investment[1] | 15.2 | 19.7 | 26.2 | 30.8 | 31.3 | 35.5 | 43.8 | 47.8 | 51.6 |
| 2 Gross Private Savings[2] | 12.9 | 16.4 | 21.3 | 25.4 | 24.0 | 27.5 | 34.6 | 37.6 | 42.6 |
| of which: Personal Savings[2] | 2.4 | 2.0 | 2.3 | 4.3 | 5.4 | 6.7 | 6.9 | 7.0 | 11.1 |
| Gross Business Savings | 10.5 | 14.4 | 19.0 | 21.1 | 18.6 | 20.8 | 27.7 | 30.6 | 31.5 |
| 3 Social Security Savings[2] | 0.5 | 1.2 | 1.8 | 1.7 | 2.4 | 2.8 | 3.3 | 3.7 | 2.7 |
| 4 Estimated Government Surplus[3] or Deficit (−) on Income and Product Transaction Account | 1.7 | 2.0 | 2.8 | 4.9 | 6.2 | 6.8 | 8.4 | 5.5 | 5.1 |
| 5 Statistical Discrepancies and other Errors | 0.1 | 0.1 | 0.3 | −1.2 | −1.3 | −1.6 | −2.5 | 1.0 | 1.2 |
| 6 Total, lines 2 to 5 | 15.2 | 19.7 | 26.2 | 30.8 | 31.3 | 35.5 | 43.8 | 47.8 | 51.6 |

[1] Calculated from table 13, includes claims against foreigners. Government capital formation calculated from M. R. Bundesbank July 1960, p. 54; St. B.R.D. Band 227, p. 18.

[2] See Table 13.

[3] Calculated from St. B.R.D. Band 227, p. 18, excluded from total expenditures and receipts are all transfer items. For similar procedure used in U.S. see: "National Income," 1954 edition, United States Department of Commerce, p. 146, exhibit I; p. 161; and table 5 p. 164.

The surplus in the income and product transaction account came about through high tax yields, the bulk from taxes on consumption. Taxes on savings were kept low, either through tax exemptions or by the outright reduction of rates. Thus, if the pursued budget policy did not increase aggregate demand, it did cause a change in its composition by cutting down the demand for consumer goods and increasing the demand for investment goods.

The purposes for which these large government savings were accumulated are shown in Table 27. The first item to be found there is government investments which amounted to 2.5 billion DM in 1949, 6.3 billion DM in 1955 and 8.1 billion DM in 1958. More than 70% of these investments were outlays for new construction, especially for road and bridge building and public enterprises.[1] Most of this new construction, 65% to 70%, occurred at the local level.[2]

As stated, the West German government has strongly favored capital formation through loans and subsidies granted for investment purposes to non-government investors. Loans to the private sector amounted to 800 million DM in 1948 and increased to 6.8 billion DM in 1958. Subsidies were as high as 650 million DM in 1958. An area in which government loans played a dominating role was residential construction. During the postwar period especially from 1949 to 1955, some sectors of the economy vital for a sustained economic growth were unable to obtain investable funds because they could not pay the high credit cost. This was especially true in the rent-controlled housing sector but it was also true in some other industries where price controls for

---

[1] "Öffentliche Anstalten und Einrichtungen."

[2] This is a disadvantage for possible anticyclical use of these large public construction outlays. Local authorities largely determine the timing of these investments in West Germany, and they are usually influenced in their decisions by factors relevant to a particular town or county, while paying little attention to the general economic situation. For the period considered here, this was not too serious, though monetary authorities have worried about poorly timed public construction as a factor increasing inflationary pressures under full employment conditions. A well-coordinated general plan for construction expenditures at all fiscal levels could contribute greatly to the country's economic stability, but it has not been achieved so far.

## TABLE 27

### Gross Investments, Loans and Subsidies for Investments Granted by Government 1948. 2d Half Year to 1958 Millions of DM. Current Prices.[1]

| Year | Construc-tion | Purchase of Equip-ment | Reinvest-ment in Fixed Assets | Loans | Sub-sidies | Partici-pations | Gross Invest-ment in Fixed Assets 1 + 2 + 3 | Loans, Subsidies and Partici-pations 4 + 5 + 6 | Total 7 + 8 |
|---|---|---|---|---|---|---|---|---|---|
|  | (1) | (2) | (3) | (4) | (5) | (6) | (7) | (8) | (9) |
| 1948 2.H.Y. | 880.1 | 114.4 | 523.6 | 800.2 | 10.0 | 8.8 | 1548.1 | 819.0 | 2367.1 |
| 1949 | 1628.4 | 250.6 | 627.2 | 1903.7 | 20.0 | 14.2 | 2506.2 | 1937.0 | 4444.1 |
| 1950 | 2070.7 | 272.0 | 603.7 | 2160.9 | 120.0 | 106.3 | 2946.4 | 2387.2 | 5333.6 |
| 1951 | 2518.4 | 429.9 | 680.7 | 3022.4 | 160.4 | 120.3 | 3629.0 | 3303.1 | 6982.1 |
| 1952 | 3009.4 | 435.6 | 789.4 | 3905.4 | 153.4 | 119.8 | 4234.0 | 4178.6 | 8413.0 |
| 1953 | 3438.7 | 472.1 | 868.5 | 4280.4 | 206.6 | 93.1 | 4779.0 | 4580.1 | 9359.4 |
| 1954 | 3786.1 | 492.2 | 875.7 | 5317.1 | 412.2 | 154.6 | 5154.0 | 5883.9 | 11037.9 |
| 1955 | 4816.3 | 548.1 | 957.2 | 5143.0 | 444.1 | 223.0 | 6321.6 | 5810.1 | 12131.7 |
| 1956 | 5508.0 | 587.0 | 1050.0 | 6111.0 | 629.8 | 244.0 | 7145.0 | 6984.1 | 14129.8 |
| 1957 | 5495.0 | 635.0 | 1120.0[2] | 6824.0 | 611.0 | 479.0 | 7250.0 | 7914.0 | 15164.0 |
| 1958 | 6300.0 | 650.0 | 1200.0[2] | 6800.0 | 650.0 | 440.0 | 8150.0 | 7890.0 | 16040.0 |

[1] Sources: 1948 2.H.Y. to 1956. St. B.R.D. Bank 227. Until 1950 exclusive, for later years, inclusive of West Berlin. Deutscher Bundestag 3. Wahlperiode, Anlage zur Drucksache 300 p. 72 f.

[2] Own estimates.

social or other reasons could not be abolished at once. Government loans were granted in these cases very often at more favorable terms than were available through normal commercial channels. In some instances subsidies were also granted. A distribution of loans by economic sectors for 1955 is shown in Table 28.

### f. *Social Security Savings*

The contribution the Social Security System made to West German reconstruction has received relatively little attention. This system, whose origin dates back for some of its insurances to the time of Bismarck, and which consists of old age insurances, unemployment, accident, and sickness insurances, is well established and comprehensive. It has aided the economic revival and growth of the country in two different ways.

First, Social Security has prevented extreme hardships for those population groups which suffered most from war and postwar events. It served in many cases to prevent persons from falling into economic annihilation by guaranteeing at least a minimum existence.[1] During the early '50's, when the accent was on efficiency and equity considerations were secondary in West Germany, the system acted as a mitigating element. This floor under the peoples' economic existence served to reduce discontent and social tension. Of course, this contribution is difficult to evaluate and more will be said about it in a later chapter dealing with the burden aspects of capital formation.

The second important function of the system was its role as a supplier of investable funds. After the currency reform in 1948, the system had an excess of current receipts over current expenditures. It contributed about 27.9 billion DM to capital formation between 1948 and 1960.[2] The largest asset increases occurred in pension insurances. Those for workers, salaried employees, and mining employees alone had accumulated more than 10 billion

---

1 "Die Sozialen Leistungen" article, *Mitteilungen des Wirtschaftswissenschaftlichen Instituts der Gewerkschaften,* No. 12, Dec., 1951; DIW, *Wochenberichte,* 1957, No. 41, p. 165.
2 This refers to all insurances shown in Table 29.

TABLE 28

Percentage Distribution of Loans Made by
Government According to Economic Sectors
in 1955[1]

| Sector | Percentage |
|---|---|
| Residential Construction | 56.2 |
| Loans made for the benefit of the economy (agriculture, industry, etc.) | 20.1 |
| Transportation, roads, bridges | 1.5 |
| Schools | 0.3 |
| Science, art, churches | 0.1 |
| Social institutions | 3.6 |
| Local institutions and Public enterprises of a local character | 17.7 |
| Other Sectors | 0.5 |
| Total | 100.0 |

[1] All levels of government. *Deutscher Bundestag, 3. Wahlperiode, Anlage zur Drucksache 300, p. 74.*

in DM assets between 1950 and 1956. Unemployment insurance, with assets totaling 3.9 billion DM in 1958, was another important supplier of investable funds. With rising incomes in the economy, gross Social Security receipts increased constantly, but so did payments. A reform in 1957 raised Social Security benefits substantially, correcting a situation under which the poor received the fewest benefits from the rapid income increases and wealth formation.[1] Annual payments to rent receivers were increased under the rent reform by 5.9 billion DM.[2] Since then, the capital formation of the system has decreased. It should be mentioned at this point that late in the '50's the reserves of the system relative to the annual outpayments were still much lower than they were before the war.[3]

The various insurance institutions are restricted in their in-

[1] Ursula Niemann, Die Wirtschaftliche und soziale Lage der Empfänger von Renten und Unterstützungen," *Mitteilungen des Wirtschaftswissenschaftlichen Instituts der Gewerkschaften, 1956,* p. 270.

[2] *M. R. B.D.L.,* June 1957, February 1957.

[3] *M. R. Bundesbank,* August 1959.

vestments by special laws, such as the Reich Insurance Code. Investments are permitted, in most cases, only in projects which serve the public interest, e.g., social housing or investment by local governments. The insurances are no longer required, as they were during the Nazi era, to buy governments bonds, but they have done this anyway. Under existing rules and regulations insurances do not directly support private investments. However, business does receive indirectly some funds from the system. The Social Security System holds a large part of its assets in the form of bank deposits, usually of a long-term nature. In addition, unearmarked loans have been granted to banks. Through financial intermediaries the insurances have greatly contributed to financing in the private sector. Direct loans have been granted to state (Länder) as well as local governments. Public enterprises, such as the federal railroad and the postal system, have also received loans. The system has always been a heavy buyer of mortgage and municipal bonds. At the end of 1958, it held 26% of all mortgage bonds and 17% of all municipal bonds. The system has been a supplier of funds for the security markets since the currency reform in 1948.

Data on the savings of the system and kinds of assets held may be found in Tables 29 and 30.

### g. *Bank Credit*

An analysis of a country's savings would be incomplete if bank credit were excluded. In modern financial systems banks are not only channeling devices for savings made in the various sectors of the economy, but they may also augment or decrease savings volume. Due to their ability to create credit they can smoothe the flow of funds and offset temporary deficiencies in sector savings. The old idea that credit creation by banks affects the money but not the capital market should be qualified. Today, financial institutions with highly diversified portfolios containing securities of all maturities are the great link between these different markets. Banks may react very sensitively to changes in credit conditions in the money market and there may be a quick transmission

TABLE 29

The Savings of the Social Insurance System.
1948, 2nd Half Year to 1957[1]
(Current prices—Millions of DM)

| Year | Sickness Insurances | Unemployment Insurance | Accident Insurance | Family[2] Aid |
|------|------|------|------|------|
| | (1) | (2) | (3) | (4) |
| 1948 2.H.Y. | n.a. | n.a. | n.a. | — |
| 1949 | n.a. | n.a. | n.a. | — |
| 1950 | 144 | 151 | 72 | — |
| 1951 | 188 | 330 | 111 | — |
| 1952 | 66 | 234 | 91 | — |
| 1953 | 55 | 524 | 64 | — |
| 1954 | 108 | 480 | 51 | — |
| 1955 | −10 | 483 | 57 | 2 |
| 1956 | −9 | 531 | 57 | 6 |
| 1957 1.H.Y. | 11 | −85 | 86 | 11 |
| 1957 | n.a. | n.a. | n.a. | n.a. |
| Sum 1950–1956 | 542 | 2733 | 503 | 8 |
| % distribution 1950–56 | 3.2 | 16.2 | 3.0 | .0 |

1 "Arbeits-und Sozialstatistische Mitteilungen," Bonn, April 1958, p. 113.
2 Kindergeldgesetz.
3 Knappschaftliche Rentenversicherung.

to the long end of the market—the capital market. Monetary policy and bank behavior can therefore greatly influence capital formation. A tight monetary policy, intended to keep prices constant, may have a highly unfavorable effect on capital formation even if savings are sufficient. On the other hand, in a period of monetary ease, investment may be kept at a high level even with savings in short supply. To what extent bank credit should be used depends on the prevailing economic conditions. Too liberal lending policies may be inflationary, while very conservative views on lending can severely restrain a country's capital formation. Bank credit is in a strategic position to affect capital formation. A review of the development in this field in West Germany between 1950 and 1960 follows.

There have been great structural changes in West German bank lending during the last ten years. The general tendency has

TABLE 29 (*cont.*)

|  | | Old Age Insurance | | Other[4] | Total Savings[5] |
|  | Workers | Salaried employees | Mining[3] employees | Insurances | (col. *1* to *8*) |
|---|---|---|---|---|---|
|  | (5) | (6) | (7) | (8) | (9) |
| 1948 2.H.Y. | n.a. | n.a. | n.a. | n.a. | 100[6] |
| 1949 | n.a. | n.a. | n.a. | n.a. | 500[6] |
| 1950 | 302 | 119 | 22 | 390 | 1200 |
| 1951 | 486 | 168 | 73 | 444 | 1800 |
| 1952 | 548 | 243 | 37 | 481 | 1700 |
| 1953 | 900 | 487 | 65 | 305 | 2400 |
| 1954 | 1214 | 554 | 60 | 333 | 2800 |
| 1955 | 1510 | 680 | 94 | 484 | 3300 |
| 1956 | 1623 | 732 | 139 | 621 | 3700 |
| 1957 1.H.Y. | 603 | 152 | – | n.a. | n.a. |
| 1957 | n.a. | n.a. | n.a. | n.a. | 2700 |
| Sum 1950–1956 | 6583 | 2983 | 490 | 3058 | 16900 |
| % Distribution 1950–56 | 38.9 | 17.7 | 2.9 | 18.1 | 100.0 |

4 Special Social Insurances, e.g., for railroad employees. Information, "Bundesbank." Determined as residual.
5 "Bundesbank" M.R., June 1958.
6 Own estimate.

been away from short-term and toward long-term lending. This reflects partly the increased liquidity of business and partly a larger supply of long-term loanable funds. The changes in total assets are shown in Table 31.

The volume of short-term bank credits increased continuously between 1950 and 1960, but the rise was largest in the early years. A considerable part of investments at that time was financed with short-term loans,[1] something of which Central Bank authorities strongly disapproved.[2] There was a decline in short-term lending after 1950, both absolute and relative, until 1958;

---

1 For the experience of West German banks to grant short-term credits for investment purposes, see H. Rittershausen, in "The Supply of Capital Funds for Industrial Development in Europe and in the United States," Supplement II, OEEC, Paris, Project No. 292, pp. 46–47.
2 BDL, *Annual Report,* 1948 and 1949, p. 6.

## TABLE 30

### Increases in Assets of West German Social Security System, 1950 to 1958, Millions of DM[1]

| Year | Deposits[2] (1) | Short-Term Securities (2) | Securities[3] (3) | Claims Against Federal Government (4) | Loans[4] (5) | Mortgages (6) | Real Estate and Equipment (7) | Total[5] 1 to 7 (8) |
|---|---|---|---|---|---|---|---|---|
| 1950 | 530 | 30 | 110 | – | 80 | 50 | 60 | 860 |
| 1951 | 460 | 30 | 440 | – | 180 | 40 | 70 | 1220 |
| 1952 | 230 | –20 | 390 | 110 | 280 | 60 | 70 | 1120 |
| 1953 | 490 | 100 | 380 | 590 | 390 | 50 | 100 | 2100 |
| 1954 | 280 | –60 | 690 | 270 | 1260 | 60 | 70 | 2570 |
| 1955 | –10 | 40 | 710 | –10 | 2000 | 50 | 110 | 2890 |
| 1956 | 680 | 50 | 870 | –20 | 1090 | 140 | 110 | 2920 |
| 1957 | 260 | –20 | 350 | 70 | 740 | 250 | 110 | 1760 |
| 1958 | 460 | –140 | 150 | –20 | 240 | 220 | 110 | 1020 |

1 M.R. March 1959, Bundesbank, p. 21, refers to rent insurance, unemployment, health and accident insurances.
2 Mostly long-term bank deposits.
3 The bulk of this consists of mortgage bonds and communal bonds.
4 Includes loans to banks.
5 There are slight discrepancies between these totals and the sum of columns 1 to 7 in Table 29. Some smaller items have been omitted in this table.

TABLE 31

## Changes in Main Assets and Liabilities of Banking System 1950 to 1960,[1] Billions of DM.

| | 1950 | 1951 | 1952 | 1953 | 1954 | 1955 | 1956 | 1957 | 1958 | 1959 | 1960 |
|---|---|---|---|---|---|---|---|---|---|---|---|
| *Increase in Assets:* | | | | | | | | | | | |
| Short-Term Bank Credit | 5.29 | 2.57 | 3.22 | 2.91 | 3.78 | 2.92 | 1.82 | 3.22 | 1.15 | 4.65 | 4.22 |
| Long-Term Bank Credit | 4.89 | 4.45 | 4.65 | 7.39 | 8.93 | 10.82 | 9.00 | 7.45 | 10.72 | 14.13 | 11.57 |
| Acquisition of Securities | 0.51 | 0.20 | 0.64 | 0.96 | 1.88 | 1.70 | 0.23 | 1.37 | 4.92 | 4.82 | 0.45 |
| Gold and Exchange Holdings of Bundesbank | −0.56 | 2.04 | 2.76 | 3.61 | 2.78 | 1.85 | 5.09 | 5.12 | 3.19 | −2.21 | 8.01 |
| Total | 10.11 | 9.26 | 11.27 | 14.87 | 17.37 | 17.29 | 16.14 | 17.17 | 19.97 | 21.39 | 24.20 |
| *Increase in Liabilities:* | | | | | | | | | | | |
| Demand Deposits, Notes and Coins | 1.87 | 2.89 | 2.67 | 3.49 | 4.55 | 3.81 | 3.22 | 1.28 | 4.42 | 1.70 | 4.46 |
| Time Deposits | 2.04 | 1.48 | 2.06 | 2.18 | −0.15 | 0.03 | 1.70 | 3.44 | 0.99 | 1.63 | 0.94 |
| Savings Deposits | 1.01 | 0.90 | 2.42 | 3.84 | 5.48 | 3.95 | 2.70 | 4.81 | 6.48 | 7.95 | 7.65 |
| Other Funds Received: | 4.78 | 3.34 | 3.11 | 3.54 | 3.92 | 6.34 | 6.88 | 5.16 | 3.76 | 4.26 | 7.68 |
| of which from: | | | | | | | | | | | |
| a. government | 2.55 | 2.22 | 1.35 | 1.41 | 3.25 | 4.55 | 4.49 | 2.79 | 1.64 | 1.27 | 2.61 |
| b. enterprises[2] | 1.59 | 1.02 | 1.67 | 1.62 | 0.01 | 1.26 | 1.05 | 1.43 | 2.10 | 2.28 | 3.34 |
| c. foreign countries | 0.59 | 0.05 | 0.03 | 0.39 | 0.58 | 0.52 | 1.13 | 0.74 | 0.02 | 0.55 | 1.39 |
| Sale of fixed interest Securities | 0.41 | 0.62 | 0.99 | 1.73 | 3.53 | 2.96 | 1.52 | 2.40 | 4.12 | 5.73 | 3.35 |
| Sale of shares | 0.01 | 0.04 | 0.03 | 0.10 | 0.05 | 0.21 | 0.13 | 0.08 | 0.21 | 0.13 | 0.12 |
| Total | 10.11 | 9.26 | 11.27 | 14.87 | 17.37 | 17.29 | 16.14 | 17.17 | 19.97 | 21.39 | 24.20 |
| *Addendum:* | | | | | | | | | | | |
| Discount rate %[3] | 4–6 | 6 | 6–4.5 | 4–3.5 | 3 | 3–3.5 | 4.5–5.5 | 4.5–4 | 3.5–3 | 2.75–4 | 5–4 |
| Bank Reserve Requirements %[3] | 10–15 | 15 | 15–11 | 10 | 10 | 10–11 | 11 | 12 | 12 | 11 | over 14 |
| Price Index G.N.P.[4] | 100 | 110.4 | 116.5 | 116.4 | 116.4 | 118.9 | 122.6 | 126.5 | 131.0 | 133.3 | 137.3 |
| Unemployment as % of Labor Force[5] | 10.4 | 8.8 | 8.4 | 7.6 | 6.7 | 4.9 | 4.2 | 3.6 | 3.5 | 2.0 | 1.5 |

[1] M. R. Bundesbank, July 1960, p. 66f. June 1961, p. 18. The values shown here are global ones and differ somewhat from those which can be derived from the consolidated balance sheet of the banking system. See: M. R. Bundesbank November 1959, p. 19. They are part of a larger system which refers to the financing of the country's capital formation and some adjustments may have been made.
[2] Includes increases in bank's capital.
[3] Bundesbank M. R. various numbers, Reserve requirements for bankplaces.
[4] See Table 3.
[5] Calculated from M. R. Bundesbank. Various numbers. Total number of unemployed as % of employed plus unemployed.

but the years 1959 and 1960 again saw large increases. Long-term lending has, on the other hand, increased both absolutely as well as relatively until 1959, the peak year with an increase of 14.1 billion DM. A leveling-off occurred in 1960.

As this is written, it is not possible to comment on future developments in either area. It is conceivable that with the establishment of a broader securities market in the second half of the '50's short-term lending will again play a larger role.

Banks themselves have been very irregular buyers of securities. In the first part of the '50's, they refused to buy because yields on taxable securities were too low. They became interested in buying after passage of the Law to Favor the Capital Market, which provided for tax-free interest. Banks bought about five billion DM of securities in 1958 and 1959, but in 1960 they cut back to 450 million DM. At the end of 1960, all banks (excluding the Central Bank) held 17.6 billion DM in longer-term securities and 5.6 billion DM in highly liquid money market papers. The latter could be used at any time to offset tight monetary policy measures. There were some fears that this could make monetary policy largely ineffective, as banks evidently had reserves enough to resist measures which they consider too restrictive. This is, perhaps, one of the reasons why monetary policy was actually of so little effect in fighting inflationary pressures in the late '50's.

The main force for monetary expansion in West Germany was the uninterrupted influx of foreign exchange due to large export surpluses. With the exception of the year 1959, there was a continuous building up of foreign exchange reserves. Increases were lowest in 1951 with 1.8 billion DM and highest in 1960 with 8.0 billion DM. Much of the prevailing inflationary pressure in West Germany can be explained through this influx, but so far no effective steps have been taken to remedy the situation. The appreciation of the DM in terms of the dollar in 1961 does not seem to have been very effective in cutting down the export surpluses.

On the liability side in Table 31, the first two items to be found are the increases in demand deposits and currency in circulation. As the data refer to the total banking system the increases in these two are equal to the change of the money supply as usually defined. But savings deposits are also highly liquid assets in West Germany. They can generally be withdrawn without notice, and rarely if ever is there a penalty imposed in the form of an interest loss. A large part (perhaps all) of savings deposits may therefore be included in the money supply. Table 31 shows that there has been a continuous monetary expansion.[1]

Main sources for long-term lending by banks have been rapidly growing time and savings deposits. The amounts shown in Table 31 include, besides individual deposits, those of the government, the Social Security System, and business. Most of the increases were due to rising individual savings, discussed earlier.

In the section dealing with government savings it was mentioned that public loans to private investors were either made directly or via financial institutions. Under special arrangements the banking system received substantial amounts of public funds. For the years 1955 and 1956 these amounted to as much as 4.5 billion DM. Public funds, augmenting those received from the private sector, allowed banks greatly to increase their long-term lending.

### h. *Foreign Funds*

Immediately after World War II, and up until 1951, the main foreign source of investable funds was the foreign aid received from the Allies. Since 1953, unilateral transfers to other countries have surpassed transfer received.[2] West Germany obtained $2,953.5 million[3] from April 1948, to December, 1954, under the Foreign Aid Program. After that date, only a small additional amount was received. Total foreign aid since 1945 amounted to $4,268.2 million.

Proceeds from the sale of imports under the foreign aid pro-

---

[1] It is not the purpose of this study to investigate the effectiveness of West German monetary policy. The interested reader will find at the bottom of Table 31 additional information about discount rates, reserve requirements, price level changes, and employment. From this, it can be seen that, though it was possible to stabilize prices with an unemployment of 7% to 8% of the labor force, with lower rates this was no longer so, in spite of monetary stringency.

[2] Table 14, Column 10.

[3] BDL, *Annual Report*, 1954, p. 94.

gram were the so-called "Counterpart Funds," which were initially administered by the Ministry of Marshall Aid in the Federal Government. The allocation of the funds to investors was, in

TABLE 32

Foreign Aid Received by West Germany
up to December, 1954[1]
(Actual deliveries. In millions of dollars)

| Period | G.A.R.I.O.A. | Marshall Aid and other Programs | Total | % |
|---|---|---|---|---|
| April 1948 to June 1949 | 964.0 | 380.6 | 1.344.6 | 45.5 |
| July 1949 to June 1950 | 353.3 | 333.8 | 687.1 | 23.4 |
| July 1950 to June 1951 | 107.5 | 414.0 | 521.5 | 17.7 |
| July 1951 to June 1952 | 2.6 | 196.3 | 198.9 | 6.8 |
| July 1952 to June 1953 | 0.0 | 98.0 | 98.0 | 3.3 |
| July 1953 to June 1954 | — | 81.6 | 81.6 | 2.8 |
| July 1954 to Dec. 1954 | — | 21.8 | 21.8 | 0.7 |
| Sum April 1948 to Dec. 1954: | 1,427.5 | 1,526.1 | 2,953.5 | 100 |
| Total Foreign Aid since 1945: | | | 4,268.2 | |

[1] BDL Annual Report 1954, p. 94. These are shipments received and not identical with allocations to various sectors. For the latter see Baumgart, *op. cit.* p. 26.

most cases, supervised by the "Bank for Reconstruction" in Frankfort.[1]

Counterpart funds amounted to 5.535 billion DM by the end of 1952.[2] Most of these were used for reconstruction. By December, 1954, 4.927 billion DM[3] of these funds had been channeled

[1] "Kreditanstalt für Wiederaufbau," Law and By-Laws, *B.G.Bl.*, 1952, I, p. 65. (For exact allocation procedure see below Chapter 4.)

[2] *Deutschland Jahrbuch, 1953*, p. 170.

[3] *St. H. B., B.D.L.* III/133, including credit for federal railway of 360 million DM and 100 million DM for Berlin in 1951 out of G.A.R.I.O.A. Funds.

into the different sectors of the economy. After the termination of the foreign aid program, the amortization of the original loans and the interest paid on them were again re-loaned. The administration of the ERP fund is now kept separately and is in the hands of the Minister for Federal Property.

No data are available about other foreign funds private or public which might have been used for investments in West Germany from June, 1948, to 1960. There is reason to assume that up to 1957, in the aggregate, these were not too large. However, the share of the West German corporations owned by foreigners—to mention one field of foreign investment—has increased since 1949. In 1936, foreigners owned 1.3 billion RM[1] in West German corporations; in 1956, 2.3 billion DM. The total capital of West German corporations was 19.2 billion RM in 1936 and 23.8 billion DM in 1956. Thus, foreigners owned 6.8% of all West German corporations in 1936 and 9.7% in 1956. This increase does not necessarily mean that there was a large inflow of additional foreign capital. The re-evaluation of assets after the currency reform, for instance, may have been partly responsible for this rise.

Lately, there have been some changes. Statistics concerning purchases of West German securities by foreigners became available for the first time in 1958.[2] They show that the latter acquired 3% of all fixed interest securities and 28% of all shares in 1958.

i. *Summary of the Government's Contribution to Savings.*

Government influence on the supply of investable funds may now be summarized. The public influence had quantitative as well as qualitative aspects, but at present we will concern ourselves with the former and answer the question: how big a saver actually was government?

Government was a strong saver through budgetary surpluses in the sense of an excess of current receipts over current expendi-

---

1 *St. B.R.D.*, Band 188, p. 6.
2 *Bundesbank M.R.*, 1959, July, p. 106.

tures, as previously stated. In the use of these funds, public authorities were the sole arbiters; that is, funds were—or could be—invested according to public preferences. If, however, the government granted tax benefits to private investors—which was very much the same as granting a subsidy—public preferences as a determinant for investments were much weaker. A mixture of private and public preferences, in most cases, decided what kinds of investments were made. Depending on the particular paragraph of the tax law the strength of public preferences differed. In order to receive tax benefits private investors in some cases had little choice but to comply with what the government wished. In other cases, investors could obtain these benefits without having to adjust their own preference pattern. This makes it difficult to determine the precise extent of the public influence on savings. As a result, three different concepts of "public savings" have been used. The first refers to savings defined as an excess of current receipts over current expenditures. The second includes, in addition to this excess, the tax benefits (taxes saved) which business or persons received when they used tax exemptions favoring capital formation. The third consists of the excess of current receipts over current expenditures as before, but added is the amount of all deductions which persons or business took when using tax exemptions for capital formation.

Included in the following calculations under government is the Social Security System, because by nature it is a public institution (no one in West Germany would argue that it is a private business) and the obligatory contributions to it are similar to taxes. Total government savings, as defined above under the different concepts, are expressed as parts of two aggregates: total gross savings, and net domestic investment plus the increase in claims against foreigners. Net domestic investment consists of domestic investments in fixed assets and inventories. As the bulk of all funds made available by the government could be used for net investments, a comparison of government savings with net domestic investment is particularly significant.

Results of the calculations are shown in Tables 33 and 34. Government gross savings between 1949 and 1957 amounted to

28.4% of all gross savings. If the budget losses through tax exemptions are added, they are 31.7%. Finally, if deductions made under the various tax exemptions for capital formation are added to government gross savings, the percentage is 36.6%. Approximately one-third of all gross savings was supplied by government. Since public corporations, the federal railway and the postal system are not included, this is a minimum.

Things look different when net government savings are compared with net savings for net domestic capital formation. The government savings, defined as an excess of current receipts over current expenditures, amounted to 46.8% of all net savings between 1949 and 1957. When budget losses through tax exemptions are included, the percentage becomes 52.5%. Finally, if

TABLE 33

Contribution of Government to Total Gross Savings.
Government Gross Savings as Percentages of Total
Gross Savings. Current Prices[1]

| Year | Government Gross Savings[2] | Government Gross Savings plus Budget Losses through Tax-exemptions[3] | Government Gross Savings plus Deductions[4] |
|---|---|---|---|
| 1948 2.H.Y. | 23.9 | n.a. | n.a. |
| 1949 | 24.6 | 31.6 | 35.7 |
| 1950 | 25.8 | 31.2 | 36.2 |
| 1951 | 26.7 | 29.5 | 33.6 |
| 1952 | 25.7 | 29.4 | 34.7 |
| 1953 | 31.9 | 36.4 | 42.4 |
| 1954 | 31.1 | 35.1 | 42.3 |
| 1955 | 29.8 | 32.2 | 37.1 |
| 1956 | 29.9 | 32.0 | 36.2 |
| 1957 | 26.5 | 28.4 | 32.0 |
| 1958 | 22.6 | n.a. | n.a. |
| 1959 | 25.0 | n.a. | n.a. |
| 1960 | 29.2 | n.a. | n.a. |
| 1949 to 1957 | 28.4 | 31.7 | 36.6 |
| 1948 2 H.Y. to 1960 | 27.4 | n.a. | n.a. |

[1] Total gross savings as shown in Table 13. Government including Social Security System.
[2] Gross Savings from Table 13.
[3] Budget losses from Tables 17 and 24.
[4] Deductions from Tables 17 and 24.

TABLE 34

Contribution of Government to Total Net Savings.
Government Net Savings as Percentage of Net
Domestic Capital Formation. Current Prices[1]

| Year | Government Net Savings[2] | Government Net Savings plus Budget Losses through Tax Exemptions[3] | Government Net Savings plus Deductions[4] |
|---|---|---|---|
| 1948 2.H.Y. | 36.8 | n.a. | n.a. |
| 1949 | 34.8 | 45.9 | 52.3 |
| 1950 | 44.9 | 55.1 | 64.4 |
| 1951 | 50.7 | 56.2 | 64.6 |
| 1952 | 45.1 | 52.2 | 62.1 |
| 1953 | 59.4 | 68.3 | 80.0 |
| 1954 | 52.0 | 59.0 | 71.8 |
| 1955 | 43.5 | 47.2 | 54.6 |
| 1956 | 47.1 | 50.5 | 57.5 |
| 1957 | 43.0 | 46.3 | 52.5 |
| 1958 | 37.4 | n.a. | n.a. |
| 1959 | 38.4 | n.a. | n.a. |
| 1960 | 43.0 | n.a. | n.a. |
| 1949 to 1957 | 46.8 | 52.5 | 61.0 |
| 1948 2.H.Y. to 1960 | 43.9 | n.a. | n.a. |

[1] Net domestic capital formation from Table 14. Government including Social Security System.
[2] Net Savings from Table 13.
[3] Budget losses from Tables 17 and 24.
[4] Deductions from Tables 17 and 24.

one adds the excess of current receipts over current expenditures and all deductions made under laws favoring capital formation, the percentage is 61%. Therefore, at least one-half, but probably more—due to omission of public corporations, railway and postal systems—of all investable funds for net domestic investment was supplied by the government.

At the beginning of this chapter, the question was asked: how could West Germany, with rather low income in the first part of the '50's generate the savings for the high rate of capital formation the country experienced? The answer to this is clear: the high rate of savings was possible because the government was a strong saver. Current government receipts substantially exceeded current expenditures. Responsible for this were high tax yields due to high tax rates and, with rising incomes, a rapidly broadening tax base; and, on the other hand, two expenditure items which were very low compared with those in other nation's budgets. These were defense expenditures and interest payments on the national debt. Defense expenditures were for years far below those of other comparable Western Countries. There was no large debt service because the national debt of West Germany is negligible compared with those of the United States and the United Kingdom.

The high rate of savings in West Germany during the crucial growth period 1949 to 1957 was definitely not due to large voluntary savings induced by high interest rates, as is sometimes assumed. The bulk of the savings were involuntarily obtained through taxes or high profits which were not taxed when invested. Without public savings, the rapid West German capital formation and the high growth rates of the economy would have been very difficult, if not impossible.

# IV. The Government's Influence on the Structure of Capital Formation

THE LAST CHAPTER pointed out that government supplied at least one-half of all net savings and about one-third of all gross savings for capital formation. These public savings resulted, no doubt, in a much larger volume of capital formation than would otherwise have been possible. With such large contributions, the government not only increased the volume of investment, but also influenced the structure of capital formation. The question now is: Was this desirable in the West German situation? Did this advance the performance of the economy by improving the quality of resource allocation, or was it a retarding element interfering with the working of an efficient market mechanism? Did this public influence on investment speed up the elimination of bottlenecks in the structure of production, or was this unnecessary because the market forces could have acted much faster, providing for higher efficiency and socially more acceptable solutions?

The study of these problems would be greatly facilitated if better data on investments and public spending in West Germany were available. There are, unfortunately, no detailed official data on investments existing by industries,[1] and it is impos-

---

[1] This handicap is now partially overcome as the Deutsche Institut für Wirtschaftsforschung in Berlin has estimated investments in fixed assets in different industries.

sible to discover from West German financial statistics the industries into which public investable funds were channeled. With these limitations, only specific investment programs in which government participated, and for which data are available, can be studied. The role of government influence on investments in the so-called "bottleneck sectors"—residential construction, shipbuilding, and agriculture—has been examined. In addition, investments in transportation and social and cultural institutions have been considered. In these sectors, government influence on investments was considerable. How these influences affected efficiency shall now be investigated.

### a. *Production Bottlenecks*

In the first chapter it was pointed out that in 1948, at the time of the currency reform, the capital stock in industry was about the same size as before the war. Unlike housing and transportation, where destruction during the war was heavy, industrial capacities were not excessively decreased, a fact which is sometimes ignored when the development of the West German economy is described. Between 1939 and 1945, large investments had been made, especially in basic industries. These offset, to a considerable extent, the losses through destruction during the war and the dismantling of industries which followed. In addition, between 1945 and 1948, there had been a small but effective volume of investments consisting largely of repairs.[1] The existence of sufficient industrial capacities was one of the main reasons why West Germany could so rapidly improve its production immediately after the currency reform. Until 1950 most industries still had idle capacities. The economy grew into these capacities and where initial bottlenecks occurred they could often be overcome through repair work requiring much less time and effort than the building of new facilities. Also, the expansion of some crucial bottleneck industries such as coal mining was favored by the occupation powers between 1945 and 1948. Coal

---

[1] It is interesting to note that investments in this period were larger than those during the years of the Great Depression.

production was somewhat ahead of production in other industrial sectors, which facilitated economic reconstruction. The essential problem in 1949 and the beginning of 1950 was using existing capacities and not the building of new ones. Under these conditions, and in view of the very high rates of unemployment, the government decided to start a public works program. This program, however, was not too vigorously pushed.[1] A restrictive money policy, pursued in an understandable fear of inflation, held back the economy in 1949 and the first half of 1950. Then came the Korean War in June, 1950. Large defense efforts in the Western world led to a rapid increase in demand for West German exportables. Domestically, under the influence of the war scare, the demand for consumer goods rose strongly. The sudden increase in aggregate demand led to a higher level of economic activity but was also accompanied by substantial price increases. Thus, a new phase in the development of the West German economy began with the Korean War.

It should be noted that, with the existing industrial capacities, by 1950 the country had already reached the 1938 level of production. For further strong expansion, however, these capacities were not sufficient. The structure of the capital stock which so far had been of lesser concern became suddenly very important.

Some of the capacities which were built during the war could not be converted quickly for civil use. War losses and dismantling had an uneven impact and often decreased capacities in some specific industrial sectors which created bothersome bottlenecks. The division of Germany had an additional effect in that some industries primarily situated in East Germany were inadequate or unavailable in West Germany. With relatively low levels of production in 1948 and 1949, all of this was not too restraining. The rapid increases in output during the Korean boom revealed, however, serious limitations.

In September, 1950, difficulties in the production of coal and steel occurred. There had been some bottlenecks in the produc-

---

[1] B.D.L., *Annual Report*, 1950, p. 29.

tion of electricity in 1949 but these became so serious in the first quarter of 1951 that the use of electric current in industry was temporarily cut by 25%. Other bottlenecks occurred in railroad transport, in the production of non-ferrous metals, and in the chemical industry.[1] Some of these difficulties were overcome through foreign trade.[2] For the more important bottlenecks in coal, steel, and electricity production, large investments were necessary to increase productive capacities.[3] If these industries themselves had to finance these investments, they would have been obliged, in view of the small volume of investable funds which could be obtained in the capital market, to finance them internally. This, in turn, would have required large price increases for these basic items. There seemed a disinclination to let this happen, because there was a fear that, with price and wage rigidities, such price rises would be rapidly propagated throughout the economy. During the Korean boom, when the economy was already experiencing substantial price pressures, this was certainly not desirable. It was preferable to give special aid to these industries.

Some critical industries (coal mining, electricity production) received large amounts of funds between 1949 and 1951 under the European Recovery Program (ERP). From the United States, under the Economic Aid Program, West Germany also received imports of various kinds. West German importers paid into a special account at the Central Bank for these U.S. imports. A fraction of the accumulated payments, or Counterpart Funds, was used by the United States government to defray the cost of transport and administration; however, the bulk was available

---

[1] R. Salomon, *Begriff und Problematik der wirtschaftlichen Engpässe,* Kiel, 1954, p. 27, *Kieler Studien No. 29,* Forschungsberichte des Instituts für Weltwirtschaft an der Universität Kiel.

[2] The removal of bottlenecks through imports became thus a balance of payments problem. For a general discussion, see W. F. Stolper, "A Note on Multiplier Flexible Exchanges and the Dollar Shortage," *Economica Internazionale,* August, 1950.

[3] "Der Investitionsmittel Bedarf in den Engpassindustrien der Bundesrepublik," *Mitteilungen des Wirtschaftswissenschaftlichen Instituts der Gewerkschaften,* Mai, 1951.

for investments in the West German economy.[1] The ERP fund, which was administered by the West German government, is still in existence. It has continued to make funds available from amortization and interest payments for investments in various sectors of the economy. ERP funds have generally been used for investments in sectors which were lagging in output and where major efforts had to be made.[2] In 1949–50, these funds were used to boost investments in basic industries. In 1950–51, they were channeled into agriculture and residential construction. They had been used to promote export industries and finance general modernization in industry.

In 1949 and 1950, ERP provided the bottleneck industries with more than 1.3 billion DM or 23% of all gross investments in fixed assets. In 1951, another 495 million DM of ERP funds were made available, of which 334 million DM were designated for railroads.[3] Still, these investments, though enormously helpful, were not sufficient for the necessary increases in output after 1950. The production of bottleneck industries had to increase substantially if the growth of the economy was not to be choked. Aid to these industries was, therefore, much debated by the government and various plans were suggested. We may refer to two: the Minister of Economic Affairs plan by Professor Erhard, and that of the Social Democratic Party.

Erhard suggested obtaining investable funds by reducing consumption through forced savings. The consumer should pay an additional amount for certain goods—which ones was never clearly spelled out, but presumably luxury items—for which he would receive coupons. These coupons would be collected and eventually exchanged for bonds. The funds obtained in this way would be channeled directly into the bottleneck industries.[4] The

---

[1] Friedrich Breckner, "ERP Finanzierung," *Handwörterbuch der Betriebswirtschaft*, Band I, Stuttgart, 1956.

[2] The German expression for these investment programs in particular sectors was "Schwerpunkt Program."

[3] Egon R. Baumgart, *Investitionen und ERP Finanzierung* (Berlin: Duncker und Humblot, 1961), p. 51, 54.

[4] Speech by Dr. Erhard, *Deutscher Bundestag, 126*, Sitzung 14, März, 1951.

argument was that the small saver would thus have an opportunity to participate in the country's capital formation. He would be forced to save but not deprived of his property as would be the case if investable funds were obtained through taxation. This was, in essence, an austerity program. It was questioned whether sufficient investable funds could be obtained in this way. The government also realized that such a forced savings program woud be highly unpopular.[1]

This plan, sometimes referred to as the "Baby Bonds Plan," was heavily attacked by the Social Democratic opposition.[2] It was argued that the government had aided capital formation in general through lavish tax concessions and excessive favoring of internal financing, often in relatively unimportant areas. The result was that the consumption goods industries and trade and services invested excessively whereas the basic industries lagged behind. The Social Democrats recommended that instead of placing an additional burden on the average consumer, whose standard of living was still very low, business in those sectors of the economy which were overinvested should be required to subscribe to a bond issue for the financing of investments in the basic industries. These funds would then be concentrated and directly allocated to those sectors where bottleneck problems were most restraining.

Aid was finally given to the bottleneck industries under the Investment Aid Law in 1952. This law closely followed the proposals of the Social Democratic opposition. All plans for Baby Bond Savings were subsequently dropped. The Investment Aid Law required that business in general had to supply one billion DM for investments in bottleneck sectors.[3] This was a massive interference of government in the working of the market system and evidently somewhat embarrassing to adherents of the free-market doctrine. The program was labeled a "Self-aid" program of the economy, and a special institution was set up to handle the

[1] Speech by Dr. Preusker, *Deutscher Bundestag, 126*, Sitzung 14, März, 1951.
[2] Speech by Dr. Nölting, *Deutscher Bundestag, 126*, Sitzung, 14, März, 1951.
[3] *Deutscher Bundestag, 1, Wahlperiode 1949, Drucksache No. 2450.*

channeling of the funds.[1] The government was not represented on the board of this institution, though the Minister of Economic Affairs certainly had some influence on the allocation of funds. The collection of the funds was supervised by fiscal authorities, and in case of non-payment the legal procedure for failure to pay taxes applied.

As a tax base the profits for the years 1950 and 1951, increased by tax deductions made under paragraphs 7a to 7e of the Income Tax Law[2] plus 4% of the turnover in 1950 and 1951, were chosen. From this amount, deductions were permitted, which, for a single proprietor, were 20,000 DM, and somewhat less for other forms of business. To the tax base thus obtained, a flat rate of 3.5% applied.[3]

The total amount actually raised under this law was 1.159 billion DM.[4] The funds were channeled into 187 enterprises: 34 in coal mining; 22 in the iron and steel industry; 34 in electricity production; 48 in gas production; 48 in water supply; and 1 in construction of railroad cars. Businesses contributing to the Investment Aid Fund received fixed interest securities issued by firms which obtained these funds. Originally, the lawmakers were uncertain as to the extent of the aid needed for the bottleneck industries and the duration of the program.[5] The law was not very enthusiastically received by many businessmen. It deprived business, especially small business, of liquidity, and in many instances Investment Aid Securities were soon resold, some at heavy discounts.[6] This may have been a major reason for terminating the program earlier than was originally intended.

In addition to this large transfer of funds between business sectors, substantial aid was given to bottleneck industries

---

[1] Kuratorium für das Industrie-Sondervermögen Investitionshilfe.

[2] For a discussion of these paragraphs, see Chapter 3.

[3] *Deutscher Bundestag, 1. Wahlperiode Drucksache No. 2758 (neu).*

[4] *"Zeitschrift für das gesamte Kreditwesen,"* 1955, p. 789; *Allgemeine Vorbemerkungen zum Bundeshaushaltsplan,* 1956, p. 300.

[5] *Deutscher Bundestag, 1. Wahlperiode Drucksache No. 2450,* p. 12.

[6] Contributing to this program were 132,000 firms. Fiscal authorities granted 116,000 requests for postponements in the payment of this levy during the time this law was effective.

through accelerated depreciation of plant and equipment under paragraph 36 of the Investment Aid Law.[1] Also, price increases for coal in May, 1952, and February, 1953, facilitated internal financing of the mining industries.

Data on the developments in the different bottleneck industries may be found in Tables 35 to 37. How these occurred may now be considered.

Production of soft coal in 1949 was 103.2 million tons, compared with 117.0 million tons in 1936 and 137.3 million tons in 1943.[2] Increases in output in this sector required large investments because most of the West German soft coal mines date back prior to 1928, and they needed large scale modernization after their excessive use during the war. Also, new mines had to be opened. Between 1949 and 1956, coal production increased to 134.4 million tons. This required an increase of only 11.6% of the labor force but nearly a tripling of gross investments. These were estimated at 470 million DM in 1949 and at 1,330 million DM in 1955. Total gross investments in fixed assets in this sector amounted to 7.8 billion DM between 1949 and 1956. Of these, 25.6% were supplied by ERP or Investment Aid funds or through internal financing favored under paragraph 36 of the Investment Aid Law. In the years 1949 and 1950 especially, investments were greatly increased through ERP funds. After 1952, support came mainly from the Investment Aid program. What other public aid this industry received is not known.[3]

It should be noted that the Federal government owns a substantial part of the soft coal mines in West Germany. In 1958, 25.7% of the total soft coal production was produced in government owned corporations.[4]

Since 1958, West German soft coal mines have had recurrent

---

[1] For a discussion of this paragraph, see Chapter 3.

[2] Richard Salomon, *op. cit.*, p. 27.

[3] Attempts were made to grant special tax exemptions for coal mining even after 1956. See: *Deutscher Bundestag 2, Wahlperiode, Drucksache 1763.*

[4] Bundesministerium für wirtschaftlichen Besitz des Bundes, "Der Bund als Unternehmer," Bad Godesberg: Verlag für Publizistik, 1961, p. 11.

TABLE 35

Production, Investments, and Employment in Coal Mining,
1949 to 1956

| Year | Production of Soft Coal[1] Mill. to. | Lignite[1] Mill. to. | Gross Investments in Fixed Assets in Coal Mining Current Prices of which Total Millions of DM.[2] | ERP Funds Millions of DM.[2] | Investment Aid Funds |
|------|------|------|------|------|------|
| | (1) | (2) | (3) | (4) | (5) |
| 1949 | 103.2 | 72.3 | 470 | 221 | |
| 1950 | 110.8 | 75.8 | 480 | 190 | |
| 1951 | 118.9 | 83.1 | 600 | 77 | |
| 1952 | 123.3 | 83.4 | 980 | 48 | |
| 1953 | 124.5 | 84.6 | 1300 | 38 | 930[3] |
| 1954 | 128.0 | 87.8 | 1345 | 17 | 440[4] |
| 1955 | 130.7 | 90.3 | 1330 | 40 | |
| 1956 | 134.4 | 95.2 | 1295 | 20 | |
| Total: 1949 to 1955 | | | 7800 | 631 | 1370 |

[1] St. J.B. 1955, p. 218. St. J.B. 1953, p. 250. St. J.B. 1958, p. 191.
[2] Egon R. Baumgart, "Investitionen und ERP Finanzierung," Berlin 1961, pp. 51, 118.
[3] Actual investment out of internal funds up to March 31, 1955, "Zeitschrift für das Gesamte Kreditwesen" 1955, p. 789.

troubles in selling their products, and output dropped to 126.0 million tons in 1960 (excluding the Saar). The decline in demand for soft coal can be explained partly by the rapidly rising use of competing sources of energy, such as natural gas or oil derivatives. Technological changes also reduced necessary coal inputs. For example, steam locomotives of the Federal railroad used 9.4 million tons of soft coal in 1956; in 1959, however, they needed only 7.6 million tons, reflecting the increased electrification of railroads and the use of Diesel engines. Traditionally, West Germany has been a net exporter of soft coal. Still, it was significant for the supply situation in soft coal that, as late as 1955, the country became for two years a net importer, buying substantial amounts of United States coal.

The argument that large public aid to coal mining during the early '50's was responsible for overproduction and excess capacities after 1958 is not very convincing. Difficulties in coal mining

TABLE 35 *(cont.)*

| Year | Employ- ment in Coal Mining 1000 Persons[5] | Production of Soft Coal | Indexes of Gross Investments | Employment | Column 4 and 5 as % of Column 3 |
|------|------|------|------|------|------|
| | (6) | (7) | (8) | (9) | (10) |
| 1949 | 512.0 | 100.0 | 100.0 | 100.0 | 43.2 |
| 1950 | 516.5 | 107.4 | 102.1 | 100.9 | 39.6 |
| 1951 | 530.1 | 115.2 | 127.7 | 103.5 | 12.8 |
| 1952 | 547.2 | 119.4 | 208.5 | 106.9 | n.a. |
| 1953 | 564.0 | 120.6 | 276.6 | 110.1 | n.a. |
| 1954 | 563.7 | 124.0 | 286.1 | 110.0 | n.a. |
| 1955 | 563.4 | 126.6 | 283.0 | 110.0 | n.a. |
| 1956 | 571.3 | 130.2 | 275.5 | 111.6 | n.a. |
| Total: 1949 to 1955 | | | | | 25.6 |

[4] Investments with Investment Aid Funds.
[5] St. J.B. 1955, p. 205. St. J.B. 1953, p. 240, for 2. H.Y. 1949, St. J.B. 1958, p. 174.

at the later date were certainly far less serious than the bottleneck situation in 1950 with its potential to delay overall economic expansion. In retrospect, public aid to this sector was necessary and wise. Without it, the bottleneck could not have been overcome as rapidly, and there might have been serious repercussions.

There were several reasons for the bottlenecks in the West German iron and steel industry prior to 1954. West Germany produced 16.9 million tons of ingot steel in 1936.[1] During the war, production was substantially increased, as is indicated by the rise of the index of production for iron and steel making and the metal goods industries. With 1936 equal to 100, the index reached 216.9 during the war.[2] This increase in produc-

[1] B. Gleitze, *op. cit.,* p. 193 f.
[2] Gleitze, *op. cit.,* p. 169.

TABLE 36

Production, Investments, and Employment in the Iron and
Steel Industry, 1949 to 1956

| Year | Production of | | GROSS INVESTMENTS IN FIXED ASSETS IN IRON AND STEEL INDUSTRY Current Prices of which | | |
|---|---|---|---|---|---|
| | Ingot Steel[1] Millions of to. | Rolled Steel[1] Millions of to. | Total Millions of DM.[2] | ERP Funds Millions of DM.[2] | Investment Aid Funds Millions of DM. |
| | (1) | (2) | (3) | (4) | (5) |
| 1949 | 9.0 | 6.3 | 280 | — | |
| 1950 | 11.8 | 8.2 | 380 | 68 | |
| 1951 | 13.1 | 9.4 | 600 | 84 | |
| 1952 | 15.3 | 10.7 | 950 | 19 | |
| 1953 | 14.9 | 10.2 | 1190 | 27 | 530[3] |
| 1954 | 17.0 | 11.5 | 1500 | 60 | 440[4] |
| 1955 | 20.7 | 14.2 | 2050 | 139 | |
| 1956 | 22.6 | 15.6 | 1670 | 18 | |
| Total: 1949 to 1955 | | | 6950 | 397 | 970 |

[1] St. J.B. 1955, p. 218. St. J.B. 1953, p. 251. St. J.B. 1958, p. 192.
[2] Source: See Table 35, footnote 2.
[3] Actual investment out of internal funds up to March 31, 1955. Source: See Table 35, footnote 3.

tion required large investments and these more than offset the war losses. According to a West German source, productive capacities in the iron and steel industry were still 10% higher in 1947–48 than in 1936; dismantling hit this industry with its capacities for war production especially hard. Shortly before the currency reform in 1948, only about 85% of the 1936 capacity existed.[1] For example, a number of key facilities for the production of rolled steel, tubes, and high quality steel were eliminated.[2] Yet, until 1950, one could not talk of a serious bottleneck in production because demand from the iron and steel-using industries was still at a low level. After 1950, with rising exports consisting largely of steel products and an increased domestic

[1] Bremer Ausschuss für Wirtschaftsforschung, "Am Abend der Demontage," *op. cit.*, p. 26.
[2] Salomon, *op. cit.*, p. 38.

TABLE 36 (*cont.*)

| Year | Employ- ment in Iron and Steel Industry 1000 Persons[5] | *Indexes of* Production of Ingot Steel | Gross Investments | Employment | Column 4 as % of Column 3 |
|------|------|------|------|------|------|
|      | (6) | (7) | (8) | (9) | (10) |
| 1949 | 181.2 | 100.0 | 100.0 | 100.0 | .0 |
| 1950 | 204.5 | 131.1 | 135.7 | 112.9 | 17.9 |
| 1951 | 212.6 | 145.6 | 214.3 | 117.3 | 14.0 |
| 1952 | 227.9 | 170.0 | 339.3 | 125.8 | n.a. |
| 1953 | 229.8 | 165.6 | 425.1 | 126.8 | n.a. |
| 1954 | 231.2 | 188.9 | 535.8 | 127.6 | n.a. |
| 1955 | 251.2 | 230.0 | 732.3 | 138.6 | n.a. |
| 1956 | 273.2 | 251.1 | 596.5 | 150.8 | n.a. |
| Total: 1949 to 1955 |  |  |  |  | 19.7 |

[4] Investments with Investment Aid funds.
[5] St. J.B. 1953, p. 241. St. J.B. 1955, p. 206. St. J.B. 1958, p. 175.

demand due to the Korean boom, shortages occurred. Disproportions between blast furnace and rolling mill capacities became
very restraining. In addition, an insufficient supply of coal became a handicap. Still, part of the bottleneck was temporarily
overcome through larger imports. In 1951–52, it became obvious
that increases in production were possible only through the
building of new capacities, and this required large amounts of
investable funds. Though the need for these investments was
recognized early, their financing remained a problem for some
time.[1] Until 1953, iron and steel prices remained controlled.
This meant that the industry, which for years had enjoyed a

---

[1] Speech by representative Scheel (F.D.P.), 2. Deutscher Bundestag, 34,
Sitzung 19 Juni 1954. Interpellation der SPD Fraktion, betreffs Wiederaufbau
von Betrieben der eisenschaffenden Industrie, *Deutscher Bundestag 1.
Wahlperiode, Drucksache No. 2896.*

## TABLE 37

### Production and Investments in the Electric Power Sector

| Year | Production of Electricity[1] Billions of Kwh | Gross Investments in Fixed Assets in Electricity Production, Current Prices, of which | | | Indexes of | | |
|---|---|---|---|---|---|---|---|
| | | Total Millions of DM.[2] | ERP Funds Millions of DM.[2] | Investment Aid Funds Millions of DM. | Production | Gross Investment | Columns 3 and 4 as % of Column 2 |
| | (1) | (2) | (3) | (4) | (5) | (6) | (7) |
| 1949 | 39.1 | 890 | 157 | | 100.0 | 100.0 | 17.6 |
| 1950 | 44.4 | 1150 | 292 | | 113.6 | 129.3 | 25.4 |
| 1951 | 51.4 | 1260 | 334 | | 131.5 | 141.6 | 26.5 |
| 1952 | 56.2 | 1440 | 89 | | 143.8 | 161.9 | n.a. |
| 1953 | 60.4 | 1530 | 76 | 610[3] | 154.5 | 172.0 | n.a. |
| 1954 | 67.9 | 1830 | 36 | 540[4] | 173.7 | 205.7 | n.a. |
| 1955 | 75.8 | 2100 | 24 | | 193.9 | 236.0 | n.a. |
| 1956 | 84.3 | 2160 | 13 | | 215.6 | 242.8 | n.a. |
| Total 1949 to 1955: | | 10200 | 1008 | 1150 | | | 21.2 |

[1] St. J.B. 1955, p. 235, p. 54°. St. J.B. 1958, p. 54°.
[2] Egon R. Baumgart, op. cit., p. 71.
[3] Investments out of internal funds up to March 31, 1955. Source: Table 35, footnote 3.
[4] Investments with Investment Aid funds.

strong seller's market, could not obtain the necessary large volume of investable funds through internal financing. As a consequence, public funds were necessary to finance investments. The industry received 152 million DM of ERP funds for investments in the years 1950 and 1951. From 1952 on, substantial additional aid was provided under the Investment Aid program. In total, between 1949 and 1956, 6.95 billion DM were invested, of which 19.7% was provided through ERP and Investment Aid funds. This public aid to the iron and steel industry was very crucial for the development of the total West German economy. It not only assured a sufficient steel supply for domestic uses, but also facilitated rising exports of such steel using industries as the automotive industry, machine building, shipbuilding, and the electrotechnical industry.

The third large bottleneck in the structure of West German production was the output of electricity. Three factors were responsible for this, two on the supply side and one on the demand side. On the supply side, there was a lack of generating capacity which could be overcome only through new investments. In addition, there was a coal shortage which occasionally severely restricted the use of existing capacities. The shortage of coal in West Germany was especially curtailing, since about 85% of all electricity is generated with soft coal or lignite as energy source. These limitations in supply occurred simultaneously with a rapid increase in the demand for electric power. West Germany produced 31.1 billion kwh in 1938 and 41.5 billion kwh in 1943, but this jumped to 60.4 billion kwh in 1953. The sharp increase in the consumption of electric energy has continued. In 1960, the country generated 113.2 billion kwh.

The supply of electricity was insufficient between 1948 and 1951, but when the production of coal increased, the situation improved temporarily. Still, the long-run problem of augmenting generating capacities for future demand increases remained to be solved. Investments in the electricity industry in West Germany before the war were usually financed through issues of long-term bonds. After the war, the industry faced a difficult situation because long-term investable funds could not be obtained on the capital market. Internal financing was very difficult, as the price of electricity was controlled and could not be raised very much for social reasons.[1] Profit margins were therefore slim, especially as the price of coal inputs rose. In view of the importance of the electrical power industry to the total economy, it was necessary to finance a large part of investments with public funds. Up to 1951, these were made available under the ERP; later under the Investment Aid program. These two sources financed about 21.2% of all gross investments between 1949 and 1955.[2]

Other bottlenecks occurred in railroad transport, which was greatly impeded after the last war through losses in rolling stock, especially railroad cars.[3] The Federal railroad was not in a position to finance the building of needed new equipment out of its own earnings. Contrary to the former Reichsbahn, the Federal railroad operated for many years at a loss. Although it made a profit on the transport of goods this was not sufficient, in many cases, to offset deficits in passenger traffic where, for social reasons, large numbers of special low tariffs are granted. Both ERP and Investment Aid funds were made available for investments in this sector.

It should be noted that the above bottlenecks were interdependent to a considerable degree. Lack of coal caused lower steel and electricity production which in turn interfered with output of transport equipment. Elimination of one bottleneck helped to overcome others. The efficiency of funds used to eliminate bottlenecks, in terms of increases in production, must therefore be rated very high.[4]

### b. *Residential Construction*

The housing shortage in postwar West Germany was a serious sociological and economic problem. Even before the war, Ger-

---

1 Baumgart, *op. cit.*, p. 81.

2 For special tax privileges to hydro-power plants, see: *Deutscher Bundestag, 2. Wahlperiode Drucksache 3426.*

3 *Deutscher Bundestag, 1. Wahlperiode 1949 Drucksache No. 573.*

4 *Allgemeine Vorbemerkungen zum Bundeshaushaltsplan*, Berlin: Bundesdruckerei, 1956, p. 298.

many needed 1.5 million dwellings. With about 2.3 million apartments destroyed in West Germany between 1939 and 1945, and an influx of more than 10 million refugees, the housing situation became desperate. In an effort to control existing housing space, the occupation powers enacted the Control Council Law No. 18 which later became part of the West German legal system.[1] Up to 1950, about 1 million apartments were added through repairs or new construction, but the deficit in apartments at the end of that year still amounted to 4.5 million units. Many of the refugees had to live under rather crowded conditions, often sharing kitchens and tables with those in whose homes they were quartered. Relations were often far from pleasant under these circumstances and all sorts of social problems and conflicts arose, especially in areas which had received a very strong influx of refugees. Providing decent housing for refugees contributed greatly to their integration and, at the same time, eliminated a lot of antagonistic feelings.

Not only refugees needed homes. Quite a large part of the indigenous population had lost its dwellings during the war and were not much better off.

In view of the extremely high demand for housing and its overall social significance, it was considered impossible to let market forces alone determine the progress in this area. The Federal Government did not abolish existing housing controls but introduced a dual policy. All dwellings erected before the currency reform in 1948 remained under control. For houses which were built later, the situation was different. Three categories of new houses were established: first, houses built with public funds known as "social housing construction"; second, tax-favored housing construction; third, housing financed without any public assistance.[2]

Social housing was promoted with public funds, usually in the form of loans or subsidies. These public funds largely replaced

---

[1] *The West German Economy*, Köln: Deutsches Industrie Institut, Köln, 1959, p. 175.

[2] *Allgemeine Vorbemerkungen zum Bundeshaushaltsplan*, Bonn, 1955, p. 192.

the owner's capital in normal financing of residential construction. First mortgages for these houses were usually obtained on the capital market. For dwellings built with public funds, the government stipulated certain minimum standards as to size and equipment, and apartments could not be rented to people with annual incomes of more than 9,000 DM. For those in lower income brackets, low rent units were reserved, and rent allowances made. The government decided on tenancy as well as on rents for houses to accommodate the lower income brackets.

No tenancy control existed for houses which were built with tax-favored funds, but to some degree rent controls prevailed. No controls of any kind applied to dwellings which were built without public aid.

In addition to the above programs, the government promoted a number of special housing programs for miners, refugees, agricultural workers, and public employees.

West Germany built 5.2 million new dwellings between 1949 and 1959, of which more than 50% were built under the social housing program. In 1960, the deficit in dwellings was reduced to about 1 million units.

Gross investments in residential construction accounted for about 25% of all gross domestic investments in fixed assets, and they increased from 2.5 billion DM in 1949 to more than 15.0 billion DM in 1959. According to an estimate made by the ministry of finances in Bonn, the government contributed to this large residential construction program a total of about 52 billion DM or about 55% of total investments between 1950 and 1959. These contributions took the form of loans, subsidies, or tax exemptions. A large part of these funds (between 50% to 60%) will eventually be repaid and does not constitute a definite budget loss. Still this fact should not detract from the eminent importance of government aid in this field. It allowed West Germany nearly to overcome one of its greatest problems within one decade.

To what extent this government sponsored housing program increased efficiency in general is difficult to say. Since in our industrial societies the ability to work depends to a considerable

## TABLE 38

### Residential Construction in West Germany—1949 to 1959. Number of Apartments Built, Gross Investment in Residential Construction

| Year | Apartments Built 1000[1] | Apartments Built with Public Aid[1] (Social Housing) 1000 | Gross Investments in Residential Construction[2] Current Prices Billions of DM. | Gross Investments in Residential Construction[3] Current Prices Billions of DM. | Gross Investment in Residential Construction as % of Gross Domestic Capital Formation in Fixed Assets |
|------|-----|-----|-----|-----|-----|
| | (1) | (2) | (3) | (4) | (5) |
| 1949 | 215 | n.a. | 2.5 | n.a. | 16.6 |
| 1950 | 360 | n.a. | 3.6 | 3.8 | 20.9 |
| 1951 | 410 | n.a. | 4.7 | 4.7 | 20.9 |
| 1952 | 443 | n.a. | 5.5 | 6.3 | 24.3 |
| 1953 | 518 | 287 | 7.0 | 7.8 | 26.6 |
| 1954 | 543 | 285 | 8.2 | 9.0 | 27.4 |
| 1955 | 542 | 269 | 9.1 | 10.1 | 24.6 |
| 1956 | 559 | 286 | 9.9 | 10.9 | 24.2 |
| 1957 | 529 | 274 | n.a. | 11.5 | 24.7 |
| 1958 | 486 | 255 | n.a. | 12.3 | 24.5 |
| 1959 | 556 | 294 | n.a. | 15.1 | 26.5 |

1 Finanzbericht, Bundesminister der Finanzen, Bonn, 1961, p. 99.
2 Baumgart, op. cit. p. 118.
3 Finanzbericht 1961, p. 100. Further source: Bundesbaublatt, Heft 6/1958, Heft 5/1960, p. 247.

TABLE 39

Public Aid to Residential Construction—1949 to 1959.
Current Prices, Millions of DM.[1]

| Year | Loans, Premiums and direct Investments (1) | Interest Subsidies[2] (2) | Budget Losses[3] Through Tax Exemptions (3) |
|---|---|---|---|
| 1949 | 1397 | 25 | 215 |
| 1950 | 1740 | 85 | 375 |
| 1951 | 2364 | 160 | 420 |
| 1952 | 3170 | 270 | 520 |
| 1953 | 3216 | 400 | 685 |
| 1954 | 3735 | 540 | 855 |
| 1955 | 3446 | 685 | 845 |
| 1956 | 4226 | 835 | 920 |
| 1957 | 4299 | 1000 | 1055 |
| 1958 | 4533 | 1165 | 1135 |
| 1959 | 4904 | 1335 | 1290 |
| 1949 to 1959 | 37030 | 6500 | 8315 |

[1] Estimate by Bundesministerium der Finanzen "Finanzbericht 1961," p. 116, 117.
[2] Calculated as difference between interest rate on loans and market rate of interest.
[3] Refers to paragraphs 3a, 7b, 7c, 10. E. St. G. and some other laws.
[4] This is a rough estimate only. Actual budget losses are very difficult to estimate as

extent on relaxation and on a certain degree of comfort in spare time, the availability of good housing was certainly very important.

Though it is not easy to evaluate the general effects which better housing had on the labor force and production, construction of houses did overcome some structural rigidities, which led directly to higher output.

Specifically, residential construction has greatly increased the efficiency of the West German economy by making the West German labor force more mobile. After 1945 large numbers of refugees found shelter in agricultural areas but these areas could not, however, offer them employment. With an increase in economic activity in industrial areas, where housing was extremely short, additional labor was needed. In many cases, people willing to work in industry had to return to agricultural areas because

TABLE 39 (*cont.*)

| Year | Total Aid (4) | Of which estimated as definite Budget Loss[4] (5) | Total Public Aid as % of Gross Investment in Residential Construction[5] (6) |
|------|------|------|------|
| 1949 | 1637 | 518 | 64.6 |
| 1950 | 2200 | 679 | 61.2 |
| 1951 | 2944 | 829 | 62.5 |
| 1952 | 3960 | 1087 | 62.5 |
| 1953 | 4301 | 1322 | 55.1 |
| 1954 | 5130 | 1663 | 56.6 |
| 1955 | 4976 | 1758 | 49.3 |
| 1956 | 5981 | 2133 | 55.0 |
| 1957 | 6354 | 2464 | 55.1 |
| 1958 | 6833 | 2820 | 55.5 |
| 1959 | 7529 | 3163 | 49.6 |
| 1949 to 1959 | 51845 | 18436 | 55.1 |

they depend on future tax rates, and, if the present value of the loss is to be calculated, on future interest rates.

[5] Column 4 as percentage of column 4 table 38.

no apartments were available for housing families. Coal mining, an industry in which output increases were imperative, had special troubles in getting labor. To increase coal production, additional housing was needed.[1] In the beginning of 1950, there was a shortage of 115,000 dwellings in the Ruhr area and, in spite of rapid construction in 1951, about 50,000 miners still remained separated from their families. This lack in housing for miners was considered so important that some experts felt residential construction for miners should have been given priority over all other investment projects.[2] Subsequently, the government did aid housing for miners through a special coal levy which raised

[1] "Entwurf eines Gesetzes zur Förderung des Bergarbeiterwohnungsbaues im Kohlenbergbau," *Deutscher Bundestag, 1, Wahlperiode, 1949, Drucksache No. 2388.*

[2] Alvin H. Hansen, Richard A. Musgrave, *Fiscal Problems of Germany*, Bonn, 1951, p. 105.

the price of each ton of coal by 1 DM. Between 1952 and 1957, 1,031 billion DM were obtained from this levy and channeled into residential construction for miners.[1]

Nor was coal mining the only industry faced with a housing problem. Residential construction in areas in which employment could be offered made it possible to draw upon labor locked in rural areas and helped greatly to overcome regional structural unemployment. In March, 1951, 9.9% of the West German labor force was unemployed. At the same time the rate was 25.6% in Schleswig Holstein, a rural state which received a large number of refugees. North Westfalia (Ruhr area) had an unemployment rate of only 3.8%, and in some professions labor shortages had already occurred.[2] In view of these differences, resettlement of part of the labor force was an urgent matter.[3] Resettlement, of course, depended to a very large extent on the availability of dwellings. Government aid for the construction of houses therefore greatly facilitated efficient use of manpower resources.[4]

West Germany has effectively eliminated unemployment pockets. This has been mostly the result of the general economic expansion, but in some cases structural difficulties existed which could only be eliminated through selective measures. To make it possible for a man willing to work to find the right house in the right place was certainly such a measure.

### c. *Shipbuilding*

A sector which received especially large government support in postwar West Germany was shipbuilding. Before the war, in 1939, Germany as a whole had a merchant fleet of about 4.5 million Gross Register Tons. Losses during the war and later reparation deliveries reduced this fleet to about 100,000 Gross

---

1 Bauwirtschaft im Bundesgebiet, Jahreszahlen IV/2, Bundesbank, collected from *Bundesbaublatt*.

2 Salomon, *op. cit.*, p. 79.

3 "Die Förderung der Umsiedlung durch den Wohnungsbau," in *Der Wohnungsbau in der Bundesrepublik, Zwischenbilanz und Vorschau*, Bad Godesberg: Bundesminister für Wohnungsbau, n.d.

4 *Deutscher Bundestag, 2, Wahlperiode Drucksache 2524.*

**TABLE 40**

**Reconstruction of Merchant Fleet. Investments and Financing of Investments in Shipbuilding—1949 to 1956, Millions of DM. Current Prices**

| Year | Gross Register Tonnage of Merchant Fleet[1] 1000 Tons (1) | Gross Investment[2] (2) | ERP Funds[2] (3) | Government Loans[3] (4) | Special Bank Credit[4] (5) | Tax-exempt loans under paragraph 7d E.St.G.[4] (6) | Other Funds (7) |
|---|---|---|---|---|---|---|---|
| 1949 | n.a. | 75 | — | | | 11 | not available |
| 1950 | 742 | 255 | 90 | | | 48 | |
| 1951 | 1162 | 425 | 53 | 450 | | 275 | |
| 1952 | 1499 | 480 | 22 | | | 300 | |
| 1953 | 1912 | 755 | 72 | | | 325 | |
| 1954 | 2345 | 855 | 58 | | 330 | 319 | |
| 1955 | 2887 | 750 | 52 | | | 100 | |
| 1956 | 3453 | 720 | 27 | | | 100 | |
| Total 1949 to 1956 | | 4315 | 373 | 450 | 330 | 1478 | 1684 |

[1] Seagoing vessels for mercantile purposes only. Baumgart *op. cit.* p. 86, further source, "Die Verkehrspolitik in der Bundesrepublik Deutschland 1949 bis 1957." Bd. 15. Schriftenreihe Bundesminister für Verkehr, Bielefeld 1957, p. 199.
[2] Baumgart *op. cit.* p. 118, 121.
[3] For 1950 and 1951. Allgemeine Vorbemerkungen zum Bundeshaushaltsplan, 1956, p. 289–290.
[4] See Table 23.
[5] For 1950 to 1955.
[5] See Table 23. These are equal to deductions.

Register Tons. The merchant fleet had been practically wiped out, and most of what was left consisted of small vessels. Its reconstruction did not start until 1951 because Allied restrictions on shipbuilding were kept in force until that time.

Since then, a rapid comeback has occurred. In 1956, the country had a fleet of 3.5 million Gross Register Tons and in 1959 the total had risen to 4.9 million Gross Register Tons.[1] West Germany today possesses one of the most modern and efficient merchant fleets in the world. In 1956, 53% of all West German ships were less than five years old. At the same time, 23% of Great Britain's fleet was in this age bracket and only 4% of the United States.[2]

In face of the catastrophic losses during and after the war, shipping companies were in no position to finance the construction of new ships internally. Borrowing of long-term funds in capital markets, in the face of the lack of long-term investable funds, was equally out of the question.

Without public aid, and in this case extremely large scale public aid, the reconstruction of the merchant fleet would have been greatly delayed—perhaps impossible. Between 1949 and 1956, about 4.3 billion DM in gross investments, nearly all of it actual net investment, were made in the construction of seagoing and inland waterway vessels.[3] In 1950 and 1951, the Federal government granted a first 460 million DM in credits for shipbuilding. An additional 373 million DM were made available from ERP funds. Also, a special credit for shipbuilding was opened at the West German central bank. The total volume of bank credit, at what was called a "bearable" rate of interest, was 313 million DM. This special credit constituted only a temporary source of funds. It was successively decreased and amounted to only 20 million DM in 1955.

All of these funds made directly available were still not suffi-

---

[1] *St. J. B.*, 1958, p. 303; *St. J. B.*, 1961, p. 352.

[2] Baumgart, *op. cit.*, p. 85, 87.

[3] Baumgart, *op. cit.*, p. 118, Jelke Wilts, *Die Anlageinvestitionen im Westdeutschen Verkehrswessen*, Münster, no date, p. 15.

cient to finance the large construction programs. Special aid had to be provided through tax exemptions. Private loans made to shipbuilding were tax free under paragraph 7d of the income tax law.[1] Similarly, accelerated depreciation for new ships was granted and later, fixed interest securities floated for the financing of shipbuilding were tax-favored. According to an estimate made by the West German finance ministry, between 1949 and 1955 about 2.6 billion DM of funds were, through one government action or another, channeled into the construction of seagoing vessels.[2] Inland waterway shipping, which had suffered much less during the war than ocean shipping, received during the same time 148 million DM, and the fishing fleet about 55 million DM in public aid. About 65% of all gross investments in this sector were made with public funds. It is no exaggeration to say that the tax payers in West Germany have to a very large extent financed the rebuilding of the merchant fleet.

### d. *Agriculture*

The whole problem of West German agriculture is special and complex, and any attempt here to investigate all its aspects would be inadequate. A few general observable trends in this sector may be indicated, however, before discussing that part which is of main interest, namely, government aid to agriculture and, especially, aid to agricultural investments.

Agriculture in West Germany at the present time produces about 25% more food than in 1938–39. Between 1949 and 1959, the fraction of Gross National Product originating in this sector increased from 10.1 billion DM to 17.1 billion DM,[3] but this rise in output was achieved with fewer farms and less people working in agriculture. Since 1949, the number of agricultural establishments decreased by 140,000 and the labor force shrank from 5.1 million to 3.8 million. The rise in output was possible only

---

[1] See Chapter 3.

[2] *Allgemeine Vorbemerkungen zum Bundeshaushaltsplan, 1956, op. cit.,* p. 289.

[3] For this value expressed as a percent of GNP see Table 4.

through better production techniques, such as high quality ferti-
lizing and substantial improvements in capital equipment, especially agricultural machinery. To offset the loss in labor, large
investments in this sector were necessary. Between 1949 and 1957,
according to an estimate furnished by the Ministry of Agriculture in West Germany, 23.7 billion DM were invested in fixed
assets in this sector. Of this, about 43.6% was made in machinery,
14.2% in new buildings, and 6.3% in livestock. Other investments
were made in land improvement, water regulation, reforestation,
and the fishing industry.

The trend in West German agriculture is toward increased
productivity, especially in view of the imminent realization of
the European Economic Community.[1] To continue this increase,
a number of structural changes will be inevitable. At the present
time, 56.2% of the 1.77 million farms have less than 5 hectares of
usable land, 36.3% have between 5 and 20 hectares, and only
7.5% have more than 20 hectares.[2] One of the necessary adjustments must be the elimination of small farms to permit efficient
use of machinery. This will, in many instances particularly in
Southwestern Germany, require consolidation of land to eliminate fragmentation, one of the basic defects of German agriculture. To some extent, redistribution of land may also be possible.
After the war, under Allied laws, a land reform was attempted,
limiting the size of farms to 100 hectares and making land available to other smaller farms. Later, a voluntary rehousing program was launched to provide more space in crowded villages
and permit farmers to be nearer their fields.

These are positive measures geared to increase productivity,
and should make West German agriculture more competitive in
the long run. Public aid for these purposes is desirable and will
facilitate any necessary adjustments.

The various price supports agriculture has received so far are a
different matter. German agriculture has lived under strong protection for about a century, and there is a long history of stabiliz-

---

1 "Entwurf eines Gesetzes zur Förderung landwirtschaftlicher Investi-
tionsvorhaben zum Zwecke der Vorbereitung auf die Europäische Wirtschafts-
gemeinschaft," *Deutscher Bundestag 3, Wahlperiode, Drucksache 193.*
2 *The West German Economy*, Deutsches Industrieinstitut, *op. cit.*

ing low incomes—the latter very often the result of low efficiency. Income stabilization schemes led to price supports or special subsidies for necessary inputs. These still exist. For instance, the federal government paid 727.4 million DM in subsidies for milk, fertilizers, and potatoes in 1957.[1] It will probably be impossible to reduce this support substantially in the coming years. What will ultimately happen, under the future European Economic Community, is impossible to predict.

With the large number of programs designed to aid agriculture in West Germany, it is not possible to trace exactly what fraction of total investments in this sector was financed with public funds, yet an estimate can be made.

According to information from the Ministry of Agriculture in Bonn, this sector received 699 million DM in ERP funds between 1949 and 1957.[2] About 3.0 billion DM was made available for investments by the government between 1949 and 1956. To speed up structural adjustments in agriculture, a special aid program called the "Green Plan" (Grüner Plan) was launched in 1956. Under this plan, an additional 1 billion DM annually has been channeled into agriculture since 1957.

Little information is available on the extent to which agriculture benefited from special tax exemptions. In 1950, exemptions under the paragraphs 7a to 7e E.St.G. totalled only 12.5 million DM.[3] Agriculture did not benefit much from this set of paragraphs used so extensively by industry. This does not mean that this sector did not receive other tax advantages. In a special study made by the Ministry of Finances,[4] an indication is given as to what indirect tax benefits accrued to agriculture under the various laws. For 1959, a year in which many special tax exemptions had ceased to exist, they were estimated at 499 million DM.

Using these figures, it is reasonable to assume that between 700

---

1 *Finanzbericht, 1961, op. cit.,* p. 312.

2 This is higher than ERP funds shown in Table 42, probably because of a somewhat different definition of investment.

3 *St. B. R. D.* Volume 125, p. 36. Income tax payers.

4 "Subventionen im Bundeshaushalt," *Deutscher Bundestag 3, Wahlperiode, Drucksache 1229,* p. 7.

## TABLE 41

### Development of West Germany Agriculture—1949 to 1959. Production, Gross Investment and Labor Force[1]

| Year | Gross National Product in Current Prices Originating in Agriculture Billions of DM[2] | Gross Investment in Fixed Assets in Current Prices[3] | | | | | | Fishery Millions of DM | Agriculture Labor Force Millions of Persons[6] |
| | | Total Millions of DM | Construction[4] Millions of DM | Machinery[4] Millions of DM | Livestock[4] Millions of DM | Other Investments[5] Millions of DM | Reforestation Millions of DM | | |
| | (1) | (2) | (3) | (4) | (5) | (6) | (7) | (8) | (9) |
| 1949 | 7.6 | 1410 | 108 | 420 | 650 | 275 | 50 | 30 | n.a. |
| 1950 | 10.1 | 1700 | 110 | 508 | 309 | 467 | 70 | 40 | 5.11 |
| 1951 | 11.8 | 2150 | 165 | 725 | 412 | 571 | 120 | 100 | 4.85 |
| 1952 | 12.8 | 2200 | 256 | 1063 | 86 | 743 | 120 | 100 | 4.69 |
| 1953 | 12.9 | 2260 | 300 | 872 | −108 | 955 | 120 | 100 | 4.54 |
| 1954 | 13.7 | 2790 | 310 | 857 | −61 | 1103 | 120 | 100 | 4.40 |
| 1955 | 14.5 | 3380 | 386 | 1320 | 125 | 1340 | 80 | 100 | 4.29 |
| 1956 | 15.0 | 3800 | 530 | 1475 | −105 | 1540 | 85 | 80 | 4.18 |
| 1957 | 15.6 | 3960 | 580 | 1517 | 202 | 1580 | 80 | 80 | 4.10 |
| 1958 | 16.5 | n.a. | 605 | 1554 | −18 | n.a. | n.a. | n.a. | 3.98 |
| 1959 | 17.1 | n.a. | n.a. | n.a. | n.a. | n.a. | n.a. | n.a. | 3.82 |

1 Includes Forestry and Fishery.
2 St. J.B. 1953, p. 544; St. J.B., p. 478; St. J.B. 1961, p. 545.
3 Data was supplied by Bundesminister für Landwirtschaft und Ernährung, Bonn. Courtesy Dr. Padberg.
4 Refers to agricultural year. The value for 1949 refers to 1948/49, for 1950 to 1949/50, and so on.
5 Partly housing, consolidation of land programs, and regulation of water.
6 Including working family members. (Erwerbspersonen) St. J.B. 1958, p. 110; St. J.B. 1961, p. 142.

TABLE 42

Public Aid to Agriculture—
1949 to 1960. Current Prices. Millions of DM.[1]

| Year | E.R.P. Funds[2] | Other Public Funds for Investments[3] | Funds Made Available under "Grüner Plan"[4] |
|------|------|------|------|
|      | (1)  | (2)  | (3)  |
| 1949 | 18.8 | 92.9 | — |
| 1950 | 150.9 | 124.0 | — |
| 1951 | 39.9 | 301.3 | — |
| 1952 | 60.1 | 300.9 | — |
| 1953 | 36.3 | 401.1 | — |
| 1954 | 22.5 | 510.3 | — |
| 1955 | 59.3 | 602.0 | — |
| 1956 | 45.7 | 684.0 | 429.7 |
| 1957 | n.a. | n.a. | 1134.0 |
| 1958 | n.a. | n.a. | 1121.2 |
| 1959 | n.a. | n.a. | 1192.4 |
| 1960 | n.a. | n.a. | 1471.0 |

[1] These are only part of the funds which were publicly provided. Includes Forestry and Fishing.
[2] Baumgart, *op. cit.*, p. 96, includes fishery.
[3] All levels of government for 1949 to 1956. Calculated from St. B.R.D. volumes 19, 54, 57, 58, 88, 99. For 1954, St. B.R.D. volume 59, page 50. For 1955, 1956, St. B.R.D. volume 227, page 34.
[4] Contribution of Federal Government only, Finanzbericht 1961, page 312.

million DM and 900 million DM annually of public funds were, in one way or another, made available for investments in agriculture, forestry, and fishing in most of the years since 1949. At least 30% of all gross investments in this sector, but probably more, were publicly promoted. After residential construction, agriculture was the sector enjoying the heaviest public support. In the near future, this will probably have to continue.[1] It is difficult to say to what extent the total public aid to agriculture increased efficiency in production, or if it would have been wiser to invest some of these funds in other sectors of the economy. The fear of some possible future food shortage and the importance of a domestic food supply have induced outlays in many instances which may not have been the most efficient. Equally important, social

[1] "Die Kredithilfen des Bundes und der Länder an die Landwirtschaftlichen Betriebe," *Zeitschrift für das gesamte Kreditwesen*, Sonderausgabe, 1961.

and political considerations have certainly influenced investment decisions. Still, the fact cannot be ignored that the West German government has become increasingly resistant to excessive agricultural support, and the government expects that West German farmers, after a period of readjustment, will be able to compete within the European Economic Community. Efforts in this direction will invariably stress the need for increased efficiency.

As matters now stand, neither the domestic problems of West German agriculture nor the larger question of its integration into the Common Market have been solved, and much larger public aid may temporarily be necessary.

### e. *Communication and Transport*

It is now widely recognized that for growing economies an efficient transportation and communication system is indispensable.[1] However, the nature of production in these industries is such that public regulations are often needed. Construction, maintenance, and improvement of nationwide transportation and communication systems are usually costly. The benefits from these systems, though often very high, may not be too apparent. Due to these particular features and the overall importance of the transportation and communication sector for the total economy in more countries, many of these systems have become either government controlled or government owned.

In West Germany the railroad (Bundesbahn) and the postal system (including telephone and telegraph systems) are publicly owned. Also, radio and television stations are the property of the government. The building and maintenance of streets, waterways, and bridges is, with some unimportant exceptions, a public task. The government has a decisive influence in these areas. Previously mentioned were two particularly critical areas in the field of transportation: bottlenecks in railroad transportation

---

[1] See for instance: Holland Hunter, "Resources, Transportation and Economic Development," in Joseph J. Spengler, editor, *Natural Resources and Economic Growth,* distributed by Resources for the Future, Inc., Washington, D.C., 1961.

## TABLE 43

### Development in Transport and Communication—1949 to 1956. Production, Gross Investment and Employment[1]

| Year | Gross National Product, Current Prices, originating in Transport and Communication Billions of DM.[2] (1) | Gross Investment in Transport and Communication Millions of DM. Current Prices[3] of which in | | | | Additional Information: Gross Investment in Roads and Waterways Current Prices[3] Millions of DM (6) | Employment in Transportation and Communication 1000 Persons[4] (7) |
|---|---|---|---|---|---|---|---|
| | | Total (2) | Postal System (3) | Federal Railroad (4) | Other Public Transportation (5) | | |
| 1949 | 7.0 | 1965 | 245 | 1250 | 120 | 405 | 1160 |
| 1950 | 8.3 | 1890 | 340 | 800 | 125 | 465 | 1180 |
| 1951 | 9.4 | 2140 | 430 | 735 | 145 | 650 | 1195 |
| 1952 | 9.7 | 2500 | 440 | 885 | 160 | 805 | 1213 |
| 1953 | 10.2 | 3260 | 505 | 1150 | 200 | 1035 | 1217 |
| 1954 | 12.0 | 3400 | 625 | 1050 | 230 | 1115 | 1242 |
| 1955 | 13.1 | 4130 | 805 | 1550 | 245 | 1600 | 1273 |
| 1956 | 14.2 | 4550 | 710 | 2040 | 265 | 1860 | n.a. |

[1] Includes Postal System, Federal Railroad, Private Railroad, Other Public Transportation, Ocean Shipping, Inland Waterway Shipping, Harbors and Private Transportation. For specific discussion of shipping, see p. 182–85.
[2] St. J.B. 1958, p. 478. St. J.B. 1961, p. 544.
[3] Baumgart, *op. cit.*, p. 118.
[4] Baumgart, *op. cit.*, p. 127.

## TABLE 44

### The Extent of Public Influence on Gross Investment in Transportation and Communication 1949 to 1956, Current Prices

| Year | Government Investments in Transport and Communication[1] Millions of DM | Public Investments in Roads and Waterways[2] Millions of DM — Total | of which in roads Millions of DM | Public Investments as Percentage of Total Investments in Transport, Communication, Roads and Waterways (excluding shipping) |
|---|---|---|---|---|
| | (1) | (2) | (3) | (4) |
| 1949 | 1615 | 596 | 319 | 96.3 |
| 1950 | 1265 | 583 | 426 | 88.0 |
| 1951 | 1310 | 651 | 580 | 82.9 |
| 1952 | 1485 | 880 | 693 | 83.7 |
| 1953 | 1855 | 1090 | 877 | 83.2 |
| 1954 | 1905 | 1244 | 1027 | 86.0 |
| 1955 | 2600 | 1779 | 1395 | 87.9 |
| 1956 | 3015 | 2095 | n.a. | 89.8 |

[1] Includes Postal System, Federal Railroad and other public transportation. See Table 43. For government aid to shipping, see Table 40.
[2] Includes roads, bridges, harbors and smaller amounts for other transportation. All fiscal levels. Sources: St. B.R.D. Volumes 19, 57, 58, 59, 88, 99, 227.
[3] Jelke Wilts, op. cit., p. 13.

## TABLE 45

### Indexes to Development in Transportation and Communication—1949 to 1956 Output, Gross Investment, Employment. 1950 = 100

| Year | Total Gross National Product[1] Current Prices | Gross National Product Originating in Transportation and Communication Sector[2] Current Prices | Total Gross Investment in Fixed Assets in West German Economy[3] Current Prices | Gross Investment in Transport and Communication Sector[2] Current Prices | Gross Investments in Roads and Waterways[2] Current Prices | Employment in Transport and Communication[2] |
|------|-----|-----|-----|-----|-----|-----|
|      | (1) | (2) | (3) | (4) | (5) | (6) |
| 1949 | 82.1 | 84.3 | 83.0 | 104.0 | 87.1 | 98.3 |
| 1950 | 100.0 | 100.0 | 100.0 | 100.0 | 100.0 | 100.0 |
| 1951 | 122.0 | 113.3 | 123.6 | 113.2 | 139.8 | 101.3 |
| 1952 | 139.5 | 116.9 | 142.3 | 132.3 | 173.2 | 102.8 |
| 1953 | 149.7 | 122.9 | 161.6 | 172.5 | 222.6 | 103.1 |
| 1954 | 160.9 | 144.6 | 180.8 | 179.9 | 239.8 | 105.3 |
| 1955 | 183.4 | 157.8 | 225.3 | 218.6 | 344.2 | 107.9 |
| 1956 | 202.1 | 171.1 | 247.3 | 240.8 | 400.1 | n.a. |

[1] Calculated from Table 3.
[2] Calculated from Table 43.
[3] Calculated from Table 11.

and shipbuilding. We may now review the total efforts which were made in these sectors.

Besides housing, transportation and communication facilities were among the areas most damaged during the war. Soon after 1945, efforts were made to repair roads and important bridges, though many projects had to be postponed because the necessary resources were lacking. With increased economic activity after 1948, it became imperative greatly to improve the existing facilities, especially railroad transportation. Since 1950, gross investment in both transportation and communication has risen at roughly the same rate as total gross investments in the economy. Investments in roads, harbors, and waterways have increased much faster. Between 1950 and 1956, the latter quadrupled, whereas total gross investments only doubled.

The output of the transportation and communication sector could be increased only through additional investments. This becomes apparent when the output increases and the increases in employment are compared. Such a comparison shows that employment in this sector increased by only 7.9% between 1950 and 1956. Output, in terms of the share of gross national product originating in this sector, rose by 71.1%.[1] In 1950, 1.96 billion DM was invested in transportation and communication to which another 405 million DM of gross investments in roads, waterways, and bridges must be added. The corresponding values for 1956 were 4.55 billion DM and 1.86 billion DM. Between 1949 and 1956, 14% of all gross domestic investments in fixed assets was made in this sector.

From available data it is impossible to determine exactly what the government contributions to these investments were. To get an approximate idea of the magnitude of the public contributions, gross investments of the Federal railroad, the postal system (including telephone, television, telegraph, and radio systems) and other public transportation, consisting mainly of urban transportation, have been totalled. These alone amounted to 1.6 billion DM in 1950 and to 3.0 billion DM in 1956. Additional

---

[1] No allowances are made here for the use of roads and waterways. Wilts, *op. cit.,* p. 26.

public investments in roads and waterways have been estimated
from fiscal data which diverge somewhat in coverage, as well as
in the definition of investment, from those of other estimates.
Allowing for these differences, and eliminating shipping from the
transportation sector—about which more detailed information
has already been given—it is found that between 1950 and 1956,
public funds financed about 88% of all gross investments in
transportation, communication, roads, and waterways. This high
percentage is due to the fact that investments in roads and
waterways in West Germany are almost exclusively a responsibility of the government.

Were the aforementioned investments high enough? Studying
the development of the transportation and communication sector
of the West German economy, the conclusion must be that the
capacity increases were barely sufficient for the expanding economy.[1] Serious bottlenecks have been avoided so far, but it is
certain that additional efforts will have to be made in the future
to prevent restraints on economic growth due to lack of transportation or communication. Road building especially must be
accelerated in view of the rapidly rising number of automobiles.[2]

There can be no doubt that the funds invested greatly increased the efficiency of the economy. From the long-run growth
viewpoint, investments in this sector were somewhat low and
public efforts should have been greater in this area.

f. *Capital Investments in Social and Cultural Institutions*

Public influences on investments which contributed to physical
production have been investigated. Now attention should be
given to investments which were made in social and cultural
institutions.

As explained in the beginning of this study, in West Germany

---

[1] *Allgemeine Vorbemerkungen zum Bundeshaushaltsplan,* 1958, p. 285;
*Finanzbericht,* 1961, p. 133.

[2] To prevent bottlenecks in road traffic, efforts were made to reduce transportation of goods by trucks and increase the proportion carried by the
railroad. This is at best a palliative measure and will not solve the problem.
It is, however, not without tradition; as the railroad system is government
owned there has long been a tendency to protect it from the competition of
private highway transport.

after World War II there was no scarcity of social capital in the sense of education and professional skills. Compared with other productive capital, these skills were relatively abundant and, in the short run, could be freely drawn upon. In the long run, social capital must, of course, be regenerated and increased through the difficult and time consuming process of education, research, and all the other endeavors necessary to transform raw labor into highly skilled professionals. It would require special research beyond the scope of this study to investigate the developments in this area in West Germany. This text must be limited to inquiring about the investments in cultural and social institutions during the first part of the '50's. The question to be answered is whether these investments, so vital for the long run growth of an economy, were adequate and had necessary government support. Since the first concern in West Germany after 1948 was to increase material production, this might not have been the case.

As a starting point, it may be useful to review quickly public expenditures for social and cultural purposes. To evaluate the achievements of West Germany in these fields, a comparison should be made with those of the democratic Germany of the Weimar Republic. In Table 46, data on expenditures are given for the years 1925 to 1957. The reader will observe that in Germany, as in all other Western countries, total expenditures by all levels of government rose strongly during the period considered. In 1929—to choose a year in which income was high—Germany as a whole had 20.8 billion RM of total public expenditures, which compares with 66.1 billion DM expenditures in West Germany in 1957. Since 1929, there have been price increases, and to obtain a meaningful comparison the figures for 1957 should be deflated.[1] After these adjustments, it is found that, in real terms, public expenditures in West Germany are still about twice as high as they were for all of Germany in the Weimar Republic. To what extent did these increased expendi-

---

[1] For this purpose, a weighted price index is used which allows for cost of living and building cost.

tures go into education, social care, health care, and cultural institutions?

In the Weimar Republic, about 12% of all public expenditures was used for public schools, high schools, and vocational schools, even during the deep depression in 1932. After the last war, this percentage dropped and was not more than 8.8% until 1957. In real terms, the per capita expenditures for schools in 1955 had risen about 50% above the 1929 level. Universities in Germany, in the period considered, received between 1.2% and 1.5% of all public expenditures. In 1929, they received 253 million RM, and in 1957, 991 million DM. In real terms, this is an increase of about 250%. Nevertheless, in spite of this increase, the needs of higher education were barely met in 1957. For health care, no prewar figures are available. In 1957, 3.9% of all public expenditures were used for this purpose.

The column headed, "Other Social Tasks" in Table 46, represents transfers and not investments. However, it is appropriate to mention them here. They comprise payments to victims of war, to the unemployed, and various other social benefits. These figures are very revealing because they reflect the enormous social cost of the aftermath of two wars and the greatest depression the country ever experienced. In 1925, with a heavy burden left over from World War I, 21.6% of all expenditures were used for these payments and benefits. Increasing unemployment brought the percentages to 22.8% in 1929 and to nearly 34% in 1932. In 1951, these items amounted to 26.7%, and in 1957 to 25.1%, of all public expenditures.

Also worth mention here are the outlays for local service which are in a sense also social and cultural expenditures. They include such items as fire protection, street cleaning, construction and maintenance of sewage systems, and other general sanitation. Since the days of the Weimar Republic between 3.3% and 3.8% of all public expenditures have been allocated for these purposes. In real terms, expenditures in this field have tripled.

Only a small part of the expenditures in the aforementioned fields (between 6% and 7%) were new investments. For the postwar years, detailed information is available, and the data are

## TABLE 46

### Development of Public Expenditures for Social and Cultural Purposes and Local Services by All Levels of Government—1925 to 1957. Current Prices[1]

| Year | | Schools[2] (1) | Universities (2) | Health Care (3) | Other Social Tasks[3] (4) | Local Services[4] (5) | Total Expenditures (6) |
|---|---|---|---|---|---|---|---|
| 1925 | Millions of RM | 1823 | 170 | n.a. | 3130 | 486 | 14484 |
| 1925 | per capita RM | 28.9 | 2.7 | n.a. | 49.5 | 7.7 | 229.3 |
| 1925 | % of total expenditures | 12.6 | 1.2 | n.a. | 21.6 | 3.4 | 100 |
| 1929 | Millions of RM | 2618 | 253 | n.a. | 4751 | 793 | 20871 |
| 1929 | per capita RM | 40.4 | 3.9 | n.a. | 73.4 | 12.2 | 322.4 |
| 1929 | % of total expenditures | 12.5 | 1.2 | n.a. | 22.8 | 3.8 | 100 |
| 1932 | Millions of RM | 1740 | 179 | n.a. | 4912 | 484 | 14492 |
| 1932 | per capita RM | 26.5 | 2.7 | n.a. | 74.7 | 7.4 | 220.5 |
| 1932 | % of total expenditures | 12.0 | 1.2 | n.a. | 33.9 | 3.3 | 100 |
| 1951 | Millions of DM | 2761 | n.a. | 1186 | 9796 | 1220 | 36677 |
| 1951 | per capita DM | 50.9 | n.a. | 23.6 | 194.9 | 24.3 | 729.7 |
| 1951 | % of total expenditures | 7.5 | n.a. | 3.2 | 26.7 | 3.3 | 100 |
| 1955 | Millions of DM | 4598 | 719 | 1996 | 13841 | 2115 | 51388 |
| 1955 | per capita DM | 88.1 | 13.8 | 38.2 | 265.2 | 40.5 | 984.7 |
| 1955 | % of total expenditures | 8.9 | 1.4 | 3.9 | 26.9 | 4.1 | 100 |
| 1957 | Millions of DM | 5607 | 991 | 2549 | 16607 | 2479 | 66075 |
| 1957 | per capita DM | 104.9 | 18.5 | 47.7 | 310.6 | 46.4 | 1235.9 |
| 1957 | % of total expenditures | 8.5 | 1.5 | 3.9 | 25.1 | 3.8 | 100 |

[1] St. B.R.D. Vol. 59, page 31; Vol. 227, page 20. Refers to current and capital expenditures. For 1925 to 1932 former Reich. For 1951 to 1957, West Germany including West Berlin.
[2] Public schools, high schools, and vocational schools.
[3] Includes support for unemployed, contributions to social security system, payments to victims of war.
[4] Includes local fire, police, street cleaning, street lighting, sanitation, construction and maintenance of sewage system and others.

presented in Tables 47 and 48. Between 1949 and 1957, gross investments in fixed assets in schools, universities, theaters, churches, hospitals and other buildings used for health care, and other institutions rendering social services amounted to 16.6 billion DM. Of this, approximately 75% was financed with public funds. Investments in schools are almost entirely publicly financed. Investments in other areas, such as health care and social institutions, are partly financed publicly. It is interesting to observe at this point that, between 1949 and 1957, gross investment in all of the above discussed fields rose somewhat more sharply than total gross domestic investments in the West German economy.

From available data, it is evident that the need for investments in the social and cultural institutions was by no means neglected by public authorities. This fact should be stressed. Investments in the above fields on the whole were adequate during the last decade, and the social and cultural sectors of the economy were by no means starved for public funds. This is remarkable in view of the many other urgent investment problems faced by the West German government.

### g. *Public Guideposts to Private Investment*

There were many different programs existing under which private firms could obtain government aid for investments. Before the more technical details are investigated, a general observation may be made. To anyone who is studying the West German attempts to boost private domestic capital formation, the vagueness which often surrounded these attempts is striking. There were many efforts, and they were often quite extensive. Yet, no precise investment criteria were ever established. In most cases, no quantitative estimates existed as to the effects of government aid to investments. Sometimes, there was no sign of any direction to aid plans. Sometimes, aid was tightly organized and supervised. Frequent shifts in policy, *ad hoc* decisions, and temporary measures indicate that there must have been conflicts and, to a certain extent, an actual dilemma in policy. This was evidently true because West Germany's Free Market economy (Freie Markt-

TABLE 47

Gross Investments in Fixed Assets in Social and Cultural
Institutions—1949 to 1957. Millions of DM, Current Prices[1]

| Year | Schools[2] | Science, Art, Churches[3] | | Health Care[4] | Social Institu- tions[5] | Total Column 1, 2 4 and 5 |
| | | Total | of which Science | | | |
|------|-----------|-------|---------|---------|---------|---------|
| | (1) | (2) | (3) | (4) | (5) | (6) |
| 1949 | 215 | 195 | 80 | 180 | 160 | 750 |
| 1950 | 335 | 250 | 105 | 245 | 200 | 1030 |
| 1951 | 460 | 295 | 115 | 340 | 240 | 1335 |
| 1952 | 555 | 350 | 135 | 405 | 260 | 1570 |
| 1953 | 680 | 430 | 160 | 450 | 295 | 1855 |
| 1954 | 750 | 495 | 185 | 500 | 305 | 2050 |
| 1955 | 845 | 555 | 205 | 595 | 340 | 2335 |
| 1956 | 1035 | 650 | 250 | 685 | 400 | 2770 |
| 1957 | 1070 | 695 | 280 | 715 | 430 | 2915 |
| Total | 5950 | 3915 | 1525 | 4115 | 2630 | 16610 |

[1] Horst Seidler and Oskar de la Chevallerie, "Die Anlageinvestitionen der sozialen und kulturellen Bereiche in der Bundesrepublik von 1949 bis 1957," p. 43, Table 10. D.I.W. Sonderhefte, Neue Folge Nr. 48. Duncker und Humblot, Berlin 1960.
[2] Includes public schools, high schools, and vocational schools.

wirtschaft) required that in as many sectors as possible resources should be allocated according to private preferences. This basic conviction became more or less a guide for economic policy. At the same time, it cannot be ignored that after 1948 the solutions which a free market system could offer under the existing economic conditions for social and structural reasons were, in many cases, unacceptable. Temporarily, some sectors of the economy were taken out of the free market system. In these sectors, price controls continued to exist, and they received special public aid or tax benefits. If this was inevitable, the final aim remained; to reintegrate these sectors into the market system as soon as possible.

TABLE 47 (*cont.*)

| Year | Schools | Science, Art, Churches | Science | Health Care | Social Institutions | Total Column 1, 2 4 and 5 | Additional Information: Index of Gross Domestic Investments in Fixed Assets. Total Economy |
|------|---------|----------|---------|-------------|---------------------|--------------------------|-------------------------------------------------------------------------------------------|
| | | INDEXES TO GROSS INVESTMENT IN | | | | | |
| | (7) | (8) | (9) | (10) | (11) | (12) | (13) |
| 1949 | 64.2 | 78.0 | 76.2 | 73.5 | 80.0 | 72.8 | 83.0 |
| 1950 | 100.0 | 100.0 | 100.0 | 100.0 | 100.0 | 100.0 | 100.0 |
| 1951 | 137.3 | 118.0 | 109.5 | 138.8 | 120.0 | 129.6 | 123.6 |
| 1952 | 165.7 | 140.0 | 128.6 | 165.3 | 130.0 | 152.4 | 142.3 |
| 1953 | 203.0 | 172.0 | 152.4 | 183.7 | 147.5 | 180.0 | 161.6 |
| 1954 | 223.9 | 198.0 | 176.2 | 204.1 | 152.5 | 199.0 | 180.8 |
| 1955 | 252.2 | 222.0 | 195.2 | 242.9 | 170.0 | 226.7 | 225.3 |
| 1956 | 308.9 | 260.0 | 238.1 | 279.6 | 200.0 | 268.9 | 247.3 |
| 1957 | 319.4 | 278.0 | 266.7 | 291.8 | 215.0 | 283.0 | 256.6 |

[3] Includes science, theatre, music, and other cultural institutions including churches.
[4] Includes physical education.
[5] Includes buildings for Social Security System and those for other social purposes.

The question now was how to facilitate such a reintegration. On the one hand, interference with the market system was called for if structural disturbances were to be quickly overcome. On the other hand, too much interference was to be avoided because it was feared that this would aggravate the situation and delay the moment when the laws of supply and demand would again predominate.

Politically, there was little agreement in this matter. Not only did differences in opinion exist as to just what were structural disturbances and to what extent these could be overcome by market forces, but also on the way in which government support was to be implemented. One group in the Bundestag (which

TABLE 48

Public Funds Used in the Financing of Gross Investments in
Fixed Assets in Social and Cultural Institutions. 1949 to 1957.
Millions of DM, Current Prices.[1]

| Year | Schools | Science, Art, Churches | Health Care | Social Institutions | Total Column 1 to 4 |
|------|---------|------------------------|-------------|---------------------|---------------------|
| | (1) | (2) | (3) | (4) | (5) |
| 1949 | 211 | 119 | 150 | 145 | 625 |
| 1950 | 334 | 140 | 189 | 144 | 807 |
| 1951 | 454 | 156 | 241 | 169 | 1020 |
| 1952 | 544 | 172 | 285 | 221 | 1222 |
| 1953 | 663 | 203 | 326 | 210 | 1402 |
| 1954 | 722 | 227 | 362 | 195 | 1506 |
| 1955 | 813 | 257 | 418 | 206 | 1694 |
| 1956 | 998 | 332 | 466 | 251 | 2047 |
| 1957 | 1029 | 348 | 495 | 252 | 2124 |
| Total 1949 to 1957 | 5768 | 1954 | 2932 | 1793 | 12447 |

[1] Seidler, Chevallerie, *op. cit.*, p. 44. Table 12 includes funds made available by Social Security System.
[2] Calculated from M. R. Bundesbank, August 1959, p. 11. Consists of own investments

perhaps could be identified with the Social Democratic Party)
would have preferred more centrally planned and guided programs,[1] directly eliminating structural disturbances. Another
group (a large part of the Christian Democrats, but especially the
right wing Free Democrats) was usually much more in favor of
general "marktkonforme" measures, preferring that business initiative cure the situation. The outcome was a mixture of policies
and the absence of any well-defined, clear, long-range program.
In some cases, especially in the first years after 1948, widely distributed aid was given through generous tax exemptions for capital formation. In other cases, such as the ERP program and the

[1] Gerhard Weisser, "Kapitallenkung," *Handbuch Sozialdemokratischer Politik*, Bonn, 1953.

TABLE 48 (*cont.*)

| Year | Indexes to Public Financing of Investments in | | | | | Additional Index of Total Public Financing of Investments[2] |
|------|---------|-----------------------|----------------|------------------------|------------------------|--------------------------|
|      | Schools | Science, Art, Churches | Health Care | Social Institutions | Total Column 1 to 4 | |
|      | (6)     | (7)     | (8)     | (9)     | (10)    | (11)    |
| 1949 | 63.2    | 85.0    | 79.4    | 100.7   | 77.4    | 72.3    |
| 1950 | 100.0   | 100.0   | 100.0   | 100.0   | 100.0   | 100.0   |
| 1951 | 135.9   | 111.4   | 127.5   | 117.4   | 126.4   | 131.9   |
| 1952 | 162.9   | 122.9   | 150.8   | 153.5   | 151.4   | 161.7   |
| 1953 | 198.5   | 145.0   | 172.5   | 145.8   | 173.7   | 180.8   |
| 1954 | 216.1   | 162.1   | 191.5   | 135.4   | 186.6   | 212.8   |
| 1955 | 243.4   | 183.6   | 221.2   | 143.1   | 209.9   | 231.9   |
| 1956 | 298.8   | 237.1   | 246.6   | 174.3   | 253.7   | 278.7   |
| 1957 | 308.0   | 248.6   | 261.9   | 175.0   | 263.2   | 300.0   |

plus loans and subsidies. Eliminated is acquisition of land. Not including Social Security System.

Investment Aid Program, the allocation of funds was tightly organized and controlled.

Some kind of investment planning became inevitable in West Germany when it received aid under the ERP program. The purpose of this aid was rapidly to increase the country's production and thus diminish dependence on outside aid. In the Economic Cooperation Agreement (ECA) Act, the West German government pledged itself to use available counterpart funds towards these ends. A special control system for the use of these funds was developed.[1] Given the objectives stated in the ECA act, it was inevitable that the government had to allocate directly

[1] "Abkommen über wirtschaftliche Zusammenarbeit zwischen der Bundesrepublik Deutschland und den Vereinigten Staaten von Amerika," reprinted in Dieter Carstens, *Der Bund als Finanzier*, Bad Godesberg, 1960, p. 248.

part of the available ERP funds. The methods which were developed for this purpose evidently later served as a model for other programs; for instance, the Investment Aid Program.[1] Studying the direct allocation of funds under the ERP program should provide some insight to the effectiveness of public influences on private investment.

Two methods were used in West Germany for the allocation of investable ERP funds: a planned allocation (Einplanungsverfahren) for credits over 100,000 DM; and, a global method (Globalverfahren) for smaller investment projects.[2]

In each year in which ERP funds were made available, the West German government—in the first years of the ERP program in cooperation with ECA administration—decided in what sectors of the economy investments should be concentrated. A number of so-called "points of main effort" (Schwerpunktprogramme) were established. These of course changed frequently. In some years, they were in coal mining, transportation, and the iron and steel industry; in other years in housing or in export industries. The choice of these sectors apparently was determined mainly by considerations of overall increases in output and productivity. Following this sectoral allocation an expenditure plan was set up to distribute the available funds. This plan was then submitted to the lower house of the government (Bundestag), and after the upper house (Bundesrat) agreed to it, it became law. Before 1954, these expenditures were part of the federal budget; after that they were shown separately in a special ERP fund.

It is not known what were the exact criteria for the selection of the "points of main effort." Apparently the various wishes and suggestions of the different states (Länder) were first collected and surveyed in the federal ministries. After this, special commissions, consisting of engineers as well as economists, examined

---

[1] *Deutscher Bundestag, 1, Wahlperiode, 1949, Drucksache*, No. 2450, p. 18.
[2] Friedrich Breckner, "ERP Finanzierung," *Handwörterbuch der Betriebswissenschaft*, Band, 1, Stuttgart, 1956; Friedrich Breckner, "Zehn Jahre Öffentliche Finanzierungshilfen," *Zeitschrift für das gesamte Kreditwesen*, Heft 3, 1960; Friedrich Breckner, "Neue ERP-Schwerpunkte," *"Volkswirt,"* 13, Jhrg. No. 40/59, p. 2180.

the various suggested programs. This work was especially difficult in the years immediately after 1948, because adequate statistics on production were lacking. Estimates had to be made which were often so bold that the economists who made them were sometimes referred to as the "club of courageous estimators." There seems to have been no detailed theory or guide stating how the funds should be allocated. In the first years, the opinion must have been that if misallocations occurred, they could not be too serious because practically everything was needed. With rapidly increasing economic activity, capacities could be easily adjusted.

This does not mean that there were no differences in opinion. These existed for some time between U.S. economists and the West Germans. The former wished to increase production in basic industries first, whereas the West Germans stressed the need to invest in manufacturing. Among the West Germans, differences in opinion seem to have existed as to duplication in industry. A minority group believed that the best resource use would be assured by having a few large producers in a given industry. The majority, however, favored a widespread competitive build up.[1]

After the distribution of investable funds by economic sectors, a more detailed allocation by firms occurred. Private firms in the selected sectors could apply for public credits—or subsidies—granted at much more favorable terms than market funds. Information about the various kinds of credits available was provided in special guides.[2]

If firms requested more than 100,000 DM, a direct allocation

---

[1] This information was received from West German civil servants who participated in the planning procedure.

[2] This was also the case for other government credits. Such "Richtlinien für die Gewährung von Krediten" were issued by the Federal Government as well as the governments of the Länder. For ERP credits available in 1960, see Dieter Carstens, *Der Bund als Finanzier, op. cit.* For government credits to private non-agricultural firms, Heinrich Dittes, "Die Kredithilfen des Bundes und der Länder an die gewerbliche Wirtschaft," Sonderausgabe der *Zeitschrift für das gesamte Kreditwesen*, 1961. A summary of all public credits and guarantees, from 1959 to 1961, is given in Konrad Nischk, *Die öffentliche Kredite und Bürgschaften*, Bonn; Stollfuss Verlag, 1959.

took place. The applying firm had to give detailed information on the kind of investment project, its asset structure, and its ability to obtain market funds. This information was first submitted to the commercial bank with which the firm conducted its usual business. There, the proposal was scrutinized from a banker's point of view and endorsed. After this, it was forwarded to the competent ministry at the state level (Land) where the project was examined from the overall economic point of view. With these two evaluations, the proposal, if recommended, went to the Federal Ministry for Economic Cooperation. At this level, the various investment projects were compared and a certain number selected.

For smaller investments, global allocation method was used. In these cases, the decision whether or not to grant credit rested with private banks. Since 1956, this has been practically the only method used.

In the case of planned allocation, a list recommending the various projects was forwarded to the main lending institutions through which ERP funds were channeled, especially the Bank for Reconstruction. Instruction was given as to the amount of funds to be drawn from the Central Bank's counterpart funds account, what interest rates should be charged, and in what way the credits should be amortized. The main lending institutions then contacted the firms recommended for credits. After submittal of credit credentials and guarantees given by a private bank, the firm would finally get the requested funds. The procedure was similar for firms receiving funds under the global method.

When general aid was given for capital formation public authorities had relatively little influence on investment patterns. This was the case in 1949 and 1950, when all firms could take advantage of tax exemptions. Very often the benefits would accrue to those sectors, trade and services for example, where capacities were already large enough. In addition, the higher the income tax liability the larger the tax savings. Thus, inequities arose. The original idea that the government should favor capital formation in general[1] through tax exemptions was soon revised. Restrictions were imposed on those groups qualified for tax exemptions. Also, the purposes for which these tax benefits were granted was narrowed. The government has slowly decreased tax exemptions, and they will probably completely disappear in the near future.

From this West German experience with tax exemptions for capital formation, the obvious conclusion is that they had distinct disadvantages. Granted on a large scale they were very expensive in terms of budget losses. Administratively they involved considerable difficulties. The legal provisions were complicated and unstable. Auditing personnel of the internal revenue service suddenly had to decide on matters which did not ordinarily fall within their purview; namely, what kind of properties qualified for accelerated depreciation, or what savings were tax deductible. Whether or not the recipients of tax benefits actually acted in the way the government desired was very often impossible to control. This uncertainty as to the effect of these tax subsidies was, without doubt, most discouraging.

---

[1] See: Representative Blücher, *Wörtlicher Bericht über die 34. Vollversammlung des Wirtschaftsrates des Vereinigten Wirtschaftsgebietes,* Frankfurt, n.d., p. 1453f.

# V. Equity, Government and Capital Formation

GOVERNMENT INFLUENCE on capital formation, it was found in previous chapters, contributed greatly to the efficiency and growth of the West German economy, both in general as well as in selective ways. The general effect of public policy was to repress consumption and increase overall capital formation. Through selection of investment programs eligible for public aid, structural rigidities were quickly overcome and output strongly increased. From the viewpoint of efficiency, the necessary resource transfer from the private to the public sector advanced West Germany's economic growth and was justifiable. However, other factors besides efficiency must be taken into consideration when such transfers occur. Of equal importance is the equity problem. Equity is important because great efficiency and a high rate of economic growth, in terms of increases in total output, may be doubtful achievements if they lead to large inequities in income and property distributions.

Since the last century, the public consensus in many Western countries has been that income distribution should not be determined solely by market forces. This consensus is evidenced by the existence of progressive income taxes, transfer payments to the underprivileged, and, in many countries, comprehensive Social Security Systems. One of the important functions of a government's budget in democratic nations is the prevention through redistribution of too large inequalities in income, with social tension a potential result. Redistribution of income may be a deliberate policy and implemented through tax and expenditure policy; but it may also be a by-product when other fiscal policy objectives are pursued.[1]

In West Germany, rapid capital formation was greatly facilitated through very high profits due to the wage lag during most of the 1950's. The question is, to what extent did tax and expenditure policy act as a corrective under these circumstances? To answer this difficult question, one has to know more about the net burden distribution of public capital formation. For this, a number of estimates are necessary.

As a first step, a gross tax burden distribution for the year 1950 will be estimated. In addition, a separate estimate will be made for the distribution of contributions to social insurances in the same year. A summary showing the combined burden distributions of taxes and contributions to social insurances will conclude the discussion of the gross burden in 1950. As a second step, changes in taxes and in incomes for later years and their bearing on the gross burden distribution will be investigated. As a third step, a distribution of the benefits from public capital formation will be estimated. In a last step, both the gross burden distribution and the benefit distribution will be combined resulting in an estimate of the net burden distribution.

### a. *Tax Burden Distribution—1950*

The question may be asked, why has the year 1950 been chosen for an estimate of the tax burden distribution? There are several reasons for this. The first, and most compelling one, is the fact that for other years insufficient data exist. It is true that even the 1950 data are somewhat crude, affecting the accuracy of the estimate; yet the results are reasonably realistic. A second reason for

---

[1] Theoretically, the case can be construed where changes in taxes and expenditures would leave income distribution the same. In practice, there will probably be always some redistribution effects.

the choice of this year is that it has an advantage over, for example, one year of the 1960's. 1950 was an early year in Germany's postwar economic growth. A main feature, namely a tax structure favorable to capital formation, was already fully developed and, at the same time, the distribution of wealth was not yet affected by the impact of this tax structure on income. In later years, the tax structure was somewhat modified. The income distribution itself reflected, then, the skew distribution of wealth which was at least partly attributable to the special treatment accorded large incomes in the early '50's.

Let us start with the estimation of the household income distribution for 1950.

*The Income Distribution*

As the income distribution is very crucial for a tax burden distribution estimate, it is necessary to explain in some detail how this estimate was derived and what sources were used.

No official data concerning the income distribution of households for the year 1950 could be found. For the entire period since the Currency Reform in 1948 there is a regrettable absence of official income distribution data in West Germany—the exception being a distribution of personal incomes by the *Statistische Bundesamt* for 1950. However, a few private studies were made to fill this gap,[1] and some of these give information on personal income distributions, some on household income distributions. In addition, detailed tax statistics on the wage tax and the assessed personal income tax are available for some years.[2] For 1950, data are also available on the structure of West German households.

From these different sets of data we can estimate a household income distribution for 1950, using as a basic guide two house-

---

[1] Deutsches Institut für Wirtschaftsforschung Berlin, *Wochenberichte*, 8, 16, 1957; 10, 11, 1957, 12, 13, 1957; Gerhard Göseke, *Die Einkommensschichtung in der Bundesrepublik*, DIW, Berlin, 1957; Paul Jostock und Albert Ander, "Konzentration der Einkommen und Vermögen," *Schriften des Vereins für Sozialpolitik*, NF Band 20/1, Berlin: Duncker und Humblot, 1960, p. 179. Also literature cited in this article.

[2] *Statistisches Jahrbuch*, 1955, pp. 413–415; 1958, pp. 383–385.

hold income distributions for 1953 and 1956 published by the "Gesellschaft für Konsumforschung" in Nüremberg.[1]

It is well known that household incomes changed rapidly with rising national income in West Germany after 1950. Since then there has been a strong upward shift of low income households into medium income brackets, and a similar, though somewhat less pronounced, shift of medium income units into higher brackets. As a first approximation, it was assumed that household incomes increased pari passu with the rise in personal income.[2] If, in 1956, a certain fraction, A per cent, of all persons had incomes below 2,400 DM and if, at the same time, the bracket from 0 to 2,400 DM contained B per cent of all households, it was assumed that this percentage differential $(X = A - B)$ was the same for 1950. Thus, if in 1950 C. per cent of all persons fell into the bracket below 2,400 DM, the fraction of households falling into this bracket would be $C - X$. Proceeding in the same way for all brackets, a percentage distribution of households by income brackets was derived. This had to show, if reasonably correct, more households in the lower brackets than the distribution for 1953. This is the case. In fact, the bulk of the households fall in this distribution into the income bracket below 2,400 DM. Experts on income distribution in West Germany, who were consulted on this problem, felt strongly that this was the case in 1950.

To test the distribution derived in this way, a second method was used. The structure of households in West Germany is known for 1950, in the sense of size and wage earner composition. In addition, tax statistics give information on the number of taxpayers and numbers of exemptions granted. As can be seen in Appendix Table 3 the majority of all West German households had one income receiver. For this group of households, our assumption of a parallel upward shift for personal incomes and household incomes is correct. Making various assumptions—

---

1 Gesellschaft für Konsumforschung, *Bedarfsstruktur,* 1956, Nüremberg, 1956, p. 14.

2 For a relationship between personal and household incomes in Germany before the war, see *Wirtschaft und Statistik,* 22; Jahrgang, 1942, p. 120f.

partly based on special information about the incomes of second and third income earners—as to the incomes of additional earners in households, we reconstructed the incomes of households by adding the incomes for the various members and determining in what brackets the households would then fall. Though this method was regarded as merely a check, not free from errors, its result seems to confirm our first estimate. After further comparison of the resultant distributions with data for the distribution of gross wages, it seems reasonable to assume that, for 1950, at least 40 per cent of all West German households fell in an annual income bracket below 2,400 DM or had less than 200 DM before taxes per month. On the other hand, 10 per cent of all households had incomes in the bracket above 6,000 DM. The distributions given in Appendix Table 1 are therefore the best estimates which could be made.

To obtain the total incomes received by each income bracket, we multiplied the number of households in each income bracket, except the highest, by the mean bracket income. Mean bracket incomes were estimated from budget studies of households.[1] At the same time, data are available on aggregate personal income and expenditure patterns. Using both sets of data it is possible to estimate as a residual the total income of the open-end upper bracket. As noted, this bracket begins with 6,000 DM, which was certainly not a high income. It would have been desirable if the lower limit of the top bracket could have been fixed at a higher level, say at least 20,000 DM, to provide information on those income groups in the medium range who had already begun to participate in the formation of capital and to bring into sharper focus the open-end upper bracket where capital formation was extremely heavy. For this there are unfortunately no data available, and the income and spending habits of the high and highest income brackets in West Germany must remain in doubt.

It should be pointed out that the derived income distribution refers to money income plus some imputed income from the use

---

[1] *Statistisches Jahrbuch,* 1953, p. 536f.

of gardens and the raising of smaller domestic animals. From the data it is not clear whether an allowance was made for imputed rent for owner-occupied houses. However, the error involved through a possible omission of this item cannot be too large.

TABLE 49

Distribution by Income Brackets of: Households, Income, Taxes Paid, Tax Exemptions and Tax Benefits to Favor Capital Formation. West Germany 1950.

| | Household Income Brackets 1000 DM. | | | | | |
|---|---|---|---|---|---|---|
| | 0–2.4 | 2.4–3.6 | 3.6–4.8 | 4.8–6.0 | 6.0 + | Total |
| 1. Distribution of Households[1] | 40.0 | 24.0 | 14.0 | 12.0 | 10.0 | 100 |
| 2. Distribution of Income[2] | 17.5 | 15.8 | 12.7 | 12.3 | 41.8 | 100 |
| 3. Distribution of Taxes Paid (Without Social Security Taxes) | 14.3 | 16.1 | 13.6 | 12.7 | 43.3 | 100 |
| 4. Distribution of Deductions (Sondervergünstigungen) to favor capital formation[3] | 4.7 | 4.7 | 5.6 | 5.9 | 79.1 | 100 |
| 5. Distribution of Special Tax Benefits under various exemptions to favor capital formation[3] | 3.3 | 3.7 | 3.7 | 4.3 | 85.0 | 100 |

[1] See Appendix Tables 1 and 3.
[2] Total Income, see Appendix Table 2, line 4.
[3] For absolute values, see Appendix Table 9.

Nothing has been said so far about corporate retained earnings after taxes. These amounted in 1950 to 1.5 billion DM and are not accounted for in the above incomes. Retained earnings constitute income, of course, and were therefore imputed to households in the various income brackets. More problematical is the treatment of part of the corporate income tax. There seems to be a consensus nowadays, reinforced through findings in recent empirical studies, that the corporate income tax is only partly borne by the owners of capital. A substantial part is thought to be shifted onto the consumer and another may be shifted, though this is less likely, backward to wage earners. The non-shifted part of the tax is, then, the only burden on owners of capital. To obtain income before taxes one has to impute this non-shifted part of the tax to the various income brackets. In Appendix Table 2, lines 2 and 4, two income distributions are shown, one without corporate retained earnings after taxes and non-shifted part of corporate income tax, the other including these two items.

### Tax Allocation by Income Brackets

The second step in our estimate involved the allocation of taxes, (actual cash receipts by the three government levels) to the different income brackets. Some of the taxes were allocated directly if it could be assumed that the household which had the tax liability carried the ultimate burden. On the other hand, for those taxes where there is a strong indication that the payer of the tax does not bear the ultimate burden, the incidence was estimated. Shifting assumptions were made in accordance with present economic theory about the incidence of taxes, but generally held incidence assumptions were modified when the economic conditions prevailing in West Germany in 1950, or particular features of the West German tax system, seemed to warrant this.

Technically, two procedures were involved in the allocation of each tax. In a first step, the total tax yield was allocated to the various groups in the economy which were believed to carry the burden. In a second step, each of these different components into which the tax was split—providing there was reason to assume shifting—was then distributed to the different household income brackets. For this purpose, special distributions, derived from a variety of West Germany statistics on income, taxes, and consumptions, were used.[1] Before we discuss the details of the estimating procedure, a few general remarks may be appropriate to indicate some particular features of our results.

---

[1] *Statistik der Bundesrepublik Deutschland,* Band 97, 125; *Statistisches Jahrbuch,* 1953, p. 536f.

The resulting distribution is, in its very nature, "macro-economic" if one wishes to use this expression. It is not the tax burden of one particular household in each income bracket which is analyzed, but that of all households. An aggregate estimate like this cannot, unfortunately, take into account such important characteristics as size of household and different consumption patterns within the same income bracket, which create special problems. Though shortcomings of this nature are not too great an obstacle for the allocation of direct taxes to the various income brackets, difficulties arise when indirect taxes, which vary with household size, are to be allocated. In our estimate it is implicitly assumed that there is an "average" household, representative in its size and consumption pattern for all households in a particular income bracket. Multiplying the tax burden on such a household resulting from an indirect tax by the number of households in the bracket results in an estimate of the total burden the particular bracket has to carry.

Students of tax burden distributions have often debated whether the aggregative approach is the most useful. It seems that the choice between the aggregative or the "selective" approach— "selective approach" being understood to mean the analysis of one household of a specific size in each bracket—depends on the purpose for which one wishes to use the distributions. Most important and compelling for the choice is also the question of availability of data. With the existing information on the West German income distribution and consumption by households, it was felt that an estimate by large income brackets was the only feasible one.

In the calendar year 1950, the total tax revenue (cash receipts) at the federal, state, and local government level was 19.971 billion DM. This revenue was received from about forty different taxes. The eight largest taxes, however, accounted for about 80 per cent of the total yield. They were, in the order of yield, the Turnover Tax (4.595 billion DM), Tobacco Tax (2.059 billion DM), the assessed Individual Income Tax (2.062 billion DM), the Immediate Aid Levy (1,876 billion DM), the Wage Tax (1.707 billion

DM), the Corporate Income Tax (1.429 billion DM), the Local Tax on Business (Gewerbesteuer) (1.250 billion DM), and, finally, the Local Real Estate Tax (1.078 billion DM). The allocation of these eight taxes will be discussed in detail. The large number of remaining smaller taxes, grouped together under "All other Taxes and Customs" in Table 50 are separately listed in Appendix Table 4, where their yields are shown. In Appendix Table 8 it is indicated how they were allocated.

*The General Turnover Tax*

The German turnover tax is imposed at different levels of production. The tax, if passed on to other levels of productions, pyramids, and the total amount of turnover tax contained in the final price of products varies with the structure of production and the way in which the product reaches the final consumer. In general, integrated firms under this tax have had an advantage over non-integrated firms. Here seems to lie one of the greatest disadvantages of this tax; namely, that it is not neutral as to the manner in which production occurs. The tax is very complicated and it is difficult to estimate its ultimate impact. It may be mentioned that because of its complications it is likely that in the near future it will be considerably changed—or even disappear—in favor of a value added tax under the "Harmonization of Taxation Program" within the framework of the European Common Market.

West German scholars in public finance have written extensively about the probable incidence of this tax.[1] Attempts have been made to estimate the amount of turnover tax contained in the purchase of various commodities and its variation with changes in the composition of the consumers' market basket. It is

---

[1] H. Schlesinger, "Die Steuerliche Belastung des Arbeiterhaushaltes," *Finanzarchiv*, Neue Folge, Band 12, Heft 3, p. 537. *Statistisches Reichsamt, Einzelschrift*, No. 21. *Die steuerliche Belastung des Haushaltsbedarfs durch Verbrauchsabgaben und Zölle*, Berlin, 1932. IFO Institut, München, *Untersuchungen zur Grossen Steuer-Reform*, München, 1953. W. Schubert, "Die Kumulativwirkung der deutschen Umsatzsteuer," *Finanzwissenschaftliches Forschungsinstitut*, Köln, 1951.

believed that this tax, very much like a sales tax imposed at the retail level, is completely shifted forward to the consumer.

As a first approximation one may assume that the tax is finally borne by income brackets according to their total expenditures for consumer goods.[1] In recent years, however, more information has become available concerning the effects of this tax on various sectors of the economy. In a very interesting study made in West Germany by Dr. G. Zeitel in 1959,[2] an attempt was made to analyze the transmission of the tax with the aid of an input-output table. The tax was traced from sector to sector and its impact shown on the vectors of final output. According to this study, in 1954 about 69 per cent of the tax ended up in consumer goods, 27 per cent in investment goods, and 3.6 per cent in exports. It can be assumed that in 1950, due to West Germany's weak position in international trade, the part passed on in exports was relatively small, and it can be neglected here. On the other hand, turnover tax on investment goods will, with some time lags, also reach consumer goods. We may therefore, without making too great an error, restrict ourselves to the vector of consumer goods, which contain in their prices turnover taxes both transmitted directly and those transmitted indirectly in depreciation charges of capital goods. Combining the results of that study with an independent estimate of each income bracket's distribution of consumer goods purchases (by industry) permitted us to derive a distribution of the final tax burden of the turnover tax. It was found that this distribution was not very much different from that of total consumer expenditures (compare lines 8 and 9 in Appendix Table 8). This confirms the view of those economists who have long maintained that, in the end, there is no great difference between the incidence of a general

---

[1] Inquiries at a number of German firms were made as to the businessman's behavior towards this tax. It was found that business people in general think of this tax as a burden which should be passed on.

[2] Gerhard Zeitel, *Die Steuerlastverteilung in der Bundesrepublik Deutschland*, Tübingen: J. C. B. Mohr, Paul Siebeck, 1959. In this study the "formal incidence" was of interest not, as in this one, the "effective incidence." The results, therefore differ substantially.

sales tax imposed at the retail level and that of the capricious pyramiding German general turnover tax.[1]

## The Tobacco Tax

The tobacco tax is imposed on cigarettes, cigars, pipe tobacco, and chewing tobacco. For these products the tax rates are different. There was no information available, however, concerning consumption of each of these products by income brackets. This tax was, therefore, allocated in accordance with total expenditures by household income brackets for tobacco products in general.

## The Assessed Individual Income Tax

This tax is paid by "entrepreneurs"—the large number of shop owners, business representatives, farmers, and independent professionals. In economic theory it is generally assumed that a personal-income tax is not shifted, although some economists have voiced doubts on this proposition.[2] We feel that in the West German case a slight modification to this generally-held incidence assumption is necessary.

A closer investigation of those groups liable to pay this tax shows that they were not only single proprietors but also, especially for the higher income brackets, co-owners of non-corporate companies such as the German OHG (general partnership), G.m.b.H. (Society with limited liability), and KG (limited partnership). These societies numbered about 40,000 in 1950 (compared with only 1,700 corporations) and they employed nearly as many people as the corporations. Some of these companies were and are very large. In our opinion it is justifiable to assume that these large companies—and for that matter also large single proprietorships whose owners very often are in the higher

---

1 Alvin H. Hansen, Richard A. Musgrave, *Fiscal Problems of Germany*, Bonn, 1951, pp. 224ff.

2 Richard A. Musgrave, *The Theory of Public Finance*, New York: McGraw-Hill, 1959, p. 355–362; Richard A. Musgrave and D. W. Daicoff, "Who Pays the Michigan Taxes?" *Michigan Tax Study*, Staff Papers, East Lansing, Michigan, 1958, p. 146.

income brackets—behave much like corporations. Like corporations, these companies will try to shift part of the personal income tax onto other groups in the economy. Strong market positions may facilitate this. This is an argument for the shifting of a part of the personal income tax; the fact cannot be ignored, however, that 1950 was a year of fairly stable prices in West Germany. Until the end of the year, most industrial, but not agricultural, prices remained stable and even showed slight declines. Therefore the general economic situation may have severely limited any shifting. We feel, however, that to account properly for the West German situation some shifting should be assumed. We therefore decided to distribute 80 per cent of the personal income tax as it was actually paid by the different income brackets. The remaining 20 per cent was distributed in the same manner as the Corporate Income Tax.

*The Immediate Aid Levy*
The "Immediate Aid Levy" (*Soforthilfe*) was, in 1950, a special levy to speed up the "Equalization of Burden Program (*Lastenausgleich*). Under this program, specific groups of the population which had suffered economic losses during the war (and later losses caused by the Currency Reform in 1948) were entitled to receive partial indemnification. Under this law, which became a very complicated one, 50 per cent of all real estate existing at the time of the Currency Reform was to be redistributed. The total amount of this redistribution has been quoted as 80 billion DM, and the program is supposed to run until 1980. Prior to 1958, 31 billion DM had been redistributed.

In 1950, the total revenue of this levy was 1,876 billion DM. This was essentially received from industry, agriculture, and owners of residential real estate. According to an estimate made by the West German Ministry of Finance, industry paid about 70 per cent, agriculture 10 per cent, and owners of real estate 20 per cent. We assumed that this capital levy could not be shifted, at least not in 1950. The three components were distributed in the following manner.

For business it was especially difficult to shift this imposed levy, because only old firms existing before the Currency Reform had to pay it. New firms established after the Reform were exempt. As both kinds of firms competed strongly in 1950, there was little hope of passing on this new burden. Half of the levy was therefore distributed by income bracket like the distribution of income from capital, to account for that part paid by corporations, and half like the distribution of income from business, to account for non-corporate business.

Similarly, it was assumed that the part paid by agriculture was not shifted. Some experts disagreed with this on the ground that most of the farms which had to pay this levy were old farms and the whole agricultural sector was evenly affected—unlike the other sectors, where the levy had a differential impact. In addition to this, it was argued that there existed strong sellers' markets for a number of agricultural products, making it easy to recover the tax. There may be merits in this argument, but it seemed to us unlikely that there was much shifting. We therefore distributed the contribution of agriculture to this levy in the same manner as the distribution of income from agriculture.

There remains, finally, the part paid by owners of residential real estate. Since rents for old apartments remained frozen in 1950—new apartments were free of rent control but to these the levy did not apply—this new tax was difficult to shift onto tenants. We distributed this part of the tax, therefore, like rental income.

### The Wage Tax (Lohnsteuer)

The wage tax is paid by wage earners and salaried employees and is essentially paid by low and medium incomes. In 1950, only 4.5 per cent of all persons contributing to this tax had gross wages over 6,000 DM. About 1 per cent had incomes over 9,000 DM.[1] In accordance with the economic theory about the incidence of personal income taxes, it was assumed that there was no shifting of this tax. The tax was therefore allocated to wage earners and salaried employees in different income brackets as indicated in

---

[1] *Statistisches Jahrbuch,* 1955, p. 413.

official tax statistics. It should be noted here that these statistics give the wage tax paid by persons and not by households. Therefore, a slight error is involved in our distribution. A household with two income receivers, for instance, both in the lowest income bracket, may not fall in the same bracket. The tax burden in this case would be too high for the lowest income receiver and too low for the bracket to which the household belongs. To account for this we allocated 15 per cent of each bracket's tax burden to the next higher bracket. Most households with two or more income receivers were taxed under the wage tax and belonged to the lower income brackets. It should be mentioned that the same error is contained in the distribution of the assessed Personal Income Tax, however to a much smaller extent. No correction was therefore made for the distribution of the Personal Income Tax.

### The Corporate Income Tax

The incidence of a corporate income tax is a widely discussed problem in literature of public finance.[1] No consensus seems to exist on this problem. One opinion is that the tax is fully borne by capital owners. Another opinion is that there is substantial shifting and that capital bears only a fraction of the tax. Detailed empirical studies about the incidence of the corporate income tax, at the present time under way in the United States, give strong support to the view that there is, on the average, a large amount of shifting, even in the short run. This shifting of the tax burden seems to occur mainly over prices.[2] In our estimate we assumed that capital bore 40 per cent of the tax burden. Another

---

[1] B. U. Ratchford and P. B. Han, "The Burden of the Corporate Income Tax," *National Tax Journal,* December 1957. Carl Shoup, "Incidence of the Corporation Income Tax: Capital Structure and Turnover Rates," *National Tax Journal,* Vol. I, No. 1, March 1948. Reprinted in AEA *Readings in Economics of Taxation,* Vol. IX, Musgrave and Shoup (editors), Homewood, Ill., 1959.

[2] Peter Briant, Marian Krzyzaniak, and Richard A. Musgrave, "An Econometric Approach to the Incidence of the Corporation Income Tax, A Preliminary Report on a Research Project," Mimeographed, 84 pp., August 31, 1959.

40 per cent we supposed to have fallen on consumers and the remaining 20 per cent on wage earners. The reason for the assumption that consumers were burdened is the fact that there were in West Germany in 1950 strong sellers' markets, which permitted firms if not to raise prices, at least to keep them close to the initial, extremely high, post-Currency Reform levels. The assumption that there was strong backward shifting of the burden towards labor is based on the fact that wages, because of large-scale unemployment, could be kept from rising, while at the same time labor productivity increased rapidly.

*The Local Tax on Business (Gewerbesteuer)*
On the local level, business in West Germany, both incorporated and non-incorporated, has to pay the *Gewerbesteuer* which is a kind of business activity tax. The tax is based on the amount of capital employed and on earnings. Local authorities are free to set the tax rates, and they are often higher in large cities than in smaller ones. (After the last war, local governments often tried to attract new firms to a specific area by exempting them from this tax for a number of years.)

In 1937, about 50 per cent of this tax was paid by corporations.[1] After the war this share probably rose slightly, and it was estimated to be in the neighborhood of 55 per cent. The rest is paid by other businesses, which include in West Germany the large number of very shall enterprises.

In West Germany this tax is considered a "cost tax" which is supposed to be recovered in prices. Whether this can be done depends of course on the existing market situation. In our opinion, and also in that of various West German tax experts consulted, it is reasonable to assume that 90 per cent of the total burden was shifted in prices.

*The Local Real Estate Tax*
The local real estate tax has two components. One tax is levied on building and land for agricultural use (*Grundsteuer* A), and

---

[1] *Statistisches Reichsamt, Gewerbesteuerstatistik, 1937 and 1938, Band 537.*

## TABLE 50

### Estimated Distribution of the Tax Burden in West Germany in 1950. Calendar Year. Cash Receipts
### Millions of DM.

| | Tax Revenue | Tax Burden by Household Income Brackets, 1000 DM | | | | |
| --- | --- | --- | --- | --- | --- | --- |
| | | 0–2.4 | 2.4–3.6 | 3.6–4.8 | 4.8–6.0 | 6.0 + |
| 1. Wage Tax | 1706.8 | 116.0 | 361.4 | 386.6 | 246.2 | 596.6 |
| 2. Personal Income Tax | 2062.5 | 61.8 | 90.7 | 101.1 | 125.9 | 1683.0 |
| 3. Corporate Income Tax | 1429.0 | 154.3 | 174.3 | 152.9 | 144.3 | 803.2 |
| 4. Turnover Tax | 4595.5 | 836.4 | 799.6 | 629.6 | 675.5 | 1654.4 |
| 5. Tobacco Tax | 2059.2 | 444.8 | 537.5 | 374.8 | 339.8 | 362.3 |
| 6. Real Estate Tax | 1078.1 | 220.3 | 177.5 | 154.4 | 133.4 | 392.5 |
| 7. Local Tax on Business | 1250.2 | 223.7 | 204.7 | 170.0 | 169.2 | 482.6 |
| 8. Immediate Aid Levy | 1876.9 | 173.7 | 150.8 | 171.3 | 141.4 | 1239.8 |
| Sum 1–8 | 16058.2 | 2231.0 | 2496.5 | 2140.7 | 1975.7 | 7214.4 |
| 9. All other Taxes and Customs | 3913.0 | 632.6 | 708.6 | 576.1 | 560.3 | 1435.6 |
| 10. Total Tax Burden | 19971.2 | 2863.6 | 3205.1 | 2716.8 | 2536.0 | 8650.0 |

another tax is imposed on all other real estate (*Grundsteuer* B). In 1950, the yield of the first was 287.6 million DM whereas the second amounted to 786.1 million DM. Thus agriculture paid about one-quarter of the total tax.

It was assumed that the tax on agricultural property was borne 50 per cent by farmers and that the other 50 per cent was shifted onto the consumer. In the sellers' markets for agricultural products existing in 1950, this seems to be a justifiable assumption.

The rest of the tax, mainly paid by owners of houses, was allocated somewhat differently. In 1950, when rent controls still existed, the argument was often heard, "Do not increase the real estate tax if rents cannot be increased." It would, however, be wrong to infer that this tax was completely shifted in 1950. Rent controls only froze a situation as it existed before the war. It is estimated that at that time probably 50 per cent of the tax was shifted towards tenants and the rest borne by owners of houses. We therefore allocated this part of the tax 50 per cent to tenants, 30 per cent to receivers of rental income, and 20 per cent to receivers of capital income.

*Other Taxes*

The remaining taxes—some of them with very small yields—are mainly excise taxes and customs. Their total yield was only 3.9 billion DM, or scarcely 85 per cent of the yield of the general turnover tax. Of the total, 1.9 billion DM could be allocated to the different brackets relatively easily, because data are available on household consumption of such commodities as sugar, tea, coffee, beer and alcoholic beverages. The remaining 2.0 billion DM tax yield, received from a number of smaller excise taxes and taxes on property, was allocated to income brackets according to special estimates which need not concern us here.

*Incidence of Tax Structure*

After the allocation of all taxes levied in 1950, we are now in a position to show the total tax burden distribution. In Table 49, line 3, a percentage distribution of the total tax bill (without social security taxes) is presented. We found that the lowest in-

TABLE 51

Estimated Effective Tax Rates in West Germany 1950
(without contributions to Social Insurance)

| Household Income Bracket 1000 DM. | 0–2.4 | 2.4–3.6 | 3.6–4.8 | 4.8–6.0 | 6.0 + |
|---|---|---|---|---|---|
| 1. Effective Tax Rate[1] | 20.5 | 25.5 | 26.8 | 25.9 | 25.9 |
| 2. Hypothetical Effective Tax Rate[2] if no special tax exemptions had been granted. | 20.7 | 25.7 | 27.1 | 26.3 | 27.9 |

[1] Line 10, Table 50 divided by line 4, Appendix Table 2.
[2] See text. Line 10, Table 50 plus line 6, Appendix Table 9 divided by line 4, Appendix Table 2.

come bracket with annual incomes below 2,400 DM contributed 14.3 per cent of total tax revenues. Our highest bracket, over 6,000 DM annual income, contributed 43.3 per cent. Income receivers with less than 500 DM monthly income, paid therefore 56.7 per cent of all taxes.

This is certainly very remarkable. The lower income brackets, which comprised mostly workers, salaried employees, and social security benefit receivers, evidently footed most of the tax bill and must have been severely restrained in their consumption.

Most significant for a tax structure analysis are the effective tax rates expressed for each income bracket—the ratio of total tax burden to income received. If these ratios are rising as income increases, one speaks of a progressive, if they are falling, of a regressive, and if they are constant, of a proportionate tax structure. In Table 51, line 1, the effective rates for the West German tax structure are shown. For the lowest income bracket, this was 20.5 per cent, for the bracket over 6,000 DM annual income, 25.9 per cent. We found that there was a steep increase in the effective rate immediately after the lowest bracket. The effective rates rose to an income level of 4,800 DM but declined slightly thereafter. The interesting question is now how far did this regressive range extend? Tentative estimates showed that it continued at least to the 8,000 DM income level before a mild progression occurred. Responsible for this feature of the West German tax structure were the turnover tax, the tobacco tax, and excises which were either regressive or proportionate in the income range considered. (See Appendix Table 7.) The weight of the income taxes in 1950 (since then the progression of these taxes has been strongly diminished) was not large enough to make for a strong progression.

So far we have discussed the distribution of the actual tax burden. As we have seen, the West Germans made extensive use of tax exemptions to favor capital formation, and it is particularly interesting to investigate what effect these special tax exemptions had on the tax burden distribution. Deductions made under special exemption provision of the income tax law amounted to about 2.3 billion DM in 1950, and the budget loss connected with this is estimated at 800 million DM (see Appendix Table 9). We asked what the hypothetical incidence of the tax structure would have been without such special exemptions. It was assumed, for the sake of simplicity, that total income and, thus tax yield, in 1950 would not have been appreciably lower without them. As can be seen in Table 51, line 2, the effective rates would have risen very little for the lower and medium brackets, but there would have been a pronounced increase for the higher ones. The effect of these exemptions, in essence, was to extend slightly the regressive range, but most important, to diminish greatly the progression for high and highest income brackets.

b. *Distribution of Contributions to Social Insurance*

The distribution of contributions to social insurances could have been included in the previous section. Many economists have argued that compulsory contributions to social insurances are really taxes, irrespective of the fact that they may establish immediate or deferred contractual obligations. Since the social security system in West Germany is institutionally distinct from the fiscal system, it is treated separately in the estimate of the distribution of the tax burden. This allows the important contributions of social insurances to West German capital formation to be brought into sharper focus. In this way, the income brackets which carried the burden when investments were financed with social security funds can be shown.

As was already stated, the social security system was a large saver during the '50's, supplying, between 1949 and 1960, approximately 27.9 billion DM of investable funds. The system consists of a number of different insurances, and not all of them have large surpluses. Sickness and accident insurances and the Family Aid program have relatively small annual excesses of current receipts over current expenditures. The large savers are the old age insurances and the unemployment insurance. Estimates, therefore, are limited to these latter two insurances.

In 1950, payments by employers and employees into old-age insurances (for workers, salaried employees, and miners) and unemployment insurance amounted to 4,545 million DM. Employers and employees each contributed in that year 5% of gross wages to rent insurance and 2% to unemployment insurance.[1] The first flat rate applied to all incomes below 7,200 DM. For unemployment insurance, the upper limit to which contributions were to be made was 4,500 DM annual income for workers and 7,200 DM for salaried employees.

It was assumed that 65% of the combined employer and employee contributions was actually borne by labor. This 65% was distributed according to estimated gross wages which households received. The remaining 35% was supposed to be shifted onto consumers, and it was distributed in the same manner as consumer expenditures. The calculated distributions may be found in Table 52. For annual incomes up to 3,600 DM, social insurance contributions were progressive, but they became strongly regressive for higher income brackets. It is estimated that in 1950, 69.1% of all contributions to rent insurance and unemployment insurance were made by households with incomes under 4,800 DM. Contributions to social insurance imposed a burden on low income brackets in West Germany which was heavier than income taxes. The burden of investments financed with surpluses

---

[1] The rates were different for insurances for miners. G. Zeitel, *op. cit.*, p. 38.

TABLE 52

Estimated Distribution of Contributions to Social Insurance by Income Brackets in 1950. Contributions to Old Age Insurance and Unemployment Insurance.

| Household Income Bracket 1000 DM. | 0–2.4 | 2.4–3.6 | 3.6–4.8 | 4.8–6.0 | 6.0 + | Total |
|---|---|---|---|---|---|---|
| Contributions Millions of DM. | 814 | 1305 | 1014 | 539 | 873 | 4545[1] |
| Contributions to Total Social Insurance Bill % | 17.9 | 28.8 | 22.4 | 11.9 | 19.3 | 100 |
| Contributions as % of Income. (Income exclusive of employers contribution to Social Insurance) | 5.9 | 10.3 | 9.9 | 5.4 | 2.6 | 5.7 |
| Additional Information: Distribution of Gross Wages, %[2] | 18.5 | 34.5 | 24.6 | 9.4 | 12.1 | 100.0 |

[1] Arbeits-und Sozialstatistische Mitteilungen, Bonn April 1958, No. 3, p. 112. Contributions of employees and employers.
[2] St. J.B. 1955, p. 413.

of social insurances fell, consequently, squarely on low income brackets.

### c. *Total Burden Distribution—1950*

To obtain a distribution of the total gross burden in Table 53, the tax burden distribution (Table 49) and the distribution of contributions to social insurances (Table 52) were combined. In part A of Table 53 the household income percentages exclude employer contributions to social insurances. Since it may be argued that these constitute income, they have been included in income in part B of the same table.

A comparison of effective tax rates in Tables 49 and 53 reveals the heavy impact of contributions to social insurance. The West German tax structure (exclusive of social security contributions) has been described as progressive for annual incomes up to 4,800 DM and then slightly regressive up to 8,000 DM, before a moderate progression sets in. The inclusion of social-insurance contributions strongly accentuates this feature of the tax structure. Using a broader income concept, which includes employer contributions to social insurances, it is found that the lowest income bracket had an effective tax rate of 25.6% (line 14, Table 53). This rose steeply to 34.7% for incomes between 3,600 DM and 4,800 DM. The income bracket between 4,800 DM and 6,000 DM had an effective tax rate of 30.6%, and for incomes over 6,000 DM it was only 28.3%. Since contributions to social insurance rapidly diminished for higher incomes, and as the progressive elements in the tax structure were rather weak, there must have been a slight decrease in the effective rate, perhaps even up to 10,000 DM annual income. The ensuing progression was probably rather mild.

Inclusion of contributions to social insurances in the tax burden also changed the contributions the various income brackets made to the total tax bill. Brackets under 4,800 DM contributed relatively more to the total burden, whereas the contributions of the 4,800 DM to 6,000 DM bracket slightly declined. For the top bracket above 6,000 DM the decrease became substantial. It contributed 43.3% to the tax bill without social insurance contributions, but only 38.8% if the latter are included.

In the light of this, it is interesting to set up two broad income brackets: those under and those above 6,000 DM annual incomes. This division is dictated by data and not intended to separate the poor from the rich. Indeed, as was pointed out earlier, 6,000 DM annual income was by no means very high. Still, the division is not without economic and sociological interest since the bulk of all workers, employees, and receivers of social security benefits had incomes below 6,000 DM.

In 1950, this lower group, with under 6,000 DM income, paid 61.2% of all taxes and contributions to social insurances. The effective tax rate (all taxes and contributions to social insurances divided by income) was 30.8% for the lower group and 28.3% for the higher group. The gross burden was thus placed on those in the lower brackets.

This is, however, not the complete story since the benefits from public spending have not yet been considered.

d. *Total Tax Burden Distribution after 1950*

It can be argued that the burden distribution in 1950 was atypical and not indicative of distributions in later years. In 1950, an early year in West Germany's economic growth, household incomes were still very low and tax rates rather high. There is no question but that the distribution of the tax burden changed after 1950. Unfortunately, not enough information is available to trace the developments quantitatively. Nevertheless, from income changes and changes in tax rates, it can perhaps be inferred what these must have been.

First, let us examine changes in tax rates.[1] After the war, Allied authorities raised rates considerably for a number of taxes,

---

[1] For changes in tax rates see: "Verbrauch und Besteuerung von Verbrauchssteuerpflichtigen Waren 1925 bis 1938 und 1949 bis 1955," *St. B.R.D.*, Band 133. "Allgemeine Vorbemerkungen zum Bundeshaushaltsplan 1959," Bonn: Bundesdruckerei pp. 161, 169, G. Zeitel, *op. cit.*, p. 19f; Dreissig, Wilhelmine, "Die Finanz-und Steuerpolitische Entwicklung in der Bundesrepublik im Jahre 1954 und 1955," *Finanzarchiv*, Band 16, Heft I, 1955.

## TABLE 53

Summary Tables: Distribution of Tax Burden and Contributions to Social Insurances in 1950. Household Income, Tax Burden, Contributions to Social Insurances, and Effective Tax Rates.

### A. Income without Employer Contributions to Social Insurances

| Household Income Bracket 1000 DM | 0-2.4 | 2.4-3.6 | 3.6-4.8 | 4.8-6.0 | 6.0 + | Total |
|---|---|---|---|---|---|---|
| 1. Household Income Million of DM | 13950 | 12590 | 10150 | 9810 | 33400 | 79900 |
| 2. Tax Burden Million of DM | 2683 | 3205 | 2716 | 2536 | 8650 | 19971 |
| 3. Contributions to Social Insurance Million of DM | 814 | 1305 | 1014 | 539 | 873 | 4545 |
| 4. Total Burden Million of DM[1] | 3677 | 4510 | 3730 | 3075 | 9523 | 24516 |
| 5. Distribution of Income % | 17.5 | 15.8 | 12.7 | 12.3 | 41.8 | 100.0 |
| 6. Distribution of Total Burden % | 15.0 | 18.4 | 15.2 | 12.6 | 38.8 | 100.0 |
| 7. Effective Tax Rate % (Total Burden divided by Income) | 26.4 | 35.8 | 36.7 | 31.3 | 28.5 | 30.7 |

### B. Income Inclusive Employer Contributions to Social Insurance

| Household Income Bracket 1000 DM | 0-2.4 | 2.4-3.6 | 3.6-4.8 | 4.8-6.0 | 6.0 + | Total |
|---|---|---|---|---|---|---|
| 8. Household Income Million of DM | 13950 | 12590 | 10150 | 9810 | 33400 | 79900 |
| 9. Employer Contribution to Social Insurances Million of DM | 393 | 792 | 608 | 242 | 239 | 2273 |
| 10. Total Income Million of DM[2] | 14343 | 13382 | 10758 | 10052 | 33639 | 82173 |
| 11. Total Burden Million of DM | 3677 | 4510 | 3730 | 3075 | 9523 | 24516 |
| 12. Distribution of Total Income % | 17.5 | 16.3 | 13.1 | 12.2 | 40.9 | 100.0 |
| 13. Distribution of Total Burden % | 15.0 | 18.4 | 15.2 | 12.6 | 38.8 | 100.0 |
| 14. Effective Tax Rate % (Total Burden divided by Total Income) | 25.6 | 33.7 | 34.7 | 30.6 | 28.3 | 29.8 |

1 Line 2 plus line 3.
2 Line 8 plus line 9.

and one of the main complaints of the West German government—repeated again and again, and becoming a sort of guide
for tax policy—was that the higher rates were detrimental to
incentives and created tax dishonesties. Attacks were especially
directed against the rates of income taxes. The conviction was
that there should be extensive cuts. After 1950, there were a large
number of tax rate changes but there was no general rate reduction. A number of tax rates were decreased, others were increased
and some remained unchanged. Yet the average tax burden was
higher in 1959 than in 1950. (See Table 54.)

Rates were sharply decreased for the wage tax and the assessed
personal income tax. This no doubt relieved lower and medium
income brackets somewhat, but it essentially favored the higher
income brackets. Income tax rate cuts for these higher brackers
more than compensated for the gradual disappearance of special
tax benefits which could be obtained in the early '50's under the
various tax exemptions for capital formation. Rates for the corporate income tax—after a temporary reduction in 1954—were
about the same for retained earnings in 1958 as in 1950. After
1953, lower corporate income tax rates were introduced for
dividends. On the average, corporate income tax rates declined as a result. The special Berlin levy (Berlin Hilfe) on
incomes rose slightly until 1956 but was later completely
dropped. Decreases in tax rates also occurred for excise taxes on
alcohol, beer, coffee, tea, and sugar. Average tax rates for the
tobacco tax, one of the most important sources of revenue in the
West German tax structure, were reduced by 30 to 35 per cent
between 1950 and 1957.

The most significant increase during the period considered was
the raising of the general turnover tax rate from 3% to 4% in
1951. This tax accounted for 23% of the total West German tax
revenue in 1950. Having such a heavy weight in the revenue
structure, the rate increase compensated, to a large extent, for the
revenue losses due to decreases in income tax rates and cuts in
the tobacco tax rate. Other rate increases occurred in the transportation and mineral oil taxes. There was also the special coal

levy introduced to finance housing for miners, and the receipts from the West German control agency for imports of agricultural products (Einfuhr und Vorratsstelle) which are in the nature of additional customs.

TABLE 54

Total Tax Revenue as Percentage of Personal Income
1950 to 1959[1]

| Year | Personal Income Definition I[2] | Personal Income Definition II[3] |
|------|---------------------------------|----------------------------------|
| 1950 | 23.8 | 25.0 |
| 1951 | 27.2 | 28.6 |
| 1952 | 28.9 | 30.4 |
| 1953 | 29.4 | 31.0 |
| 1954 | 28.6 | 30.2 |
| 1955 | 27.6 | 29.2 |
| 1956 | 27.8 | 29.4 |
| 1957 | 26.8 | 28.5 |
| 1958 | 26.0 | 27.7 |
| 1959 | 27.3 | 29.0 |

[1] Without contributions to Social Insurances.
[2] Personal Income inclusive contributions of employers to Social Insurance. Added are corporate retained earnings and 40% of assumed, non-shifted, corporate income tax.
[3] Personal Income as under definition I but contributions of employers to Social Insurance excluded.

Left more or less unchanged were the tax on local business (Gewerbesteuer), the real estate tax, and the property tax. There was also no great change in contributions to the Equalization of Burden Fund levy.

In 1957, contributions to old age insurances were raised by 4%, whereas those to unemployment insurance were lowered by 2%. This 2% net increase in contributions to the Social Security System has substantially increased the burden on lower brackets and tended to offset previous reductions in wage tax rates.

Next for consideration is the impact of income changes, which were much more important to the tax burden distribution than changes in tax rates. It is estimated that in 1950 40% of all West German households had annual incomes under 2,400 DM and only 10% over 6,000 DM. Data on household incomes for later

years indicate that just three years later only 12% of all households were still in the lowest bracket, whereas about 25% had
incomes above 6,000 DM. By 1956, there were further improvements. At that time, 8.8% of all households had incomes under
2,400 DM but 44% over 6,000 DM.[1] Data on taxpayers by income
brackets, as shown in Table 58, corroborate this upward shift in
incomes. As a result, the percentage contributions to the total tax
bill have decreased for income brackets below 3,600 DM annual
income and substantially increased for the medium incomes up
to 9,000 DM. With the strong reduction in income tax rates,
higher income brackets in all likelihood did not contribute a
much larger share to the total tax bill than they did in 1950.

Considering the importance of the various tax yields to the
total tax revenue and, further, the progressivity of each, the conclusion is that after 1950 the West German tax structure became
less progressive. (See Tables 55 to 57.) The effects of all these rate
changes and different expenditure patterns were probably the
following: The effective tax rates as calculated for 1950 for lower
income brackets may have been decreased by 1.5% or 2% in
1955;[2] increases in effective rates occurred for medium brackets
up to 10,000 DM annual income. The rate changes also reduced
the effective rates for higher income brackets. As far as the progressivity of the West German tax structure is concerned, the
range of regressive taxation in 1955 probably extended beyond
10,000 DM annual income, and the progression from there on
was a very mild one. The trend was toward a more regressive tax
structure.

There are good reasons to believe that in later years, at least
up to 1955, in spite of tax rate and income changes, the gross
burden was still very much on the consumer at the lower end of
the income scale.

---

1 *Bedarfsstruktur 1956*, p. 14, Nürnberg: Gesellschaft für Konsumforschung,
e.V., Mai 1956.
2 For later years decreases may have been somewhat larger. See: Günter
Pehl, "Indirekte Steuerbelastung von Arbeitnehmerhaushalten im Jahre 1958,"
*Mitteilungen Wirtschaftswissenschaftliches Institut der Gewerkschaften,*
December 1959, p. 307.

## TABLE 55

Total Tax Revenue (Cash Receipts) All Government Levels. 1950–1960. Millions of DM.[1] Calendar Year.

| Year | (1) Total Tax Revenue | (2) Wage Tax | (3) Assessed Personal Income Tax | (4) Corporate Income Tax | (5) Turnover Tax | (6) Tobacco Tax | (7) Real Estate Tax | (8) Local Tax on Business | (9) Local Tax Equalization of Burden |
|---|---|---|---|---|---|---|---|---|---|
| 1950 | 19972 | 1706 | 2062 | 1429 | 4595 | 2059 | 1078 | 1250 | 1876 |
| 1952 | 33023 | 3658 | 4036 | 2780 | 8381 | 2334 | 1225 | 2623 | 1806 |
| 1954 | 38084 | 3875 | 4848 | 3071 | 9593 | 2304 | 1334 | 3343 | 2187 |
| 1956 | 46969 | 5402 | 5144 | 3637 | 12184 | 2781 | 1404 | 4223 | 2438 |
| 1958 | 52260 | 5932 | 5982 | 5190 | 12963 | 3093 | 1521 | 5261 | 2072 |
| 1960 | 67813 | 7970 | 9729 | 6432 | 15871 | 3513 | 1614 | 7360 | 2023 |

| Year | (10) Trans-portation Tax | (11) Customs | (12) Automobile Tax | (13) Mineral Oil Tax | (14) Property Tax | (15) Coffee Tax | (16) Alcohol Tax | (17) All Other Taxes |
|---|---|---|---|---|---|---|---|---|
| 1950 | 240 | 604 | 339 | 67 | 106 | 329 | 480 | 1752 |
| 1952 | 355 | 1054 | 469 | 590 | 178 | 535 | 590 | 2409 |
| 1954 | 173 | 1486 | 599 | 781 | 620 | 301 | 781 | 2788 |
| 1956 | 253 | 1983 | 837 | 1415 | 758 | 405 | 684 | 3421 |
| 1958 | 544 | 2094 | 1082 | 1665 | 888 | 486 | 857 | 2630 |
| 1960 | 766 | 2775 | 1448 | 2641 | 1080 | 681 | 1012 | 2898 |

[1] St. J.B. 1955, p. 406; 1958, p. 374; 1961, p. 432.

## TABLE 56

### Changes in Tax Structure: Yield of Taxes as Percentage of Total Tax Revenue, 1950 to 1960.[1]

| Year | Total Tax Revenue (1) | Wage Tax (2) | Assessed Personal Income Tax (3) | Corporate Income Tax (4) | Turnover Tax (5) | Tobacco Tax (6) | Real Estate Tax (7) | Local Tax on Business (8) | Equalization of Burden Levy (9) |
|---|---|---|---|---|---|---|---|---|---|
| 1950 | 100.0 | 8.5 | 10.3 | 7.2 | 23.0 | 10.3 | 5.4 | 6.3 | 9.4 |
| 1952 | 100.0 | 11.1 | 12.2 | 8.4 | 25.4 | 7.1 | 3.7 | 7.9 | 5.5 |
| 1954 | 100.0 | 10.2 | 12.7 | 8.1 | 25.2 | 6.0 | 3.5 | 8.8 | 5.7 |
| 1956 | 100.0 | 11.5 | 11.0 | 7.7 | 25.9 | 5.9 | 3.0 | 9.0 | 5.2 |
| 1958 | 100.0 | 11.4 | 11.4 | 9.9 | 24.8 | 5.9 | 2.9 | 10.0 | 4.0 |
| 1960 | 100.0 | 11.7 | 14.3 | 9.5 | 23.4 | 5.2 | 2.4 | 10.9 | 3.0 |

| Year | Transportation Tax (10) | Customs (11) | Automobile Tax (12) | Mineral Oil Tax (13) | Property Tax (14) | Coffee Tax (15) | Alcohol Tax (16) | All Other Taxes (17) |
|---|---|---|---|---|---|---|---|---|
| 1950 | 1.2 | 3.0 | 1.7 | 0.3 | 0.5 | 1.6 | 2.4 | 8.8 |
| 1952 | 1.1 | 3.2 | 1.4 | 1.8 | 0.5 | 1.6 | 1.8 | 7.3 |
| 1954 | 0.5 | 3.9 | 1.6 | 2.0 | 1.6 | 0.8 | 2.1 | 7.3 |
| 1956 | 0.5 | 4.2 | 1.8 | 3.0 | 1.6 | 0.9 | 1.5 | 7.3 |
| 1958 | 1.0 | 4.0 | 2.1 | 3.2 | 1.7 | 0.9 | 1.6 | 5.0 |
| 1960 | 1.1 | 4.1 | 2.1 | 3.9 | 1.6 | 1.0 | 1.5 | 4.3 |

[1] Calculated from Table 55.

## TABLE 57

### Changes in Yields of Various Taxes 1950 to 1960.[1] 1950 = 100.

| Year | Total Tax Revenue (1) | Wage Tax (2) | Assessed Personal Income Tax (3) | Corporate Income Tax (4) | Turnover Tax (5) | Tobacco Tax (6) | Real Estate Tax (7) | Local Tax on Business (8) | Equalization of Burden Levy (9) |
|---|---|---|---|---|---|---|---|---|---|
| 1950 | 100.0 | 100.0 | 100.0 | 100.0 | 100.0 | 100.0 | 100.0 | 100.0 | 100.0 |
| 1952 | 165.3 | 214.4 | 195.7 | 194.5 | 182.4 | 113.4 | 113.6 | 209.8 | 96.3 |
| 1954 | 190.7 | 227.1 | 235.1 | 214.9 | 208.8 | 111.9 | 123.8 | 267.4 | 116.6 |
| 1956 | 235.2 | 316.6 | 249.5 | 254.5 | 265.2 | 135.1 | 130.2 | 337.8 | 130.0 |
| 1958 | 261.7 | 347.7 | 290.1 | 363.1 | 282.2 | 150.2 | 141.1 | 420.9 | 110.4 |
| 1960 | 339.5 | 467.2 | 471.8 | 450.1 | 345.5 | 170.6 | 149.7 | 588.8 | 107.8 |

| Year | Transportation Tax (10) | Customs (11) | Automobile Tax (12) | Mineral Oil Tax (13) | Property Tax (14) | Coffee Tax (15) | Alcohol Tax (16) | All Other Taxes (17) |
|---|---|---|---|---|---|---|---|---|
| 1950 | 100.0 | 100.0 | 100.0 | 100.0 | 100.0 | 100.0 | 100.0 | 100.0 |
| 1952 | 147.9 | 174.5 | 138.3 | 880.1 | 167.9 | 162.6 | 123.0 | 137.5 |
| 1954 | 72.0 | 246.1 | 176.6 | 1166.0 | 584.9 | 91.5 | 162.8 | 159.1 |
| 1956 | 105.4 | 328.4 | 246.8 | 2112.6 | 715.0 | 123.1 | 142.5 | 195.3 |
| 1958 | 226.7 | 346.8 | 319.1 | 2485.8 | 837.7 | 147.7 | 178.6 | 150.1 |
| 1960 | 319.1 | 459.5 | 427.0 | 3943.0 | 1018.9 | 207.0 | 210.9 | 165.4 |

[1] Calculated from Table 55.

e. *Distribution of Benefits from Public Investments*

In preceding sections, our inquiry concerned the gross burden distribution when the government in West Germany financed investments through taxes and from social insurance funds. The gross burden aspect of public capital formation alone is, however, insufficient for the understanding of the equity problems involved. The correlates to the gross burden were the benefits which accrued to the various income brackets. Most significant for the equity of public spending is the net burden imposed—obtained by deducting the benefits from the gross tax burden. Its derivation is necessary to comprehend the effects of public capital formation on income and property distribution.

TABLE 58

Percentage Distribution of Income Taxpayers
by Income Brackets: 1950, 1954 and 1957[1]

| Income Bracket 1000 DM. | 1950 | 1954 | 1957 |
|---|---|---|---|
| 0–3 | 50.2 | 22.6 | 28.4[2] |
| 3–5 | 36.8 | 39.9 | 30.2 |
| 5–8 | 9.1 | 28.1 | 28.5 |
| 8–12 | 2.3 | 5.6 | 8.3 |
| 12–16 | 0.7 | 1.7 | 2.0 |
| 16 + | 1.0 | 2.2 | 2.6 |
| Additional Information: Number of Taxpayers Mill. Persons | 12.8 | 16.0 | 20.5 |

[1] Persons paying wage tax (Lohnsteuer) and assessed personal income tax (Einkommensteuer). Estimated from St. J.B. 1955, p. 412, 414; St. J.B. 1958, p. 384; St. J.B. 1961, p. 444. Information Bundesminister der Finanzen, Anlage 1 und 2, Vw/4–1036–134/58.
[2] This higher percentage in the lowest bracket reflects the fact that, with reaching of the labor resource ceiling, persons hired were often low skilled and low paid.

Benefits accrued to the various income brackets in West Germany in two ways: from direct public investments and through tax exemptions as incentives for capital formation. It will facilitate this study to treat these two separately.

Estimating a tax burden distribution is difficult and painstaking work, invariably involving many questionable assumptions. An estimate of the distribution of benefits from public expenditures is even more difficult.[1] The fact is that benefits from public spending do accrue to people, in many cases irrespective of whether they pay for them, or whether or not they wish to receive them. Most important is that there is no reason to believe that these benefits accrue to everyone in the same way or to the same extent. This is quite obvious when the government makes expenditures which aid specific groups of the population, such as workers, farmers, or businessmen. In this case, one could try to impute the benefits derived directly to the group concerned. It should be noted, however, that even here such allocation may not exactly correspond to the actual distribution of benefits. If the government relieves the poor, everybody benefits in the sense that it is gratifying to see dire proverty and misery disappear. If aid to education is given, it may be true that most of the benefits accrue to students, but society also gains because it can enjoy the talents and skills of more educated people. Thus, even in cases of specific expenditures, no perfectly watertight demarcation is possible as to who actually receives the benefits.

The difficulties increase enormously when it comes to the allocation of general expenditures which, by their very nature, cannot be imputed to any specific group. Examples of such public expenditures are defense outlays, the cost of general government, or the maintenance of a police force.

One way to allocate these expenditures is to distribute them equally among households, for the reason that in a democratic society every person or household gets the same protection and services. On the other hand, it could be stated that it is the task of government to guarantee that citizens can earn their living and that its essential function is to see to it that market-determined incomes are not forcefully and illegally changed. If this is the case, the general benefits of public spending would accrue to

---

[1] In this case, a more refined analysis would have to take into account the time pattern of the services which public investments render. This could not be attempted for lack of data. It is felt, however, that the method used here is a good approximation of the actual benefit distribution.

citizens according to their incomes earned. A third, and quite defensible hypothesis, is that in a capitalistic society it is the foremost task of the government to protect property rights. In this case, the benefit of general expenditures would accrue to people according to the existing property distributions.

As the above mentioned three distributions are very different in capitalistic Western countries, it is important which one is used for the allocation of benefits. If it is the government's task to protect property, most of the benefits would go to upper income brackets. On the other hand, if everyone benefits in the same way, lower and medium income brackets will benefit most.

For an estimate of the benefit distribution, the different public expenditures were grouped. Specific expenditures, such as those for residential construction under the Social Housing Program or schools, have been distributed by income brackets according to special distributions i.e., income receivers eligible for social housing or number of children in each income bracket. As far as general expenditures are concerned, the distribution of household incomes and number of households by income brackets were used for the benefits allocation. Because it is often assumed that lower income brackets benefit most from public expenditures, this study tries not to bias estimates in favor of these, preferring the criteria of household incomes to number of households in cases where the use of the latter would have been justified. Our benefit distribution is biased in favor of higher income brackets.

The results of the computations are given in Table 60 where, in line 2, a percentage distribution of benefits from public investments, as shown in Table 59, may be found. It is remarkable that in spite of the admitted built-in bias in favor of higher income brackets the bulk of all benefits accrued to annual incomes under 6,000 DM. Half of all benefits were probably received by households with incomes slightly over 3,800 DM. Though the precise allocation of benefits to the various brackets may be questioned, it seems beyond dispute that the lower income brackets benefited most from public investments in 1950.

Since the distribution of the tax burden is known, our study now proceeds to derive a net burden distribution by combining the burden and benefit distributions. Unfortunately, effective tax rates for the various income brackets for the net burden distribution cannot be calculated, since the distribution of benefits from current expenditures were not included. Yet, given the existing revenue and spending structure, the question of who would have benefited if the government increased public expenditures or capital formation by one DM in 1950 can be answered.

### The Distribution of Benefits from Public Investments

| Category of Investment Expenditure: | Distribution by Household Income Brackets according to Distribution of: |
|---|---|
| General Government | Income |
| Public Safety | " |
| Social Institutions | " |
| Construction other than Residential Construction | " |
| Justice | 50% Income, 50% Number of households |
| Science and Arts | "          "          " |
| Waterways, Harbors | "          "          " |
| Other Transport and Traffic | "          "          " |
| Burden as a Consequence of War | "          "          " |
| Residential Construction | Income of wage earners under 9,000 DM annual income |
| Schools | 90% Number of children in income brackets, 10% income |
| Municipal Services | Number of households |
| Roads | 33% Number of households, 33% Income, 33% to upper bracket |
| Agriculture and Forestry | Income from agriculture |
| Industry, Trade and Arts | 50% Income, 30% Income from business, 20% Income from capital |

The results are shown in Table 60 in lines 5 and 6. From these it is obvious that such spending involved a redistribution to the lower income brackets. If investments were financed only out of taxes, the redistribution would have been larger than if a mixture of tax finance and financing with social insurance funds had been used. The reason for this is that contributions to social insurances were made mainly by lower income brackets. In 1950, income brackets under 4,800 DM received a net benefit from public investments, and those with higher incomes made a net

## TABLE 59

### Distribution of Gross Investments by Government in West Germany According to Economic Sectors. 1949 to 1955. Current Prices.[1]

| | 1949 | 1950 | 1951 | 1952 | 1953 | 1954 | 1955 | 1950 to 1955 |
|---|---|---|---|---|---|---|---|---|
| General Government | 3.8 | 4.3 | 3.8 | 2.6 | 2.5 | 2.4 | 2.4 | 2.8 |
| Public Safety[2] | 0.3 | 0.2 | 2.4 | 1.3 | 1.1 | 0.9 | 1.2 | 1.2 |
| Justice | 0.7 | 0.7 | 0.6 | 0.6 | 0.5 | 0.5 | 0.5 | 0.5 |
| Schools | 5.4 | 5.8 | 8.2 | 7.9 | 8.2 | 7.9 | 8.5 | 7.9 |
| Science and Arts | 3.0 | 2.6 | 2.8 | 2.7 | 2.6 | 2.6 | 2.8 | 2.7 |
| Social Institutions (including Health Care) | 7.6 | 5.6 | 6.5 | 7.3 | 6.6 | 6.1 | 6.0 | 6.4 |
| Residential Construction | } 32.3 | 24.5 | 36.5 | 33.3 | 30.4 | 28.9 | 24.5 | 29.4 |
| Other Construction | | 15.7 | 6.5 | 2.6 | 2.3 | 2.9 | 14.5 | 7.1 |
| Agriculture, Forestry | 2.6 | 2.6 | 5.0 | 3.7 | 4.4 | 5.0 | 5.2 | 4.5 |
| Industry, Trade and Arts | 5.8 | 8.6 | 10.7 | 6.6 | 7.8 | 6.6 | 12.1 | 8.7 |
| Municipal Services | 10.5 | 9.4 | 6.2 | 12.5 | 14.2 | 17.6 | 11.7 | 12.6 |
| Roads and Bridges | 8.2 | 7.3 | 6.4 | 13.5 | 14.9 | 14.3 | 7.3 | 11.0 |
| Waterways, Shipping, Harbors | 6.7 | 4.5 | 4.0 | 3.6 | 3.3 | 2.9 | 2.6 | 3.3 |
| Other Traffic and Transport | 0.3 | 0.4 | 0.2 | 0.5 | 0.4 | 0.8 | 0.6 | 0.5 |
| Burden as a Consequence of War | 12.8 | 7.8 | 0.1 | 1.3 | 0.7 | 0.6 | 0.1 | 1.3 |
| Total: | 100.0 | 100.0 | 100.0 | 100.0 | 100.0 | 100.0 | 100.0 | 100.0 |
| Gross Investments accounted for in above distribution: Millions of DM. | 3561.4 | 4770.5 | 6066.3 | 8139.8 | 9042.5 | 10470.9 | 11398.5 | 49888.5 |
| Total Gross Investment by Government: Millions of DM. | 4444.1 | 5333.6 | 6932.1 | 8413.0 | 9359.4 | 11037.9 | 12131.7 | |
| % of all Government Investments accounted for: | 80.2 | 89.5 | 87.5 | 96.6 | 96.6 | 94.9 | 93.9 | |

1 Sources: St. B.R.D., Volumes 4, 17, 19, 54, 57, 58 and 59. Includes new construction, reinvestment in fixed assets, purchase of equipment, and loans and subsidies for investments.
2 Includes for later years some investments for defense purposes.

contribution. Increases in public capital formation have, therefore, tended to mitigate inequalities in income distribution.

### f. *Tax Exemption Distribution*

Another distribution may now be considered. Tax exemptions have been discussed in preceding chapters, and their importance for West German capital formation may again be indicated by referring to their magnitude. Between 1949 and 1957, about 28.4 billion DM in special tax exemptions as incentives for capital formation were granted, which was more than 6% of the total revenues of all levels of government. Individuals as well as corporations were entitled to make use of these exemption possibilities. Fortunately, data are available on the distribution of tax exemptions by income brackets for the personal income tax for 1949 and 1954 and we can estimate what income brackets derived benefits. In addition, the total amount of tax exemptions used by corporations in these years is known. For the allocation of the latter, it is assumed that they were distributed by income brackets in the same manner as income from capital. The calculated distributions for 1949 and 1954 are shown in Table 61. They do not refer to exactly the same kinds of tax exemptions since a number of them expired before 1954 but the differences are minor. In 1949, 88.2% of all exemptions were granted to income brackets over 6,000 DM annual income. A small fraction of all households, only 0.7% in income brackets over 50,000 DM, used 41.2% of the exemptions. In 1954, the distribution was not quite as skewed, but 1.1% of households with incomes over 50,000 DM still received 33.5% of all exemptions. It should be noted that the distributions shown refer to tax exemptions and not to taxes saved. Since marginal tax rates were much higher in the upper brackets, the distribution of the actual benefits received was even more in favor of higher incomes. The distributions in Table 61 may not be perfect, but they are reliable enough to warrant one conclusion: tax incentives for capital formation overwhelmingly benefited the higher income brackets.

The effect of tax exemptions as incentives to invest was a strong diminution of the redistribution which occurred through

## TABLE 60

### Distribution of Benefits from Government Investments in 1950.
### Excess of Benefits over Burden in Income Brackets.

| Household Income Brackets 1000 DM. | 0–2.4 | 2.4–3.6 | 3.6–4.8 | 4.8–6.0 | 6.0 + | Total |
|---|---|---|---|---|---|---|
| 1. Distribution of Benefits from Government Investments: Millions DM. | 1073.6 | 1064.9 | 777.9 | 529.6 | 1324.5 | 4770.5 |
| 2. % Distribution of Benefits from Government Investments | 22.5 | 22.3 | 16.3 | 11.1 | 27.8 | 100.0 |
| 3. Distribution of Tax Burden % | 14.3 | 16.1 | 13.6 | 12.7 | 43.3 | 100.0 |
| 4. Distribution of Tax Burden and Contributions to Social Insurances %[1] | 15.0 | 18.4 | 15.2 | 12.6 | 38.8 | 100.0 |
| 5. If 1 DM. was raised through taxes for Government Investment, Brackets received (+) DM. Benefit in excess of Burden: (line 2 minus line 3) | +0.082 | +0.062 | +0.027 | −0.016 | −0.155 | |
| 6. If 1 DM. was raised through taxes and contributions to Social Insurances[1] for Government Investment, Brackets received (+) DM. Benefits in excess of Burden: (line 2 minus line 4) | +0.075 | +0.039 | +0.011 | −0.015 | −0.110 | |

[1] Only Rent and Unemployment Insurance.

public investments in favor of lower income groups, as explained above. In Table 62, line 4, the actual redistribution, as it took place in West Germany in 1950, may be found. Net benefits from total government efforts to increase capital formation were derived only by the two lowest brackets under 3,600 DM annual incomes. A comparison of lines 5 and 6 in Table 60 with line 4 in Table 62 shows that the benefits were substantially lower than without tax exemptions.

TABLE 61

Distribution of Tax Exemptions to Favor Capital Formation and Number of Taxpayers by Income Brackets in 1950 and 1954.

| Income Bracket of Taxpayer 1000 DM. | Deductions[1] 1949 % | Number of Taxpayers[2] 1950 % | Deductions[3] 1954 % | Number of Taxpayers[4] 1954 % |
|---|---|---|---|---|
| 0–6 | 11.8 | 70.9 | 17.7 | 68.6 |
| 6–50 | 47.0 | 28.4 | 48.7 | 30.3 |
| 50–100 | 13.0 | 0.5 | 13.7 | 0.8 |
| 100 + | 28.2 | 0.2 | 19.8 | 0.3 |
| Total | 100.0 | 100.0 | 100.0 | 100.0 |
| Deductions accounted for Millions of DM. | 1489 | | 2771 | |

[1] Income taxpayers and corporations. Deductions by income taxpayers distributed according to Statistisches Bundesamt VII. D. 10. Table 3. Statistik der Einkommensteuerveranlagung 1949 Bundesgebiet (unpublished). Deductions by corporations distributed like income from capital.
[2] Income taxpayers. St. J.B. 1955, p. 415.
[3] St. J.B. 1960, p. 437, for income taxpayer. Deductions by corporations distributed like income from capital.
[4] Income taxpayers, St. J.B. 1958, p. 385.

g. *Summary: Public Capital Formation and Equity*

In the preceding sections, the object was to obtain a quantitative picture of the effects of public capital formation on income distribution. It was concluded that even with a tax structure as little progressive as that of West Germany, there was still some redistribution in favor of lower income brackets. However, public investments financed with Social Security funds and the granting of special tax exemptions for capital formation diminished this redistribution. The reason for this was that contributions to social insurances were made mostly by lower and medium income

## TABLE 62

### Distribution of Benefits from Government Investment and Tax Exemptions in 1950. Benefits over Burden in Income Brackets.[1]

| Household Income Bracket 1000 DM. | 0–2.4 | 2.4–3.6 | 3.6–4.8 | 4.8–6.0 | 6.0 + | Total |
|---|---|---|---|---|---|---|
| 1. Distribution of Benefits from Government Investments and Tax Exemptions, Millions of DM. | 1103.3 | 1095.4 | 808.1 | 564.4 | 2006.8 | 5575.1 |
| 2. Distribution of Total Benefits, % | 19.7 | 19.7 | 14.5 | 10.1 | 36.0 | 100.0 |
| 3. Distribution of Tax Burden and Contributions to Social Insurance if no Tax Exemptions for Capital Formation had been granted, % | 14.6 | 17.9 | 14.9 | 12.3 | 40.3 | 100.0 |
| 4. Excess of Benefits (+) over Burden in each Bracket per 1 DM. additional Total Benefits, DM. (line 2 minus line 3) | +0.051 | +0.018 | −0.004 | −0.022 | −0.043 | |

[1] In this table, tax exemptions are treated as subsidies to the different income brackets (line 1). This requires that on the burden side it must be assumed that the full tax bill was paid (line 3).

brackets, whereas the bulk of the benefits from tax exemptions accrued to higher income brackets. As incomes rose during the '50's, households shifted into somewhat higher income brackets. With increases in incomes came an upward shift in the distribution of the tax burden and, since the structure of public investments did not change much, it is likely that a similar upward shift also occurred in the benefit distribution. Notwithstanding these changes, households at the lower end of the income scale most likely continued to benefit from public capital expenditures throughout the '50's.

This is important since there is evidence that, as a by-product of West Germany's economic growth and large capital formation, the income distribution, and even more so the property distribution, became rather unequal. This development has caused grave concern in many quarters in West Germany, and it is useful to review what has been said on this subject.

The argument is that most of the benefits from the country's rapid economic growth accrued to the upper income brackets. Since everybody is absolutely better off, the relative shifts in the income and property distribution are somewhat disguised, and perhaps also morally more tolerable than otherwise might be the case. A humorous story in West Germany points out that everybody is better off as a result of the rapid economic expansion; the worker who had one bicycle now has two, and the man who formerly owned one steel mill has another. Detailed quotes are given (all translations by the author) on what has been written on this subject.

Concerning those who carried the burden of rapid capital formation, Leitz writes about the effects of financing investments:

> It is safe to assume that especially in the first years the very high rate of internal financing hit the propertyless groups—workers, salaried employees, officials, receivers of Social Security benefits, and also the free professions. The worse their initial economic conditions the harder they were hit. The larger the pent-up demand of households, the more inelastic was their demand in goods markets and their supply in the labor markets. To some extent this may have

been mitigated by aid from the Immediate Aid and Equalization of Burden Program, but this was very often delayed and could only take care of certain minimum requirements. The main sufferers of the (capital) accumulation were, therefore, refugees and expellees, who constituted at the same time the bulk of the industrial reserve army, and the population of big cities. These groups had suffered most during the war.[1]

Professor Wallich observes that:

Ever since the Currency Reform, Germany has had a reputation for a high degree of inequality in its income distribution. For a number of years, this reputation rested largely on circumstantial evidence, but it has, on the whole, been confirmed by the income pyramid for the year 1950, finally published in 1954.[2]

Wallich believed that the adverse social effects were partly compensated by increases in, and redistribution of, income, but he admits that in spite of this:

It has probably left the inequality of incomes a good deal more pronounced than it is in most Anglo-Saxon countries.

Lohmann, who analyzes the West German postwar investments and their financing, concludes that:

As a consequence, the income distribution did not only become more unequal but remained so in the last years.[3]

Deist, a prominent Social Democratic member of the Bundestag, writes in 1960:

The uncomfortable feeling about the present property distribution increases. In fact, capital formation occurs in such a way that the existing inequality in property distribution becomes larger.[4]

---

[1] Klaus Leitz, Investitionen und Sozialstruktur in Westdeutschland, Zürich: Polygraphischer Verlag, 1956, p. 78. (Translation by author.)

[2] Wallich, *op. cit.,* p. 47.

[3] Martin Lohmann, "Die westdeutschen Investitionen und ihre soziale Problematik," *Hamburger Jahrbuch für Wirtschafts und Gesellschaftspolitik,* Tübingen: J. C. B. Mohr, Paul Siebeck, 1958, p. 45.

[4] Heinrich Deist, "Der Weg zu einer gerechten Vermögensverteilung," *Die Neue Gesellschaft,* 1960.

Criticism of the income and property distribution also comes from Catholic quarters. Paul Jostock writes about West German capital formation after 1948:

> As usual, nearly everything became the property of entrepreneurs and capital owners. It is true that workers received a nice wage, but a just participation in the gains, especially in undistributed profits, was denied to them. If one thinks how urgent the reform of our property is and what a unique opportunity the postwar developments offered, one can only call the whole process a scandal which cries for change.[1]

About the large concentration of property in upper income brackets, Professor Bruno Gleitze has the following to say:

> Owners of capital, treated generously during the currency reform, have survived the enormous destruction of capital during the last war and are stronger and more powerful than ever before. There have never been as many millionaires in West Germany as at the present. Never before has there been such a concentration of billions in property values in the hands of a few families as at the present time.[2]

Stressing that most of the new capital accrued to the same groups as before the war, something which is certainly interesting from the political as well as sociological point of view, Gleitze says:

> After the war that part of capital formation which leads to economic power accrued only to a small extent to new owners. The overwhelming part fell into the hands of old property owners.[3]

Some people even seem to think that there must have been an extreme polarization in the property distribution. Anton Reithinger writes:

> The accumulation of capital in West Germany during the decade 1947 to 1957 occurred according to the expectations

---

1 Paul Jostock, "Das Sozialprodukt und seine Verteilung," *Sozialreferat des Zentralkomitees der Deutschen Katholiken*, Paderborn, n.d., p. 38.

2 Bruno Gleitze, "Die lohnpolitische Situation," *Konjunkturpolitik 3*, Jhrg. 1957.

3 Bruno Gleitze, "Der westdeutsche Investitionsaufwand und seine Finanzierung," *Konjunkturpolitik 3*, Heft 1958.

of Karl Marx and not according to the theories of Ludwig Erhard.[1]

The Social Democratic Party gave considerable attention to the problem of income and property distribution in 1960. In a resolution of the party leadership, one reads:

> Workers as well as small entrepreneurs are mostly excluded from this capital formation which was possible through the efforts of the whole nation. This development has been favored through the policy of the government.[2]

The West German government has never really faced up to this problem until lately. It has usually questioned that such shifts in the income and property distribution actually occurred without proving the contrary or even publishing data which would make an objective assessment possible. A feeling prevails that the problem of the income and property distribution question hangs as a cloud over the West German economic growth process and the absence of any relevant official statistics on this, if not suspicious, is certainly astonishing. West German officials have been very much concerned about the sectoral distribution of capital formation and have generally stressed that it should increase in the personal sector and decrease in the business and public sector. The reason is that this allegedly would lead to a more desirable distribution of property. Interest has centered on the relative importance of the various kinds of savings and intersectoral flow of investable funds.[3] Which income brackets could and did form capital, the crucial issue, received little attention during most of the '50's. Occasionally, this problem was mentioned. In a publication of Professor Erhard's ministry in 1957 one learns about the possible sociological consequences of West Germany's capital formation through high profits:

---

[1] Anton Reithinger, "Soziale Marketwirtschaft auf dem Prüfstand," Frankfurt: Fritz Knapp Verlag, 1958, p. 26.

[2] *SPD Parteitag 21*, bis 25. November, 1960 in Hannover, Unkorrigiertes Protokoll, 4. Tag, p. 55. Antrag 46.

[3] These problems were especially discussed in connection with plans to revive the capital market.

Internal financing in the economy, on the one hand, requires high prices and leads, on the other, to a one-sided capital formation in overwhelmingly large and already highly profitable enterprises. This obvious phenomenon becomes alarming and generates social tensions which may lead to dangerous demands for co-ownership and collective property even in middle class circles and parties.[1]

The Federal Minister, Franz Blücher admits in 1957 that the bulk of income receivers did not participate in capital formation. (In his opinion, this was due to the fact that they became consumption-oriented after the war, and that they did not save, though they had the opportunity.) He writes:

Such a one-sided structure of capital formation within a Social Market Economy, which is neither market-conform nor social in the long run, has to lead to dangerous distortions of the economic and social structure.[2]

These developments could not continue unnoticed and, since 1960, the West German government has become more concerned about this problem. Professor Fritz Burgbacher, chairman of the CDU/CSU "Committee on Property," has vigorously and courageously fought for a broader distribution of property in the future. By demanding that an estimated increase of 250 billion DM in the capital stock in the next ten years should be more equally distributed, he has implied that the past distribution did have shortcomings.[3] Others, too, fought for a more equal distribution of income and property.[4] As a result of all this in 1961 the government issued a first law intended to promote capital formation by employed persons. This was a first timid effort to

[1] Der Bundesminister für Wirtschaft, *Sonderhefte zum Bericht über die wirtschaftliche Lage in der Bundesrepublik*, Heft 3, February 1957, p. 3.

[2] Franz Blücher, Bundesminister, Bad Godesberg, 16 January 1957. In so-called "Blücher Gutachten," p. 7, typewritten.

[3] Fritz Burgbacher, *Politik auf drei Ebenen*, Köln: Verlag Deutsche Glocke, 1961, p. 79.

[4] Gerhard Zweig und Hans Georg Feldhege, *Eigentum für Alle*, Bad Godesberg: Asgard Verlag, 1961, especially pp. 9–10. Oswald von Nell-Breuning, S. J., "Eigentumsbildung in Arbeiterhand," *Sozialreferat des Zentralkomitees der Deutschen Katholiken*, Paderborn, n.d. Erwin Häussler, *Der Arbeitnehmer von Morgen*, Stuttgart, 1955.

increase incomes of employees, but it is still significant as a departure from ideas and attitudes of the '50's.[1] The law was clear recognition of the fact that savings will be made only if incomes are high enough to do so. Ex-post it admits, implicitly, that this was not the case for the masses in the '50's, and that little capital formation occurred in lower and medium income brackets.

The all-out drive for economic growth has evidently led to large inequities in West Germany—a price which perhaps had to be paid. The controversy is still going on as to whether or not the price was too high.

The role of public capital formation in this process is now evident. It involved, as we have found, a redistribution in favor of lower brackets. Therefore, it must have limited inequities in income and property distribution which were inevitable as a result of a high incentive, high profit growth. With a significantly lower level of public investments, or still higher tax incentives for private business to invest, inequities would have been even larger.

If the West German worker could not participate as a shareholder in the country's growth, he was at least assured of various benefits from public spending. He could perhaps get a decent apartment under the Social Housing Program and his children could receive an adequate education. In the absence of these and other benefits, social tensions might have run very high. Public capital formation, without a doubt, acted as a strong mitigating element during the incentive growth process.

---

[1] "Gesetz zur Förderung der Vermögensbildung der Arbeitnehmer," *Bundesgesetzblatt 18*, Juli, 1961.

# Appendix Tables to Chapter V

*"The Distribution of the
Tax Burden in 1950"*

## APPENDIX TABLE 1

### Estimate of Number Distribution of Households by Income Brackets West Germany 1950

| Household Income Brackets 1000 DM. | 0-2.4 | 2.4-3.6 | 3.6-4.8 | 4.8-6.0 | 6.0+ | Total |
|---|---|---|---|---|---|---|
| Estimate I[1] | 45 | 24 | 10 | 11 | 10 | 100 |
| Estimate II[2] | 38.8 | 23.4 | 16.2 | 12.3 | 9.3 | 100 |
| Final Estimate | 40.0 | 24.0 | 14.0 | 12.0 | 10.0 | 100 |
| Number of Households Millions | 6.15 | 3.69 | 2.15 | 1.85 | 1.54 | 15.37[3] |

[1] See text.
[2] Based on income tax data and data about structure of households.
[3] "Wirtschaft und Statistik," 1954, p. 214.

APPENDIX TABLE 2

Estimate of Household Incomes and Expenditures. Reconciliation of Totals with National Income Aggregates

| | Household Income Bracket 1000 DM. | | | | | Total |
|---|---|---|---|---|---|---|
| | .0–2.4 | 2.4–3.6 | 3.6–4.8 | 4.8–6.0 | 6.0+ | |
| 1. Mean Bracket Income DM[1] | 2250 | 3400 | 4700 | 5240 | 20,077 | |
| 2. Bracket Income Billions of DM. | 13.84 | 12.54 | 10.10 | 9.70 | 30.92 | 77.10[2] |
| 3. Corporate Retained Earnings plus Non-shifted Corporate Income Tax | 0.11 | 0.05 | 0.05 | 0.11 | 2.48 | 2.80[4] |
| 4. Total Income of Bracket Line 2 ÷ 3. Billions of DM.[8] | 13.95 | 12.59 | 10.15 | 9.81 | 33.40 | 79.90 |
| 5. Total Expenditures Billions of DM. | 11.90 | 10.80 | 8.75 | 8.90 | 22.10 | 62.45[3] |
| 6. Savings, Wage and Personal Income Taxes Contribution to Social Security: Billions of DM. | 2.05 | 1.79 | 1.40 | .91 | 11.30 | 17.45 |
| of which: | | | | | | |
| Corporate Retained Earnings: (item 3) Billions of DM | | | | | | 2.80[4] |
| Savings of Persons and Non-Incorporate Business: Billions of DM | | | | | | 5.34[5] |
| Social Security Contribution of Employees and Wage Taxes: Billions of DM. | | | | | | 5.03[6] |
| Assessed Personal Income Tax: Billions of DM. | | | | | | 2.06[7] |
| Unexplained: Billions of DM. | | | | | | 2.19 |

[1] Estimated from: Statistisches Jahrbuch 1953, p. 536, 537. Statistik der Bundesrepublik Deutschland Band 97. Without employer contributions to Social Insurance.
[2] Statistisches Jahrbuch 1961. p. 551, deducted are 4.26 Bill. DM. employers contribution to Social Security Insurance.
[3] Same as 2.
[4] Corporate Retained Earnings alone 1.47 Bill. DM. Statistisches Jahrbuch 1961. p. 550.
[5] Same as 4.
[6] Same as 4.
[7] Statistsches Jahrbuch 1953, p. 451.
[8] Without employer contributions to Social Insurance.

APPENDIX TABLE 3

## Household Structure in West Germany in 1950

| House-hold Members: | No. of Households[1] 1000 | 0 | *of which with Income Receivers:* 1 | 2 | 3 | 4 | 5+ |
|---|---|---|---|---|---|---|---|
| 1 | 2.811 | | 2696 | | | | |
| 2 | 3.834 | | 2823 | 958 | | | |
| 3 | 3.588 | | 1934 | 1352 | 265 | | |
| 4 | 2.547 | | 1220 | 795 | 453 | 65 | |
| 5+ | 2.591 | | 723 | 803 | 581 | 315 | 161 |
| | 15.371 | 224[2] | 9397 | 3909 | 1300 | 380 | 161 |

[1] "Wirtschaft und Statistik" 1954, p. 214.
[2] Probably Institutions counted as households.

APPENDIX TABLE 4

## Total Tax Revenue at All Government Levels in West Germany in 1950. Calendar Year. Millions of DM.[1]

| Kind of Tax | Tax Revenue | % of Total Tax Revenue |
|---|---|---|
| *Taxes on Income:* | | |
| Payroll Tax | 1706.8 | 8.5 |
| Assessed Personal Income Tax | 2062.5 | 10.3 |
| Corporate Income Tax | 1429.0 | 7.2 |
| Local Tax on Business | 1250.2 | 6.3 |
| Berlin Levy, Employees | 192.2 | 1.0 |
| "    ", Income Tax Payer | 74.2 | 0.4 |
| "    ", Corporations | 42.0 | 0.2 |
| Sub-Total | 6756.9 | 33.8 |
| *Taxes on Property:* | | |
| Real Estate Tax | 1078.1 | 5.4 |
| Immediate Aid Levy | 1876.9 | 9.4 |
| Inheritance Tax | 22.9 | 0.1 |
| Tax on Acquisition of Real Estate | 37.9 | 0.2 |
| Tax on Transfer of Titles | 16.0 | 0.1 |
| Automobile Tax | 338.8 | 1.7 |
| Fire Protection Tax | 18.4 | 0.1 |
| Property Tax | 105.7 | 0.5 |
| Sub-Total | 3494.7 | 17.5 |

## APPENDIX TABLE 4 *(cont.)*

| Kind of Tax | Tax Revenue | % of Total Tax Revenue |
|---|---|---|
| *Sales Taxes, Excises, Customs* | | |
| Turnover Tax | 4595.5 | 23.0 |
| Customs | 604.5 | 3.0 |
| Tobacco Tax | 2059.2 | 10.3 |
| Coffee Tax | 329.0 | 1.6 |
| Tea Tax | 31.7 | 0.2 |
| Sugar Tax | 367.0 | 1.8 |
| Salt Tax | 38.9 | 0.2 |
| Beer Tax | 337.0 | 1.7 |
| Alcohol Monopoly | 480.3 | 2.4 |
| Champagne Tax | 18.9 | 0.1 |
| Tax on Matches | 60.7 | 0.3 |
| "  " Lamps | 13.9 | 0.1 |
| "  " Mineral Oil | 67.3 | 0.3 |
| "  " Beverages | 53.4 | 0.3 |
| Other Excise Taxes | 14.0 | 0.1 |
| Sub-Total | 9071.3 | 45.4 |
| *Other Taxes:* | | |
| Insurance Tax | 62.4 | 0.3 |
| Lotteries and Race Tax | 80.2 | 0.4 |
| Tax on Drafts | 44.1 | 0.2 |
| Transportation Tax | 239.7 | 1.2 |
| Berlin Levy in Postal Services | 49.8 | 0.2 |
| Amusement Tax | 113.2 | 0.6 |
| Dog Tax | 37.8 | 0.2 |
| Other Smaller Taxes | 21.2 | 0.1 |
| Sub-Total | 648.4 | 3.2 |
| Total | 19971.5 | 100 |

1 Because of rounding individual items may not add to totals.

APPENDIX TABLE 5

Estimated Distribution of Tax Payments for 1950.
(% of Total Yield Contributed by Income Brackets.)

| Household Income Bracket 1000 DM. | 0–2.4 | 2.4–3.6 | 3.6–4.8 | 4.8–6.0 | 6.0+ | Total |
|---|---|---|---|---|---|---|
| 1. Wage Tax | 6.8 | 21.2 | 22.7 | 14.4 | 34.9 | 100 |
| 2. Personal Income Tax | 3.0 | 4.4 | 4.9 | 6.1 | 81.6 | 100 |
| 3. Corporate Income Tax | 10.8 | 12.2 | 10.7 | 10.0 | 56.2 | 100 |
| 4. Turnover Tax | 18.2 | 17.4 | 13.7 | 14.7 | 36.0 | 100 |
| 5. Tobacco Tax | 21.6 | 26.1 | 18.2 | 16.5 | 17.6 | 100 |
| 6. Real Estate Tax | 20.4 | 16.5 | 14.3 | 12.4 | 36.4 | 100 |
| 7. Local Tax on Business | 17.9 | 16.4 | 13.6 | 13.5 | 38.6 | 100 |
| 8. Immediate Aid Levy | 9.3 | 8.0 | 9.1 | 7.5 | 66.1 | 100 |
| 9. All other Taxes and Customs | 16.2 | 18.1 | 14.7 | 14.3 | 36.7 | 100 |
| Total | 14.3 | 16.1 | 13.6 | 12.7 | 43.3 | 100 |

# APPENDIX TABLE 6

## Estimated Distribution of Taxes Paid by Income Brackets.
### (Tax as % of Total Tax Bill)

| Household Income Bracket 1000 DM. | 0–2.4 | 2.4–3.6 | 3.6–4.8 | 4.8–6.0 | 6.0+ |
|---|---|---|---|---|---|
| 1. Wage Tax | 4.0 | 11.3 | 14.2 | 9.7 | 6.9 |
| 2. Personal Income Tax | 2.2 | 2.8 | 3.7 | 5.0 | 19.5 |
| 3. Corporate Income Tax | 5.4 | 5.4 | 5.6 | 5.7 | 9.3 |
| 4. Turnover Tax | 29.2 | 24.9 | 23.1 | 26.6 | 19.1 |
| 5. Tobacco Tax | 15.5 | 16.8 | 13.8 | 13.4 | 4.2 |
| 6. Real Estate Tax | 7.7 | 5.5 | 5.7 | 5.3 | 4.5 |
| 7. Local Tax on Business | 7.8 | 6.4 | 6.3 | 6.7 | 5.6 |
| 8. Immediate Aid Levy | 6.1 | 4.7 | 6.3 | 5.6 | 14.3 |
| 9. All other Taxes and Customs | 22.1 | 22.1 | 21.2 | 22.1 | 16.6 |
| Total | 100 | 100 | 100 | 100 | 100 |

## APPENDIX TABLE 7

### Estimated Effective Tax Rates. (Tax As % of Incomes).

| Household Income Bracket 1000 DM. | 0–2.4 | 2.4–3.6 | 3.6–4.8 | 4.8–6.0 | 6.0+ |
|---|---|---|---|---|---|
| 1. Wage tax | 0.8 | 2.9 | 3.8 | 2.5 | 1.8 |
| 2. Personal Income Tax | 0.4 | 0.7 | 1.0 | 1.3 | 5.0 |
| 3. Corporate Income Tax | 1.1 | 1.4 | 1.5 | 1.5 | 2.4 |
| 4. Turnover Tax | 6.0 | 6.4 | 6.2 | 6.9 | 5.0 |
| 5. Tobacco Tax | 3.2 | 4.3 | 3.7 | 3.5 | 1.1 |
| 6. Real Estate Tax | 1.6 | 1.4 | 1.5 | 1.4 | 1.2 |
| 7. Local Tax on Business | 1.6 | 1.6 | 1.7 | 1.7 | 1.4 |
| 8. Immediate Aid Levy | 1.2 | 1.2 | 1.7 | 1.4 | 3.7 |
| 9. All other Taxes and Customs | 4.5 | 5.6 | 5.7 | 5.7 | 4.3 |
| Total | 20.5 | 25.5 | 26.8 | 25.9 | 25.9 |

## APPENDIX TABLE 8

### Basic Distributions Used for Allocation of Taxes

| Household Income Bracket 1000 DM. | 0-2.4 | 2.4-3.6 | 3.6-4.8 | 4.8-6.0 | 6.0+ | Total |
|---|---|---|---|---|---|---|
| 1. Payroll Tax | 8.0 | 23.5 | 22.5 | 13.0 | 33.0 | 100 |
| 2. Assessed Personal Income Tax | 1.0 | 2.5 | 3.5 | 5.0 | 88.0 | 100 |
| 3. Rental Income | 20.0 | 14.0 | 13.0 | 11.0 | 42.0 | 100 |
| 4. Income from Capital | 4.0 | 1.5 | 1.5 | 4.0 | 89.0 | 100 |
| 5. Income from Business (Gewerbebetrieb) | 7.0 | 8.0 | 10.0 | 7.5 | 67.5 | 100 |
| 6. Income from Agriculture | 14.0 | 19.0 | 25.0 | 13.0 | 29.0 | 100 |
| 7. Berlin Levy on Income Tax Payers | 5.5 | 7.5 | 8.5 | 6.5 | 72.0 | 100 |
| 8. Total Consumer Expenditures | 19.1 | 17.3 | 14.0 | 14.2 | 35.4 | 100 |
| 9. Final Burden Distribution Turnover Tax | 18.2 | 17.4 | 13.7 | 14.7 | 36.0 | 100 |
| 10. Consumption of Coffee | 14.9 | 22.6 | 18.6 | 19.7 | 24.2 | 100 |
| 11. Consumption of Tea | 10.7 | 40.6 | 16.7 | 15.0 | 17.0 | 100 |
| 12. Consumption of Sugar | 34.6 | 23.3 | 15.6 | 14.0 | 12.5 | 100 |
| 13. Consumption of Beer | 22.2 | 25.0 | 18.5 | 18.5 | 15.8 | 100 |
| 14. Consumption of Tobacco | 21.6 | 26.1 | 18.2 | 16.5 | 17.6 | 100 |
| 15. Consumption of Salt, Vinegar | 35.8 | 23.1 | 15.3 | 13.0 | 12.8 | 100 |
| 16. Consumption of Alcoholic Beverages | 11.8 | 24.1 | 22.3 | 21.4 | 20.4 | 100 |
| 17. Expenditures for Rent | 30.1 | 22.7 | 16.5 | 15.6 | 15.1 | 100 |
| 18. Expenditures for Entertainment, Education | 18.9 | 20.4 | 18.2 | 17.9 | 24.6 | 100 |
| 19. Expenditures for Heat and Light | 32.0 | 23.3 | 16.0 | 14.6 | 14.1 | 100 |
| 20. Expenditures for Insurance | 18.7 | 26.8 | 20.0 | 18.1 | 16.4 | 100 |

## APPENDIX TABLE 9

### Estimate of Distribution of Deductions and Tax Benefits by Income Brackets Under Provisions to Favor Capital Formation,[1] 1950, Millions of DM.

| Household Income Bracket 1000 DM. | 0–2.4 | 2.4–3.6 | 3.6–4.8 | 4.8–6.0 | 6.0+ | Total |
|---|---|---|---|---|---|---|
| 1. Deductions by Income Taxpayers | 59.1 | 52.2 | 80.2 | 91.5 | 1591.9 | 1874.9 |
| 2. Deductions by Corporations | 50.6 | 57.2 | 50.2 | 47.4 | 263.8 | 469.2 |
| 3. Total Deductions | 109.7 | 109.4 | 130.4 | 138.9 | 1855.7 | 2344.1 |
| 4. Taxes Saved by Income Taxpayers | 1.4 | 1.9 | 5.1 | 11.2 | 550.4 | 570.0 |
| 5. Taxes Saved by Corporations | 25.3 | 28.6 | 25.1 | 23.7 | 131.9 | 234.7 |
| 6. Total Budget Loss[2] | 26.7 | 30.5 | 30.2 | 34.9 | 682.3 | 804.7 |

[1] The exemptions included are the paragraphs 7a to 7e, 10a, 10 section 1/4 and 32a of the West German Income Tax Law. The estimate is based on an unpublished table for 1949, Statistisches Bundesamt VII, D. 10, Table 3.
[2] Budget losses were calculated with average bracket tax rates for Personal Income Tax and 50% tax rate for corporate deductions.

# VI. Lessons from the West German Experience

WHAT ARE THE main findings of this study? We have discovered that in the 1950's the West German government had an important influence on the country's capital formation and we have indicated the particular economic conditions which necessitated this influence. A number of useful lessons can be learned from the West German experience.

The first lesson is that a high level of public capital formation is compatible with the working of a vigorous free-market economy. There is no indication that it interferes with the country's economic growth. On the contrary, it contributes strongly to keep it at a high level.

In West Germany, for many years, about one-half of net domestic investments and one-third of all gross investments were financed in one way or another with public funds. This was certainly a large share, even if we admit that Germany had a long-standing tradition of public influence on capital formation. After 1948, the West Germans put their faith in the working of a free-market economy, and still the traditional public influence on capital formation not only remained but grew even larger. The reason for this was the early recognition that in many situations market forces alone could not be relied upon to produce politically and socially acceptable solutions and to generate a satisfactory rate of economic growth. In many cases, market forces

263

had to be aided and guided—if not permanently, at least temporarily. Basically, there was agreement that government had a role and responsibilities in the country's capital formation. Obviously, the large public efforts in this area did not lead to any kind of socialization.

How was the public influence on capital formation implemented? Government used a large number of different methods to assure that public preferences were not ignored. In the choice of these, compromises were, of course, to be found between what was economically desirable and politically feasible. Government had its leverage on capital formation essentially through fiscal policy and not through monetary policy, as is often assumed. West Germans evidently had much more confidence in guiding and changing income and spending streams directly than in relying on influencing asset preferences to obtain desired results.

The contribution monetary policy made to capital formation was marginal at best and is often overrated. A rather tight money policy during most of the '50's was, on the whole, unfavorable to capital formation. High interest rates increased the cost of capital goods and would have made many vital investments impossible if their impact had not been partly offset through fiscal policy. There is no evidence that high interest rates induced a large volume of additional voluntary savings. The volume of savings was largely determined by incomes. When these rose, the savings volume increased, but even then voluntary savings were only a small part of all investable funds.

This leads to the problem of the origin of savings for rapid capital formation. West Germany's capital formation was financed through "involuntary savings." The bulk of all investable funds was obtained through high profits and taxes. The trend to this pattern of savings is also observable in other countries. What made the West German case unique, however, was the large portion of savings obtained through taxes.

That government could become such a large saver in the '50's was no doubt facilitated through a number of circumstances. For example: Allied tax policy between 1945 and 1948, under which tax rates were substantially raised; the absence of large defense expenditures; and, due to the repudiation of the National Debt, practically no debt service. The most important factor however, was, that the tax revenues—and thus the tax burden—remained very high in comparison with other countries during a period of rapid growth. It is true that the distribution of the tax burden was slowly changed and the West German tax structure probably became more regressive, but aggregate tax revenue, as a percentage of total personal income, continued to be high.

From this, we can conclude that rapid economic growth and a concomitant high level of taxation are evidently not incompatible, provided the tax burden distribution is "right." What is "right" will depend on the preference between more growth or more equity. The West Germans so far have been inclined to favor the former.

Government in West Germany ran a continuous large surplus of current receipts over current expenditures which was available for direct investments by government and for loans to investors in the private sector. In addition, the government tried to stimulate savings and investments through tax exemptions. What does the West German experience show concerning the relative merits of these two methods?

Politically, tax exemptions seem to have had initial appeal. Yet they were soon reduced and are to disappear completely in the near future because of a number of distinct disadvantages. It was found that additional savings induced through tax exemptions were rather costly in terms of budget losses. Tax exemptions were difficult to control administratively and open to many abuses. In addition, and this became the most serious objection, they were highly inequitable as most benefits accrued to higher income brackets. The West German experience indicates that granting general and large tax exemptions to stimulate capital formation is a very questionable procedure which can easily become a waste of public funds. If the choice is to favor capital formation through taxes—to which the government is entitled but never receives—or through matching grants, loans, or subsidies out of taxes actually received, one should prefer the latter. The reasons for this are that, in the first place, the benefits may accrue haphazardously to sectors which are not crucial for economic growth and, in the second place, they could be made available to those industries where output is badly lagging, thus obviating the danger that sectoral imbalance will impede the growth of the whole economy. Through loans and subsidies it is easier to assure the most efficient use of public funds for capital formation. If these loans and subsidies are made available for investments in the private sector there should be some guarantee that this will actually benefit public and not private interest exclusively. This was not always the case in West Germany. The quality of resource allocation could often have been better, especially in the first years after 1948. More investment planning on a national scale would have been very beneficial.

What lesson does the West German experience offer as far as equity aspects of capital formation are concerned, and how does public capital formation fit into the picture?

A high incentive growth process, characterized by high profits and, for a long time, low wages, led to an undesirable income and property distribution during the last decade. There has been a very large capital accumulation in the higher income brackets, whereas large parts of the population participated in the new wealth only to a small extent. This was evidently the price to be paid for rapid incentive growth. If it was a high price, only the future would tell. For a country which is still struggling to cement its democracy, increasing inequality could easily prove to be a heavy burden.

Based on what information is available so far, it is the author's opinion that the large scale public capital formation favored lower income brackets especially, and thus lessened, to some extent, the impact of the changes in income and property distribution towards greater inequality. This was the case in spite of a tax structure which was only slightly progressive—in fact, over a considerable income range, regressive—because most of the benefits from public investments accrued to lower and medium income brackets.

This suggests that public capital formation can fulfill a very important function. In societies which aspire to a high level of economic growth, it is probably inevitable that conflicts will arise between different groups. One group may favor growth and efficiency with perhaps a more unequal distribution of income and property. Other groups may prefer solutions which would lead to more equal distribution of income even if it meant smaller increases in output. It is conceivable that public capital formation could act as a strong mitigating element in such conflicts and prevent them from becoming disruptive.

# Bibliography

## Books

Albers, Willi. *Die Kapitalausstattung der Flüchtlingsbetriebe in West-deutschland.* Kiel: Institut für Weltwirtschaft, 1952.

Barocka, Egon. *Kapitalmarkt und Wohnungsbau.* Köln: Deutsches Volksheimstättenwerk, Folge 13, 1958.

Baumgart, Egon R. *"Investitionen und ERP Finanzierung."* Deutsches Institut fuer Wirtschaftsforschung, Sonderhefte, Neue Folge, Nr. 56, Reihe A: Forschung, Berlin: Duncker und Humblot, 1961.

Baumgart, Egon, Krengel, Rolf, und Moritz, Werner. *Die Finanzierung der industriellen Expansion in der Bundesrepublik waehrend der Jahre des Wiederaufbaus,* Duncker und Humblot, Berlin 1960.

Binder, Paul. *Die Geldkapitalbildung.* Tübingen: J. C. B. Mohr, Paul Siebeck, 1952.

Bouman, P. J.; Beijer, G.; and Oudegeest, J. J. *The Refugee Problem in Western Germany.* The Hague: Martinus Nijhoff, 1950.

Brehmer, Ekhard. *Struktur und Funktionsweise des Geldmarktes in der Deutschen Bundesrepublik seit 1948,* Tübingen: J. C. B. Mohr, Paul Siebeck, 1956.

Carstens, Dieter. *Der Bund als Finanzier, Kredite, Leistungen und Buergschaften des ERP Sondervermögens,* Bad Godesberg: Verlag für Publizistik, 1960.

Claren, Joachim. *Die Kapitalanlagen der privaten deutschen Lebens-versicherungsunternehmen.* Berlin: Duncker und Humblot, 1955.

[Commission on Money and Credit], *Money and Credit, Their In-*

269

*fluence on Jobs, Prices, and Growth,* Englewood Cliffs, N.J.: Prentice-Hall, Inc., 1961.

[Deutsches Institut für Wirtschaftsforschung.] *Wirtschaftsprobleme der Besatzungszonen.* Berlin: 1947.

————. *Die deutsche Wirtschaft zwei Jahre nach dem Zusammenbruch.* Berlin: 1947.

————. *Die deutsche Industrie im Kriege, 1939–1945.* Berlin: Dunkker und Humblot, 1954.

Duhner. *Das öffentliche Vermögen.* Bonn: Institut für Finanzen und Steuern, Heft 35, n.d.

Edding, Friedrich. *The Refugees as a Burden, a Stimulus and a Challenge to the West German Economy.* The Hague: Martinus Nijhoff, 1951.

Ehrlicher, Werner. *Geldkapitalbildung und Realkapitalbildung.* Tübingen: J. C. B. Mohr, Paul Siebeck, 1956.

Eisendrath, Ernst. *Anlagevermögen und Dekapitalisation der deutschen Industrie.* Deutsches Institut für Wirtschaftsforschung Sonderhefte, Neue Folge Nr. 8. Berlin: Duncker und Humblot, 1950.

Erhard, Ludwig. *Germany's Comeback in the Worldmarket.* New York: Macmillan, 1954.

Esser, J. *Währungsgewinnabgaben insbesondere Obligationen und Kreditgewinnabgabe im allgemeinen Lastenausgleich.* Bonn: Institut für Finanzen und Steuer, Heft 9.

Förster, Karl Heinz. *Finanzierung durch Abschreibungen.* Stuttgart: C. H. Poeschel, 1953.

Fousek, Peter G. *Foreign Central Banking, the Instruments of Monetary Policy.* New York: Federal Reserve Bank, 1957.

Fritz, Ernst. *Die Vermögensanlagen der Versicherungswirtschaft in aufsichtsbehördlicher Sicht.* Berlin: Duncker und Humblot, 1958.

Gamerdinger, Dieter. *Der Kapitalmarkt in der Bundesrepublik und die Voraussetzungen seiner Funktionsfähigkeit.* Tübingen: Hopfer Verlag, 1959.

Gerschenkron, Alexander. *Bread and Democracy in Germany.* Berkeley and Los Angeles: University of California Press, 1943.

[Gesellschaft für Wirtschafts-und Sozialwissenschaften.] *Einkommensbildung und Einkommensverteilung.* Verhandlungen auf der Tagung des Vereins für Sozialpolitik, Köln, 1956. Berlin: Duncker und Humblot, 1957.

Gleitze, Bruno. *Ostdeutsche Wirtschaft.* Duncker und Humblot, Berlin, 1956.

Göseke, Gerhard. *Die Einkommensschichtung in der Bundesrepublik.* Berlin: Deutsches Institut für Wirtschaftsforschung, 1957.

Grüning, Ferdinand and Krengel, Rolf. *Die Expansion der west-deutschen Industrie von 1948 bis 1954.* Deutsches Institut für Wirtschaftsforschung Sonderhefte, Neue Folge, Nr. 34. Berlin: Duncker und Humblot, 1955.

Haas, Gerhard und Martin, Gustav. *Steuerermässigungen durch Son-derausgaben.* Heidelberg: Verlagsgesellschaft "Recht und Wirt-schaft," 1958.

Harmsen Report. *Am Abend der Demontage. Sechs Jahre Reparations-politik.* Bremen: Truien Verlag, 1951.

Heinze, Hellmut und Kehr, Peter. *Einkommensteuergesetze 1951, 1952, 1953, 1954, 1955.* Bonn: Stollfuss Verlag, 1956.

[IFO, Institut für Wirtschaftsforschung.] *Die Industrie Westdeutsch-lands.* München: 1950.

————. *Die Nivellierung des Lohn-und Gehaltsniveaus in West-deutschland gegenüber der Vorkriegszeit.* München: 1952.

————. *Materialien zur grossen Steuerreform.* Band 1. München: 1953.

[Institut für Finanzen und Steuern.] *Der Bundeshaushalt.* Bonn: Heft 15, Band 5, 1956.

————. *Der Bundeshaushalt am Kreuzweg.* Bonn: Heft 44, n.d.

————. *Die Finanzpolitik in der Wahlperiode 1953–1957* Bonn: Heft 50, n.d.

————. *Die heutige Steuerbelastung der gewerblichen Wirtschaft.* Bonn: Heft 26, Band 2, n.d.

————. *Gesetz über den Lastenausgleich.* Bonn: Heft 23, n.d.

[Institut für Konjunkturforschung] *"Konjunkturstatistisches Hand-buch."* Berlin, 1936.

Jaschinski, Heinrich. *Die Kapitalbildung für den Wohnungsbau, Tatsachen und Probleme.* Köln: Deutsches Volksheimstättenwerk, Folge 10, 1956.

Keynes, John Maynard. *The General Theory of Employment Interest and Money.* New York: Harcourt, Brace and Company, n.d.

Klein, Lawrence R. *The Keynesian Revolution.* New York: Macmillan, 1954.

Krengel, Rudolf. *Anlagevermögen, Produktion und Beschäftigung der Industrie in der Bundesrepublik von 1924 bis 1956.* Deutsches Institut für Wirtschaftsforschung Sonderhefte, Neue Folge Nr. 42. Berlin: Duncker und Humblot, 1958.

Lehmann, Werner. *Bauspar A.B.C.* Bonn: Domus Verlag, 1958.

Leist, Klaus *Investitionen und Sozialstruktur in Westdeutschland.* Zürich: Polygraphischer Verlag A. G., 1956.

Lukaschek, Hans. *The German Expellees, a German Focal Problem.* Bonn: Federal Ministry for Refugees, 1952.

Lurie, Samuel. *Private Investment in a Controlled Economy, Germany 1933–1939.* New York: Columbia University Press, 1947.

Martin, Gustav und Skomski, Peter Klaus. *Das Einkommensteuerrecht seit der Währungsreform.* Heidelberg: Verlagsgesellschaft "Recht und Wirtschaft," 1956.

Mehnert, Klaus und Schulte, Heinrich. *Deutschland Jahrbuch 1953.* Essen: Rheinisch-Westfälisches Verlagskontor, 1953.

Mendershausen, Horst. *Two Postwar Recoveries of the German Economy.* Amsterdam: North Holland Publishing Co., 1955.

Menges, Günter und Likbeck, Heinrich. *Löhne und Gehälter nach den beiden Weltkriegen.* Maisenheim-Glan: Anton Hain K. G., 1958.

Musgrave, R. A. *The Theory of Public Finance.* New York: McGraw-Hill, 1959.

Osthues, Heinz. *Einkommensverhältnisse und private Geldkapitalbildung in Westdeutschland 1925–1953.* Berlin: Duncker und Humblot, 1957.

Rheitinger, Anton. *Soziale Marktwirtschaft auf dem Prüfstand.* Frankfurt: Fritz Knapp Verlag, 1958.

Salomon, Richard. *Begriff und Problematik der wirtschaftlichen Engpässe.* Kiel: Institut für Weltwirtschaft, Kieler Studien, 1954.

Schlange-Schöningen, Hans. *Im Schatten des Hungers.* Hamburg, Berlin: Paul Parey Verlag, 1955.

Schmölders, Günter. *Finanzierungsprobleme im Zusammenhang mit der wirtschaftlichen Eingliederung der Heimatvertriebenen.* Berlin: Duncker und Humblot, 1955.

Seidler, Horst und de la Chevallerie, Oskar. *Die Anlageinvestitionen der sozialen und kulturellen Bereiche in der Bundesrepublik von 1949 bis 1957.* Berlin: Duncker und Humblot, 1960.

Stolper, Wolfgang F., assisted by Roskamp, Karl W. *The Structure of the East German Economy.* Center for International Studies, M.I.T. Cambridge: Harvard University Press, 1960.

Strathuis, Hans. *Der Kapitalmarkt in Westdeutschland und die Probleme seines Wiederaufbaus.* Bonn: Institut für Finanzen und Steuern, Heft 16.

Strathuis, Heinrich. *Die Finanzierung der Verteidigungsausgaben in der Bundesrepublik Deutschland.* Bonn: Institut für Finanzen und Steuern, Heft 21, 1952.

―――――. *Die langfristige Finanzierung der Wirtschaft.* Bonn: Institut für Finanzen und Steuern, Heft 20.

Vetter, Ernst Guenter. *Investitionslenkung.* Heidelberg: Quelle und Meyer, 1956.

Wallich, Henry C. *Mainsprings of the German Revival.* New Haven, Conn.: Yale University Press, 1955.

Zapf, Bernhard. *Steuerliche Finanzierungshilfen.* Köln: Schmidt, Otto, K. G., 1953

Zeitel, Gerhard. *"Die Steuerlastverteilung in der Bundesrepublik Deutschland."* Tübingen: J. C. B. Mohr, Paul Siebeck, 1959.

Zweig, Gerhard, und Feldhege, Hans Georg. *"Eigentun für alle."* Bad Godesberg: Asgard Verlag, 1961.


*Articles and Reports*


Ackley, Gardner. "Analisi Keynesiana E Problemi Economici Italiani." *Banca Nazionale del Lavoro.* Roma, 1957.

[Bank for International Settlements.] 28th Annual Report. Basle, 1958.

[Bank für Vertriebene und Geschädigte (Lastenausgleichsbank), A. G.] *Zweiter Jahresbericht,* Geschäftsjahr, Bad Godesberg, 1951.

Barna, T. "Investment in Britain and Germany, a Clue to Export Performance?" *The Banker,* January, 1958.

[Berliner Bank A. G.] "Die Börse." Annual Reports: 1952 to 1961. West Berlin.

————. "Wirtschaftsberichte." West Berlin.

————. "Zur Kapitalbildung in der Bundesrepublik." *Wirtschafts-berichte,* Heft 2/57. April, 1957.

[Bundesverband des privaten Bankgewerbes E. V.] *Berichte über die Geschäftsjahre, 1952, 1953, 1954, 1955, 1956, 1957.* Köln.

Burchhardt, F. A. and Martin, K. "Western Germany and Reconstruction," *Bulletin of the Oxford University Institute of Statistics,* Nr. 12, 1947, p. 409.

Butters, J. Keith. "Effects on Taxation on the Investment Capacities and Policies of Individuals." *Federal Tax-policy for Economic Growth and Stability.* 84th Congress, I Session. Joint Committee Print., Nov. 9, 1955.

[Deutsche Bank A. G.] "Wirtschaftliche Mitteilungen." Frankfort. a. M.

[Deutsches Institut für Wirtschaftsforschung.] *Vierteljahreshefte zur Wirtschaftsforschung.* Berlin.

————. "Wochenbericht." Berlin.

[Deutscher Raiffeisenverband, e.V.] *Jahrbuch des Deutschen Raffei-senverbandes, e.V.,* IX. Jahrgang, 1956, Bonn, 1957.

[Deutscher Sparkassen und Giro Verband.] "The German Savings Bank Organization." Bonn, n.d.

————. *Jahresberichte,* 1949 to 1960. Bonn.

————. Geschäftsstelle, "Öffentliche Bausparkassen." *Jahresberichte,* 1953, 1954, 1955, 1956, 1957.

Dreissig, Wilhelmine. "Die finanz-und steuerpolitische Entwickelung in der Bundesrepublik im Jahre 1954 und 1955." *Finanzarchiv,* Band 16, Heft I, 1955.

[Dresdner Bank A. G.] "Börsenberichte."

————. "Kapitalmarkt und Börse." 1956, 1957.

————. "10 Fragen und Antworten zum steuerbegünstigten Sparen." Dez., 1956, Nov., 1957.

————. "Wirtschaftsberichte."

[ECA.] "The Integration of Refugees into German Life." A report of the ECA Technical Assistance Commission on the Integration of the Refugees in the German Republic. Bonn: March, 1951.

*The Economist.* "No Policy in Germany." Vol. 155, 1948, p. 733.

*Europa Archiv.* "Die Rechtsprobleme der deutschen Auslandsschuldenregelung und ihre Behandlung auf der Londoner Schuldenkonferenz." Sept. 20, 1952, p. 15.

Fey, Walter. "Der Wohnungsbau in der Bundesrepublik Deutschland. Zwischenbilanz und Vorschau," Bundesminister für Wohnungsbau, Bonn, 1951.

————. "Der Wohnungsbau und seine Finanzierung in der Bundesrepublik Deutschland im Jahre 1955." *Bundesbaublatt,* Heft 4, April, 1956.

————. "Merkmale und Finanzierung des Wohnungsbaus in der Bundesrepublik Deutschland im Jahre 1956." *Bundesbaublatt,* Heft 4, June 1957.

————. "Der Eigenheimbau in der Bundesrepublik." Auszug aus *Privates Bausparwesen, 1957.* Bonn, 1957.

————. "Wohnungsverhältnisse und Wohnungsversorgung in der Bundesrepublik Deutschland." *Bundesbaublatt,* 1957, Heft 8–10 and 1958, Heft 1.

————. "Merkmale und Finanzierung des Wohnungsbaues in der Bundesrepublik Deutschland im Jahre 1957." *Bundesbaublatt,* Heft 5–6, 1958.

Fischer-Dieskau, Joachim. "Strukturwandlungen in der Finanzierung des Wohnungsbaues." *Der langfristige Kredit.* Bonn, Juli, 1953. 2. Ausgabe.

[Gesamtverband der Versicherungswirtschaft E. V.] *Geschäftsberichte für* 1950–51, 1953–54, 1954–55, 1955–56, 1956–57. Köln.

[German Federal Government.] *The Bulletin,* published by the Press and Information Office of the German Federal Government.

Gleitze, Bruno. "Der westdeutsche Investitionsaufwand und seine Finanzierung seit der Währungsreform." *Konjunkturpolitik.* Heft 3, 1958.

Gurley, John G. "Excess Liquidity and European Monetary Reforms, 1944–1952." *The American Economic Review,* March 1953, p. 76.

Hagen, Egon. "Wandlungen in den Finanzierungsformen der Aktiengesellschaften," *Weltwirtschaftliches Archiv.* Heft 2, 1955, p. 157.

Heller, Walter W. "Tax and Monetary Reform in Occupied Germany," *National Tax Journal,* 1949, p. 215.

[IFO Institut München.] "Fünf Jahre Deutsche Mark." *Der Wiederaufbau der westdeutschen Wirtschaft seit der Währungsreform.* Berlin: Duncker und Humblot, 1953.

————. "Wirtschaftskonjunktur." *Berichte des IFO Institutes für Wirtschaftsforschung.* München.

Jecht, H. "Die Bundessteuerreform 1954." *Finanzarchiv.* 1955, Band 16, Heft 1, p. 331.

Jecht, Horst. "Finanzpolitik und Kapitalbildung," Reihe *Recht und Staat,* Heft 217, Tübingen, 1958.

Keiser, Günther and Benning, Bernhard. "Kapitalbildung und Investitionen in der deutschen Volkswirtschaft 1924 bis 1928." *Vierteljahreshefte zur Konjunkturforschung.* Sonderheft No. 22, 1931.

Kindleberger, C. P. "German Terms of Trade by Commodity Classes and Areas." *Review of Economics and Statistics,* May, 1954.

Klopstock, Fred H. "Monetary Reform in Western Germany," *Journal of Political Economy,* 1949, p. 277.

[Kreditanstalt für Wiederaufbau.] *Annual Reports:* 1950, 1951, 1952, 1953, 1954, 1955, 1956, 1957. (Engl. ed.)

Lehmann, Werner. "Privates Bausparwesen 1958." Bonn: Domus Verlag.

*Lloyds Bank Review.* "Germany without Incentives." July, 1947, p. 23.

Lutz, F. A. "The German Currency Reform and the Revival of the German Economy," *Economica,* 1949, p. 122.

Mendershausen, Horst. "Prices, Money and the Distribution of Goods in Postwar Germany," *The American Economic Review,* June, 1949, p. 646.

————. "Anglo-German Export Competition," *Review of Economics and Statistics,* August, 1952.

Musgrave, R. A. "The Incidence of the Tax Structure and Its Effect on Consumption," *Federal Tax Policy for Economic Growth and Stability,* 84th Congress, 1st Session, Joint Committee Print, Nov. 9, 1955.

Musgrave, R. A. and Daicoff, D., "Who Pays the Michigan Taxes." *Michigan Tax Study, 1958,* Staff Papers, Lansing, Michigan, U.S.A.

[Norddeutsche Bank A. G.] *Das Börsenbild 1956. Das Börsenbild, 1957.*

Pederson, J. "An Evaluation of Postwar Monetary Reforms." *Weltwirtschaftliches Archiv.,* Band 62, 1959/I, p. 198.

[Rhein-Main-Bank.] "Steuersparnis durch steuerbegünstigtes Sparen." (Neubearbeitung nach dem Stande von Dezember 1952).

————. "Steuerersparnis durch steuerbegünstigtes Sparen." (Neubearbeitung, Juli, 1953).

[Rhein-Main-Bank A. G.] "Kapitalmarkt und Börse 1955." December, 1955.

Samuelson, Paul A. "New Look in Tax and Fiscal Policy," *Federal Tax Policy for Economic Growth and Stability.* Joint Committee of the Economic Report, 84th Congress, Nov. 9, 1955.

Sauermann, Heinz. "The Consequences of the Currency Reform in Western Germany," *The Review of Politics,* 1950, p. 175.

Schlesinger, Helmut. "Die steuerliche Belastung des Arbeiterhaushaltes," *Finanzarchiv,* Band 12, 1950–1951, p. 532.

Schultz, T. W. "Effects of Trade and Industrial Output of Western Germany upon Agriculture," *American Economic Review,* May, 1950.

Shelton, John P. "A Tax Incentive for Stabilizing Business Investment," *National Tax Journal,* 9, 1956, Nr. 3, 273.

Smith, Warren L., "Monetary Fiscal Policy and Economic Growth," *The Quarterly Journal of Economics,* February, 1957.

————. "The Discount Rate as a Credit Control Weapon," *The Journal of Political Economy,* April, 1958.

[Sparkassen und Giro Verband e. V.] *Sparkasse: Zeitschrift des deutschen Sparkassen und Giro Verbandes e. V.,* Bonn.

"Steuerliche Massnahmen zur Förderung der Ausfuhr," *Der Betrieb,* 1951, Nr. 24, p. 453.

[Sparkassen und Giro Verband, e. V.] "Blick auf die Wirtschaft." Bonn, n.d.

*Der Spiegel.*

Stolper, W. F., "A Note on Multiplier, Flexible Exchanges and the Dollar Shortage," *Economia Internazionale,* Vol. II, N. 3, Aug., 1950.

————. "West German Development in an Expanding World Economy," *World Politics,* Oct., 1956.

Tobin, James. "Growth through Taxation," *The New Republic,* 1960. Reprinted in Edmund S. Phelps (editor), *The Goal of Economic Growth.* New York: W. W. Norton and Co., Inc., 1962.

Unverzagt, Friedrich. *Die deutschen Sparkassen seit der Währungsreform 1948.* Stuttgart, n.d.

[Verband der privaten Hypotheken Banken e. V.] *Berichte für die Geschäftsjahre,* 1954, 1955, 1956, 1957. Bonn.

Villwock, Kurt. *Umfang und Merkmale des öffentlich geförderten sozialen Wohnungsbaues 1952–54 und seine Finanzierung.* Bundesminister für Wohnungsbau, Bonn.

*Der Volkswirt.* "Wertpapier und Sparer," "Sparen und Investieren," "Börsen und Emissionsgeschäft im Zeichen der Popularisierung des Wertpapieres." Supplements to *Der Volkswirt,* Frankfurt a. M., n.d.

Wilts, Jelke. "Die Anlage Investitionen im westdeutschen Verkehrswesen von 1949 bis 1955," Institut für Verkehrswissenschaft an der Universität Münster, Heft 13, n.d.

[Wirtschaftswissenschaftliches Institut der Gewerkschaften.] *Mitteilungen,* Köln.

## Official Publications

[Bank Deutscher Länder.] *Monthly Reports.* English Edition, 1949 to 1957.

————. *Annual Reports.* English Editions, 1948–49 to 1956.

"Bericht über die Lage der Landwirtschaft." (Grüner Bericht) 1958. Bonn, 1958.

[Bundesminister für Arbeit und Soziale Ordnung.] *Arbeits-und Sozialstatistische Mitteilungen.* Bonn.

[Bundesministerium der Finanzen.] *Allgemeine Vorbemerkungen zum Bundeshaushaltsplan.* Rechnungsjahre 1956 to 1960.

[Bundesministerium der Finanzen.] *Finanzbericht 1961 und 1962.* Bad Godesberg: Verlag Dr. Heger, 1962.

[Bundesminister für Wirtschaft.] *Sonderhefte zum Bericht über die wirtschaftliche Lage in der Bundesrepublik,* Bonn.

[Bundesminister für wirtschaftlichen Besitz des Bundes.] *Der Bund als Unternehmer.* Bad Godesberg, 1960.

[Bundesminister für wirtschaftliche Zusammenarbeit.] "Bericht der Bundesrepublik Deutschland über die wirtschaftliche Lage und die Entwickelungsmöglichkeiten bis zum Jahre 1956," ". . . bis zum Jahre 1957," ". . . bis zum Jahre 1958."

Colm, Gerhard; Dodge, Joseph M.; Goldsmith, Raymond W. "Plan for the liquidation of war finance and the financial rehabilitation of Germany," Washington, D.C. Reprinted in *Zeitschrift für die gesamte Staatswissenschaft,* III, Band 2, Heft, 1955.

[Department of Commerce.] "National Income." A supplement to the survey of current business, 1954 edition. United States Department of Commerce, Washington, D.C., 1954.

[Department of State.] "Postwar monetary and fiscal policies in Western Germany." OIR. Report 5171, May 1951, unclassified, Department of State, U.S.A.

[Deutsche Bundesbank.] *Annual Report.* English Edition, since 1957.

————. *Monthly Reports.* English Edition, since 1957.

[Deutscher Bundestag.] "Allgemeine Vorbemerkungen zum Entwurf des Bundeshaushaltsplans für das Rechnungsjahr 1958." 3. Wahlperiode Anlage zur Drucksache 300. D. Bundestag, 3.

————. "Bericht über die Lage der Landwirtschaft." Grüner Bericht, 1957, 2. Wahlperiode, Drucksache 3200. D. Bundestag, 2.

*"Die deutsche Industrie.* Gesamtergebnisse der amtlichen Produktionsstatistik. Berlin, 1939. Schriftenreihe des Reichsamtes für wehrwirtschaftliche Planung, Heft 1.

*Economic Data on Potsdam Germany.* Special Report of the Military Governor, Office of Military Government for Germany (U.S.). Sept., 1947.

*Economic Report of the President.* Washington, D.C., Jan., 1959.

*Einkommensteuer, Körperschaftssteuer, Lohnsteuer, Notopfer.* 13. neubearbeitete Auflage. München; C. H. Beck, 1953.

[Europäische Gemeinschaft für Kohle und Stahl, Hohe Behörde.] "Löhne und Sozialleistungen in der Industrie der Gemeinschaft." Luxemburg, May, 1955.

"Gutachten von Juni 1950 bis November 1952." Der wissenschaftliche Beirat beim Bundeswirtschaftsministerium, 2. Band. Göttingen: O. Schwartz, n.d.

[Gutachten des Wissenschaftlichen Beirates beim Bundeswirtschaftsminister. "Kapitalmarkt und Besteuerung." (typewritten) Bonn. Jan. 26, 1958.

"Habenzinsabkommen." *Reichsanzeiger,* Nr. 299, December 22, 1936 and Mai 29, 1943.

Hansen, Alvin H. and Musgrave, Richard A. *Fiscal Problems of Germany.* Submitted to the Minister of Finance of the Federal Republic of Germany, Sept. 24, 1951.

*Investitionshife Gesetz.* München: C. H. Beck, 1952.

Joint Report of the United States and United Kingdom Military Governors. "The European Recovery Program." Nr. 2, Dec., 1948.

[OEEC.] "The Supply of Capital Funds for Industrial Development in Europe" OEEC, project 292. Paris, 1957.

――――――. "The supply of capital funds for industrial development in Europe and the United States." OEEC, project 292, Supplement 2. Paris.

――――――. "Massnahmen zur Sicherung der inneren finanziellen Stabilität der Bizone." Aktions-Programme, 1949–50. Expose vorgelegt von der Verwaltung für Wirtschaft der OEEC in Paris im Juli 1949.

[OMGUS.] "A Year of Potsdam." OMGUS, Economic Division, Office of Mil. Gov. for Germany (U.S.).

Padberg, K. und Nieschulz, A. "Produktion, Verkaufserlöse und Betriebsausgaben der Landwirtschaft im Bundesgebiet." Sonderdruck aus *Agrarwirtschaft,* Heft 2, 1958.

*Reichsabgabenordnung, Steueranpassungsgesetz, Finanzverwaltungsgesetze.* München: C. H. Beck, 1953, 13. vermehrte Auflage.

[Statistisches Bundesamt.] "Verbrauch und Besteurung von Verbrauchssteuerpflichtigen Waren 1925–1938 und 1949–1955." *Statistik der Bundesrepublik Deutschland,* Band 133. Stuttgart: Kohlhammer.

――――――. "Der Bruttolohn der Arbeitnehmer und seine steuerliche Belastung im Jahre 1950." *Statistik der Bundesrepublik Deutschland,* Band 107. Stuttgart: Kohlhammer.

――――――. "Die öffentliche Finanzwirtschaft 1955 und 1956." *Statistik der Bundesrepublik Deutschland,* Band 227. Stuttgart: Kohlhammer.

――――――. "Der Verbrauch in Arbeitnehmerhaushaltungen 1949–1952." *Statistik der Bundesrepublik Deutschland,* Band 97. Stuttgart: Kohlhammer.

――――――. "Das Eigentum am Kapital der deutschen Aktiengesellschaften." *Statistik der Bundesrepublik Deutschland,* Band 188. Stuttgart: Kohlhammer.

――――――. "Die öffentliche Finanzwirtschaft in den Rechnungsjahren 1948 bis 1954." *Statistik der Bundesrepublik Deutschland,* Band 59. Stuttgart: Kohlhammer.

————. "Der Finanzausgleich zwischen Land und Gemeinden in den Rechnungsjahren 1951 bis 1955." *Statistik der Bundesrepublik Deutschland*, Band 125. Stuttgart: Kohlhammer, 1956.

————. "Das Einkommen der Einkommen-und Körperschaftssteuerpflichtigen und seine Besteuerung." *Statistik der Bundesrepublik Deutschland*, Band 125. Stuttgart: Kohlhammer, 1956.

*Statistisches Handbuch der Bank Deutscher Länder 1948–1954.* Frankfurt, 1955.

*Statistisches Handbuch von Deutschland, 1928–1944.* Herausgegeben vom Länderrat des amerikanischen Besatzungsgebietes, München, 1948.

*Statistisches Jahrbuch für die Bundesrepublik Deutschland*, 1952–1961.

*Statistisches Jahrbuch des Deutschen Reiches*, 1938, 1939–40.

*Umsatzsteuergesetz.* 15. ergänzte Auflage. München: C. H. Beck, 1953.

[United Nations, Economic Division.] "Economic Survey of Europe, 1949, 1955, 1957."

*Vermögenssteuergesetz, Bewertungsgesetz, Erbschaftssteuergesetz.* München: C. H. Beck, 1952, 8. vermehrte Auflage.

"Veröffentlichungen des Bundesaufsichtsamtes für das Versicherungs- und Bausparwesen." *Geschäftsberichte, 1954–1955, 1956–1957.* Berlin.

"Wirtschaft und Statistik." Wiesbaden: Statistisches Bundesamt.

[Wissenschaftlicher Beirat beim Bundesfinanzminister.] "Gutachten betreffs des weiteren Ausbaues und der rechnerischen Gestaltung der steuerlichen Sparbegünstigung im Rahmen der Einkommensteuer." (Unpublished.)


*Other Sources*


Blücher, Franz, *Überlegungen zur Frage der Sanierung des deutschen Kapitalmarktes. (Blücher Gutachten)*, Bad Godesberg, Jan. 16, 1957, (typewritten).

*The Economist.* "The German Exchange Enigma." Nov. 7, 1956, p. 264.

Gleitze, Bruno. "Die Möglichkeiten des institutionellen Sparens." Lecture given before the "Evangelische Akademie," Bad Boll, Württemberg, Nov. 9, 1957. (Manuscript)

————. *Produktivität, Lohn, Arbeitszeit.* Lecture, Heppenheim, Jan. 1957. Frankfurt: Uniondruckerei und Verlagsanstalt.

[Institut für Weltwirtschaft an der Universität Kiel.] *Deutsche Wirtschaft und Industrieplan.* Essen, 1947.

[Kreditanstalt für Wiederaufbau, Frankfurt.] "Kapitalmarkt und Investitionsfinanzierung in der Bundesrepubik." Dec. 28, 1953 (typewritten).

*London Times.* "Windfall Profits and Currency Reform." Statement by W. H. A. Bishop, Jan. 22, 1949.

Strathuis, H. *Internationaler Sparkongress 1957 in Paris.* Erster und zweiter Bericht, n.d.

[Wirtschaftsrat des Vereinigten Wirtschaftsgebietes (Amerikanisches und Britisches Besatzungsgebiet in Deutschland).] *Wörtliche Berichte über die Vollversammlungen des Wirtschaftsrates, 31–40.Vollversammlungen.* Frankfurt am Main, n.d.

# Name Index

Albers, W. 139n.
Ander, A. 210n.

Barnett, H. J. 20.
Baumgart, E. 20, 120n, 166n, 170n, 174n, 175n, 183n, 184n, 189n, 191n.
Becker, W. D. 92n.
Blücher, F. 124n, 207n, 251, 251n.
Böhm, F. 46.
Borchardt, K. 20.
Brazer, H. E. 20.
Breckner, F. 166n, 204n.
Briant, P. 221n.
Burgbacher, F. 251, 251n.

Carstens, D. 205n.
Chevallerie, de la O. 200n, 202n.

Daicoff, D. W. 218n.
Deist, H. 248, 248n.
Dittes, H. 205n.
Dohrendorf, E. M. 49n.
Dreissig, W. 139n, 230n.

Eckaus, R. 20.
Edding, F. 31n, 32n.
Eisendrath, E. 36n.
Erhard, L. 39n, 46, 166, 166n, 250.
Eucken, W. 46.

Feldhege, H. G. 251n.
Felix, D. 20.
Förster, K. H. 127n.

Gant II, A. H. 141n.
Gleitze, B. 28n, 35n, 36n, 91n, 171n, 249, 249n.
Göseke, G. 210n.

Han, P. B. 221n.
Hansen, A. H. 181n, 218n.
Häussler, E. 251n.

Hayek, F. A. 46.
Heidenheimer, A. J. 20.
Heller, W. F. 45n, 122n.
Hunter, H. 190n.

Jostock, P. 21n, 249, 249n.

Kaldor, N. 54n.
Kindleberger, C. P. 50n.
Krengel, R. 36n, 74n, 120n.
Krzyzaniak, M. 20, 221n.
Kunze, W. 41n.
Kuznets, S. 66n, 118n, 120n.

Lehman, W. 109n.
Leitz, K. 248, 248n.
Lohmann, M. 248, 248n.
Lutz, F. A. 45n.

MacBean, A. I. 25n.
Marx, K. 250.
Mendershausen, H. 20, 40n.
Metzler, L. 42n.
Mirrlees, J. A. 54n.
Molitor, B. 47n.
Möller, H. 41n.
Moritz, W. 120n.
Müller-Armack, A. 46, 46n.
Musgrave, R. A. 20, 181n, 218n, 221n.

Nell-Breuning, von, O. 251n.
Niemann, U. 148n.
Nischk, K. 205n.
Nölting, Dr. 167n.

Oliver, H. M. 46n.
Opie, R. G. 25n.
Osthues, H. 92n, 93n, 94n.

Padberg, Dr. 184n.
Pehl, G. 234n.

283

Phelps, E. S. 54n.
Preusker, Dr. 167n.

Ratchford, B. U. 221n.
Reiss, W. 126n.
Reithinger, A. 250, 250n.
Rittershausen, H. 151n.
Robinson, R. 20.
Röpke, W. 46.
Rüstow, A. 46.

Salomon, R. 165n, 169n, 172n, 182n.
Sauermann, H. 41, 41n.
Schlange Schöningen, H. 29.
Schlesinger, H. 82, 216n.
Schmölders, G. 46.
Schubert, W. 216n.
Seidler, H. 200n, 202n.
Senf, P. 20.

Shepherd, W. G. 25n.
Shoup, C. 221n.
Sohmen, E. 25n.
Solow, R. M. 54n.
Spengler, J. J. 190n.
Strathuis, H. 95n.
Stolper, W. F. 20, 30n, 165n.

Tuchtfeldt, E. 49n.

Veit, O. 46.

Wallich, H. C. 35n, 118n, 248.
Weisser, G. 202n.
Wilts, J. 184n, 192n, 194n.
Wolf, E. 39n.

Zeitel, G. 20, 217, 217n, 227n, 230n.
Zweig, G. 251n.

# Subject Index

Accelerated depreciation, 124, for industrial building 125, for housing 129, 185.
Aggregate demand, 59.
Agriculture, 62, problems 185, investments 188–189.
Alcohol tax, 138, 232.
Allied controls, 35, 43, 122, 123, 143, 177.
Armament, 70.
Artisans, 64.

Baby Bonds Plan, 167.
Bank credit, 55, 148–153.
Bank portfolios, 154.
Bank for reconstruction, 156.
Beer tax, 138, 232.
Benefit from public investments, 238–243.
Berlin, 28, levy 232, refugees 31, 81, Wall 30, 62.
Black markets, 32.
Bottlenecks in production, 125, 145, 163 f.
Budget, losses 101, 108, administrative 139, and basic law 143, effect on aggregate demand 145.
Bundesbank, 83, 141.
Bundes Finanzministerium, 101.
Business financing, general 55, external 112–113, long run trend 118–119.
Business savings, 86, 110 f.

Capital formation, general 51–52, equity problems 208–209.
Capital goods, quality 55, demand for 57.
Capital, intangible, 54, 196.
Capital market, 55, committee, 98, 132, 149, 165.

Capital stock, in industry, 35, after 1945 55, 164.
Chemical industry, 30, 36.
Christian Democratic Party, 202.
Coal mining, 165, 169–171, 181.
Communication and transportation, 190–195.
Construction, 62, 77.
Consumption, 57.
Competition, 48.
Consumer credit, 70.
Consumer demand, 66.
Corporations, 86, 157.
Corporate income tax, 123, 138, 216, incidence of 220–221, 232.
Counterpart funds, 156, 165.
Currency reform of 1948, 27, 41–46, plans 43, 122.
Customs, 138, 216.
Czechoslovakia, 31.

Debts, prewar, 79.
Defense expenditures, 70, 76.
DM opening balance sheet, 125–127.
Deutsche Bundesbank, 83, 141.
Discounts, preferential for exports, 134–135.
Dismantling, 36, 172.
Dividends, 137.
Dodge-Colm-Goldsmith Plan, 41.

East Germany, 28.
Economic Cooperation Agreement Act, 203.
Einfuhr-und Vorratsstelle, 233.
Electric Power Sector, 36, 165, 175–176.
Electrotechnical Industry, 72.
Employment, 56, 62, 180, 182, 197.
Entrepreneurs, attitude of 34.
Eröffnungsbilanz in DM, 125–127.

Equalization of Burden, law, 43, 126, 138, levy 215, levy incidence of 219–228, fund, 83.

Equity, problems in capital formation, 61, 249, 252.

European Economic Community, 186.

European Recovery Program, 157, 165, 166, 169, 175, 176, 184, 203, 204.

Exchange rate, 72, 154.

Expenditures, for schools 197, for universities 197.

Exports, 37, guarantees for, 134, surplus, 66, 71, 78, 79.

Farms, 186.

Federal Railway, 99, 159, 176, 194.

Fertilizer, 29.

Fiscal levels, 138.

Fiscal policy, 40, 46, compensatory 58, 122–123, 232.

Fodder supply, 29.

Food, drink and tobacco industry, 37.

Food, supply 28, 29, rationing 29, imports 29.

Foreign aid, 155.

Foreign exchange reserves, 71, 143, 154.

Foreign trade, 37, 165.

Free Democratic Party, 202.

Freiburg school, 46.

Germany, division of 28.

Gewerbesteuer, 138, 216, incidence of 222, 233.

Government savings, 55, 86, 138, 139–141, 157–161.

Gross National Product, 61.

Growth rates of G. N. P., 62.

Grüner Plan, 187.

Habenzinsabkommen, 98.

Hitler regime, 35, 64.

Housing, 31, 145.

Hungary, 31.

Immediate Aid Levy, 43.

Incentives, 44, 47, 49.

Imports, food 29, 37, raw materials 37, 38.

Income, before 1948 33, personal 91.

Income distribution, 48, 64, 210–214, 233.

Income taxes, 122, 138, 215, incidence of 218, 220, 232.

Industrial production, 30, 35, 62.

Inflation, 96, 97.

Inheritance tax, 123, 138.

Inter government relations, 86, 139.

Interest rate, 47, 96, 97, 98, structure 99.

Inventories, 77.

Investment Aid Law, 124, 125, 167–169, 175–176.

Investment, in equipment 77, by government 60, 238–243, in agriculture 188, in coal mining 169, in electric power sector 175, in industry 36, in iron and steel industry 173, in residential construction 178, in transportation 194.

Investment planning, 204–206.

Investment policies, 201–204.

Iron and steel industry, 30, 171–174.

J.E.I.A., 38.

Julius Tower, 143.

Korean boom, 62, 70, 77, 164.

Labor, in agriculture, 185.

Labor, attitude of, 32.

Labor force, 30 f.

Lex Preusker, 108.

Light industries, 30.

Life insurance, 94.

Loans, for capital formation 71, short-term 151.

Machine building, 36, 72.

Marshall Plan, 99, 156.

Meat production, 29.

Merchant fleet, 184.

Mining, 36, 125.

Monetary policy, 97, 155n.

Money market, 56.

Money supply, 39.

Occupation, cost of, 70.

Oder-Neisse line, 28, 31, 38, 39.

Oils and fats industry, 37.

Population, 30.
Postal system, 159, 194.
Potsdam Agreement, 41.
Preferences, private 158, public 158.
Price control, 39.
Prices, investment goods 72, cost of living 39, residential construction 72.
Price level, 39, 47, 62, 97.
Price system, 59.
Private property, 34.
Product mix, 58.
Production, structure of 62.
Property distribution, 250–251.
Property tax, 123.
Public corporations, 86.
Public sector, 60, 83.

Rationing, food 29.
Real estate tax, 138, 216, incidence of 222.
Red Army, 30.
Refugees, 31, 124, 177, 180.
Residential construction, 77, 99, 177–182, government support for 178.
Resource allocations, in capital formation, 59.
Restitution payments, 79.
Retained earnings, 111, 213.
Roads, 195.
Ruhr district, 30, 181.
Rumania, 31.
Russian occupation, 36, 39.

Savers, income brackets of 101.
Savings in building associations, 93.
Savings deposits, 43, 66, 91, 92, 93, premium payments 109, 155.
Savings, incentives, 96.
Savings in insurance companies, 91, 94.
Savings, general, 55.
Savings, government, 55, 138, 139–141, 157–161.
Savings, individual, 43, 47, 66, 83, 87, incentives for 90, 250.
Securities, 91, 94–95.
Security markets, 98.
Services, 62, 64.
Shares, 137.

Shipbuilding, 182–185.
Social Democratic Party, 166, 167, 202, 250.
Social Insurance, 49, 90, 94.
Social Insurance Contributions, incidence of 226–229, 233.
Social Market Economy, 46–50.
Social Security System, 70, 83, as saver 147–148.
Soviet Union, 57.
Sparprämie, 109.
Steel Construction, 72.
Subsidies for agricultural products, 187.
Subsidies, for capital formation, 71.
Sugar tax, 138, 232.
Switzerland, 134.

Tax burden distribution, 209–210, after 1950 234–235.
Tax exemptions, distribution of, 243–245.
Tax exemptions for individual savings, 104–107.
Tax exemptions, 123, for retained earnings, 131–132.
Tax exemptions for security purchases, 100, 101, 132.
Tax favored exports, 134.
Tax favored loans, 129–130, 145.
Tax incentives for business savings, 122.
Tax rates, 230–233.
Tax structure, incidence of, 224–226.
Technology, 54.
Textile industry, 37.
Tobacco tax, 123, 138, 215, incidence of 218, 232.
Transport and communications, 30, 62, 190.
Turnover tax, 138, 215, incidence of 216–218, 232.

United Kingdom, 161.
United States, 134, 161, government, 41, 165.

Wages, 44.
Wage share, 64.
Weimar Republic, 196.

This manuscript was edited by Robert Kanzler.
The book was designed by Sylvia Winter.
The text typeface is Linotype Baskerville
originally cut by John Baskerville in the 18th century.
The display face is Caslon Bold Condensed based on designs
originally made by William Caslon in the early 18th century.
The book is printed on S. D. Warren's Olde Style Antique paper
and bound in Joanna Mills' Parchment cloth over boards.
Manufactured in the United States of America.